THE EVERYDAY PRACTICE OF PRACTICE OF VALUATION AND INVESTMENT

THE EVERYDAY PRACTICE OF VALUATION AND INVESTMENT

POLITICAL IMAGINARIES OF SHAREHOLDER VALUE

HORACIO ORTIZ

Columbia University Press   *New York*

Columbia University Press
Publishers Since 1893
New York   Chichester, West Sussex
cup.columbia.edu

First published in French as
Valeur financière et vérité: Enquête d'anthropologie politique sur
l'évaluation des entreprises cotées en bourse
© 2014 Presses de la Fondation Nationale des Sciences Politiques

English translation copyright © 2021 Horacio Ortiz

Library of Congress Cataloging-in-Publication Data
Names: Ortiz, Horacio, 1974– author.
Title: The everyday practice of valuation and investment : political
imaginaries of shareholder value / Horacio Ortiz.
Other titles: Valeur financière et vérité. English
Description: New York : Columbia University Press, [2021] |
Includes bibliographical references and index.
Identifiers: LCCN 2021014520 (print) | LCCN 2021014521 (ebook) |
ISBN 9780231201186 (hardback) | ISBN 9780231201193
(trade paperback) | ISBN 9780231553971 (ebook)
Subjects: LCSH: Valuation—Political aspects. |
Investments—Political aspects. | Value—Political aspects. |
Finance—Political aspects.
Classification: LCC HG4028.V3 O7813 2021 (print) | LCC
HG4028.V3 (ebook) | DDC 332.63/221—dc23
LC record available at https://lccn.loc.gov/2021014520
LC ebook record available at https://lccn.loc.gov/2021014521

Columbia University Press books are printed on permanent and
durable acid-free paper.
Printed in the United States of America

Cover design: Noah Arlow

CONTENTS

Acknowledgments vii

Introduction 1

1 The Organizational Space of Financial Value 36

2 Valuation as a Personal Opinion 83

3 The Truth of Value as the Result of Efficient Markets 142

4 Financial Value as Political Assemblage 195

Conclusion 243

Notes 255
Bibliography 285
Index 303

ACKNOWLEDGMENTS

I STARTED the research presented here as a PhD project in the year 2000, first under the supervision of Michèle de La Pradelle, who passed away in 2004, and then under the supervision of Marc Abélès. In different ways, their care, support and enthusiasm helped me carry out this project. The present book is a very revised version of a book published in French in 2014 at the Presses de Science Po, with the crucial editorial support of Patrick Legalès. The French version was written when I was a post-doctoral researcher at Mines ParisTech, financed by the European Research Council, Grant number ERC-2010-StG 263529. I wrote the translation in the following years, as I had become associate professor at the East China Normal University and researcher at the CNRS, IRISSO, Université Paris Dauphine—PSL. In 2019–2020 I was a member at the Institute for Advanced Study, Princeton, a position funded by the Florence Gould Foundation Fund, and although I did not work on the manuscript during that time, exchanges with colleagues I met there were extremely useful to think about it.

In the long process since the beginning of the research presented here, many people commented on drafts, ideas, related papers and presentations. My exchanges with Keith Hart, Sabine

Montagne and Fabian Muniesa over many years have contributed to shape the main ideas presented in this book more than I could ever acknowledge properly. I have also been deeply influenced by the work of Jane Guyer and Bill Maurer, both of whom also gave me always very inspiring insights on the occasions I had the chance to exchange with them in person. This version also benefited from critiques and comments published in book reviews of the first version. With no particular order other than alphabetic, I want to thank the comments and inspiration I received from Simone Abrams, Galit Ailon, Thomas Angeletti, Guillaume Arnould, Alvaro Artigas, Máximo Badaró, Nina Bandelj, Hélène Baligadoo, Laura Bear, Marlène Benquet, David Beytelmann, Yuri Biondi, Tom Boellstorf, Hernán Borisonik, Anaïs Bouteille Bokobza, Nina Boy, Robert Boyer, Benjamin Braun, Sarah Carton de Gramont, Isabelle Chambost, Maria Chaves Jardim, Chen Jin, Sophie Chevallier, Kimberly Chong, Lily Chumley, Joseph Confavreux, Christine Cooper, Sophie Corbillé, Lynda Dematteo, Liliana Doganova, Julia Eckert, Elena Esposito, Terry Evens, Didier Fassin, Melissa Fisher, Marion Fourcade, Marie-France Garcia-Parpet, Christina Garsten, Natalia Gavazzo, Vincent Gayon, Olivier Godechot, Emiliano Grossman, Julian Gruin, Isabelle Guérin, Alya Guseva, Ellen Hertz, Karen Ho, Huang Jianbo, Deborah James, Webb Keane, Oliver Kessler, Rita Kesselring, Teresa Kuan, Marc Lenglet, Paul Lagneau-Ymonet, Pierre Lascoumes, Jeanne Lazarus, Stefan Leins, Benjamin Lemoine, Li Limei, Dominique Linhardt, Mariana Luzzi, Tom MacDonald, Liz MacFall, Donald MacKenzie, George Marcus, Sarah Mazouz, Sabrina Melenotte, Johnna Montgomerie, Birgit Müller, Lúcia Müller, Micah Murphy, Susana Narotzky, Federico Neiburg, Jorge Núñez, Erin O'Connor, Fareen Parvez, Florence Paterson, Gustav Peebles, Michael Perret, Johannes Petry, Anne Pezet, Álvaro Pina-Stranger, Martha Poon, Pierre-Charles

Pradier, Sarah Quinn, Adrienne Roberts, Fernando Rabossi, Maka Rodríguez, Enrique Rodríguez Larreta, Alexandre Roig, Janet Roitman, Akos Rona-Tas, Leslie Salzinger, Cheryl Meiting Schmitz, Mallika Shakya, Shao Jing, Sarah Sippel, Adrienne Sörbonn, Nathan Sperber, David Stark, Philippe Steiner, Yamina Tadjeddine, Bruno Théret, Noam Thuram, Chloe Thurston, Anna Tsing, Fred Wherry, Ariel Wilkis, Caitlin Zaloom, Viviana Zelizer, Zhang Hui, Zhu Jianfeng, and Zhu Yujing. All errors are of course mine.

I also thank two anonymous reviewers of Columbia University Press for their extremely useful critiques, comments, and suggestions, and the copyeditors for their magical work. Very special thanks to Eric Schwartz for his generous and enthusiastic support for this project, and to Marion Fourcade for making it possible.

And, of course, an ecstatic thanks to all those whose love inspired me all along!

THE EVERYDAY PRACTICE OF PRACTICE OF VALUATION AND INVESTMENT

INTRODUCTION

I N the forest of skyscrapers that is Midtown Manhattan, where most of the financial industry is located, the offices of Brokers Inc. take up the top floor of a twenty-six-story building. Around 9 A.M., like every morning for the last few weeks of this summer of 2002, I present my employee card to the doorman, who lets me into the elevator. At Brokers Inc., the activity has started at 1 A.M., shortly before the opening of European stock exchanges. I sit at my desk, in front of Frédéric, a young salesperson in charge of selling financial analysis. He is leaving a twenty-second message on an answering machine, explaining enthusiastically that the company Dupré will probably announce positive results soon, the consequence of an aggressive commercial strategy that seems to be bearing fruit, and inviting the absent interlocutor to call him back for more information.

Frédéric will repeat this message throughout the morning, making dozens of phone calls, most of which will not be answered. These brief financial analyses, which he leaves on the answering machines of his potential or current customers, concern companies listed on the European stock exchange Euronext and rely on information produced by Frédéric's colleagues who are financial analysts at Brokers SA, based in Paris. Earlier in the morning, around 6 A.M., he started reading the financial news of the day and double-checking data with the Paris office. He will follow up his phone calls by sending emails, using the Bloomberg communication network, which connects the terminals of thousands of financial professionals around the world.

Frédéric must filter and complement the information provided by Brokers SA's analysts in accordance with standardized procedures. The listed company is analyzed as a promise of future income for the shareholder in the form of dividends or increases in the share price. The company is also compared to other listed companies in order to establish a hierarchy among possible investment objects. The analysis also considers short-term variations in the company's stock price as possible investment bets. According to regulations, the methods used by Frédéric and his colleagues for this valuation are mandatory for their positions. These methods are taken into account in employees' labor contracts and in the commercial contracts that bind their employers, and they constitute the core of the financial theory taught at universities and business schools, such as the one attended by Frédéric before starting his professional career.

According to this financial theory, Frédéric must produce a personal opinion about the listed company using standard methods. His financial analysis must strive to come as close as possible to the supposed true value of the company, which the market price is expected to eventually reflect. If Frédéric considers the current price too high, he should advise his customers to sell before the market corrects itself. He should recommend buying in the opposite case. Still according to this theory, the mechanism called market efficiency ensures that the price, which contains all available information about the listed company and hence reflects as closely as possible its true value, can serve as a signal for all other social actors, leading to a socially optimal allocation of resources.

Frédéric graduated from a prestigious French business school, did an internship at a consulting company, and then worked as a financial analyst for a few months at Brokers SA before settling in New York as a salesperson. A little over a year ago he passed the qualifying examination required by U.S. financial authorities, and now, at twenty-seven, he can sell financial services and is officially allowed to participate in front-office activities—i.e., those performed by financial analysts, traders, salespeople, and fund managers, among others.

Leaving a twenty-second message on an answering machine is a very important moment in the attempt to attract a clientele, which, as a young salesperson, Frédéric has yet to build up. His clients, current and potential, are U.S.-based fund managers who buy stocks listed in Europe on behalf of their customers—for example, participants in a pension or a mutual fund. For the moment, most of Frédéric's interlocutors have not called back. The few clients he has already established for Brokers Inc. provide the company with more than $1 million in yearly revenue, and Frédéric hopes to receive nearly $200,000 in salary and bonus combined for 2002.[1] These money flows are supposed to pay for the quality of the information he gives to his clients.

Around noon in New York, the activity of salespeople at Brokers Inc. slows down because stock exchanges have closed in Europe. Frédéric then takes the time to read financial analyses and search for information on the internet, in the specialized press, or through discussions with his colleagues in the office, who are traders, analysts, or salespeople like him. His working day ends at around 6 P.M. unless there is an outing with customers, such as going to a restaurant, a hockey game, or a striptease show, paid for by Brokers Inc. Frédéric explains to me that he is still learning the ropes of his work, but that he does not plan to devote his entire career to it. He says his salary allows him to "earn a good living but not to become rich," and he hopes to move up in the profession, eventually becoming a partner in another company.

Brokers Inc., with its twenty-five employees, is a very small company in the financial industry. The information that Frédéric sells to his customers is only one of the multiple sources that each fund manager must use according to the terms of his[2] employment contract. Most of these fund managers are employees of companies managing money for third parties, investing their money in financial assets (equities, bonds, and credit derivatives, among others[3]) issued not only in Europe but also in the United States and in other parts of the world. These investment funds mainly collect middle-class savings from rich areas of the world and channel them to financial assets issued by companies and public institutions located mainly in these same areas but also elsewhere globally.

At the time of my observations at Brokers Inc., in the summer of 2002, the stock prices of companies listed on the major exchanges based in Europe and the United States are starting to go up. Frédéric, like his colleagues and customers, expresses some optimism: they seem to be finally out of what they call the "internet bubble." This expression refers to the period between 1996 and 2003 when the stock prices of companies involved in what were then termed the new communication technologies rose sharply and then collapsed. This price movement was described to me at the time by almost all my respondents as "the most serious financial crisis since 1929," an expression also found in the press and political speeches. The employees at Brokers Inc. tell me the industry seems to be returning to normalcy, by which they refer, mostly implicitly, to the market efficiency whose disruption was designated by the word "crisis." This indicates a situation in which the socially optimal allocation of resources brings forth economic growth, higher stock prices, more money invested in stocks, and hence an increase in the fees that constitute the income of employees like those of Brokers Inc.

In the financial industry, the decision to allocate this money to one activity rather than another is usually based on financial valuation such as that made by Frédéric. The truth of the value of listed companies, which the salesperson supposedly looks for, is part of a global setting, in which the financial industry supports some activities at the expense of others, establishing a hierarchy of access to money that state regulation justifies politically as a result of market efficiency. This book contributes to understanding how this process comes about by exploring the everyday practices of financial professionals. It analyzes how they define what they call "financial value" in multiple ways and what roles these definitions play in the distribution of money by the financial industry. In order to do so, in this introduction, I first situate the financial industry, and the practices of people like Frédéric, in the global monetary relations of which they are a part. I then clarify some of the theoretical presuppositions of the political anthropology of finance proposed in this book—in particular, those concerning the concepts of power, money, and value.

THE FINANCIAL INDUSTRY AS THE ORGANIZATION OF A GLOBAL DISTRIBUTION OF RESOURCES

The main analytic concern I address in this book is the role that the financial industry plays in the production of global social hierarchies. I use the term *financial industry* to designate a vast series of companies, like investment management companies, insurance companies, rating agencies, banks, investment banks, and brokers, among others. Through their commercial relations, these companies collect, produce, and distribute money worldwide—in particular, as they produce, define, and circulate financial assets like stocks, bonds, and derivatives. In this process, the employees of the financial industry give some activities access to money and exclude others, and those that are given access must often transform according to the industry's valuation and investment requirements.

The concept of financial value—which, when applied to listed stocks, revolves around the notion of shareholder value—is a crucial component in this process. In order to understand how these global hierarchies result from the everyday practices of financial valuation and investment of employees like Frédéric, we must consider several aspects. These practices must be analyzed as part of global historical processes and monetary flows. Their regularity is related to financial regulation and the rules organizing the relations within and between companies, including the financial methods and lines of reasoning that have technical, moral, and political meanings. Finally, these practices must be analyzed in terms of how they make sense to those who follow them in their everyday lives; i.e., they must be understood as part of the personal trajectories of financial employees.[4] Fieldwork renders observable only a fragment of global financial relations. At the same time, the standardization of procedures within the financial industry gives these observations a certain representative character, although they must be explored without simplifying the multiple social meanings of money inside and outside the financial industry.

In this section, in order to establish the political importance of practices like those of Frédéric described earlier, I first place them in the global monetary hierarchies of which they are a part. This provides the setting in which to examine how current financial regulations and professional rules organize and legitimize global hierarchies using a concept of financial value that is considered both true and fair because it results from the acts of investors meeting in efficient markets and leads to a socially optimal allocation of resources.

At the end of 2017, the four hundred biggest investment management companies managed $63.3 trillion, of which $31 trillion was managed by the twenty biggest companies.[5] But this is only a fraction of the money managed by the financial industry worldwide. The total amount can be approximated using the capitalization[6] of outstanding stocks, bonds, and derivatives, which are mainly produced and exchanged within the financial industry. At the end of 2017, the global capitalization of listed stocks was about $85.7 trillion—among which a large portion consisted of $32 trillion for the New York Stock Exchange and Nasdaq; $13 trillion for the stock exchanges of Shanghai, Shenzhen, and Hong Kong combined; and $7 trillion for Euronext and the Deutsche Börse combined.[7] There was $112.5 trillion in bonds outstanding—with $18 trillion issued by the U.S. federal government, $10 trillion by the state of Japan, $4.6 trillion by the People's Republic of China, and around $8.5 trillion by the states of the Eurozone.[8] And there was $11 trillion in financial derivatives outstanding, for a notional amount of $531.6 trillion, mostly based on short-term loans and foreign exchange transactions labeled in U.S. dollars.[9]

Thus, at the end of 2017, the financial industry controlled around $200 trillion. This can be compared to a global gross domestic product (GDP) of $80.6 trillion for that year—with $19.4 trillion attributed to the United States, $12.6 trillion to the territories of the Eurozone, and $12.2 trillion to China.[10] It can also be compared to the world aggregate for state budgets of $23.7 trillion, with $6.3 trillion for the budget of the U.S. federal government, $3.1 trillion for the Chinese government, and $6.1 trillion for the governments of the Eurozone states. The narrow measure of monetary mass for the whole world was $34.4 trillion, and the broad measure was of $86.5 trillion.[11]

These numbers describe a concentration of money in the United States, Europe, and Japan and increasingly in China. This can be compared to the number of undernourished in the world, which in 2017 rose to 821 million people, mostly situated in Latin America, Africa, and Asia.[12] According to different analyses, the amount of money necessary to ensure that enough food is distributed to all is around $100 billion.[13] The territories where the money is concentrated are also marked by strong inequalities, but these inequalities must be placed within global monetary relations, in which the resources produced and distributed by the financial industry are denied to the poorest segments of the population.[14]

The production of all these numbers poses interrelated epistemological and political questions concerning their legitimacy as representative of any relevant social reality. These numbers are accompanied by multiple expert discourses about their meaning, including official controversies about how they should be interpreted, which often hide or exclude narratives about what they occlude.[15] But they matter because, even with all their epistemological and political problems, they highlight how financial relations managed by the financial industry relate to particular geographies and activities. These forms of inclusion, exclusion, and hierarchy constitute a global political space of power relations around the distribution of money, of which the activity of employees like those of Brokers Inc. is a part.

In order to understand the specific geography of the distribution of money by the financial industry, it is important to situate it in a global historical process.[16] The geography of the current distribution of money by the financial industry is the historical result of colonial empires, the Cold War, and the development of a new global industrial center in China.

The contemporary financial industry was shaped over several centuries, playing a fundamental role in the constitution of colonial empires. Since their creation in the eighteenth and nineteenth centuries, the United States and nation-states in Europe have had a relation at once symbiotic and conflictive with the administration of global financial relations by private companies. The separation between states and the financial industry is never as clear-cut as some definitions of the concepts may suggest, and up until World War I, the expansion of the gold standard worldwide was an articulation of the intimate relation between states and financial corporations in colonial centers—in particular, for the United Kingdom and France. The period between World Wars I and II was one of confrontation around these global empires. It ended with a shift in this power relation, as the United States accumulated more gold and financial capacities than any other state, backed by military and corporate power.

After World War II and in the 1950s, many governments retained the power to direct credit in order to transform social hierarchies. This was done by mobilizing Keynes-inspired theories in western Europe and the United States, socialist theories in the territories under the influence of the Soviet Union, and developmental theories in many of the poorest territories of the world, some of which were marked by decolonization and the creation of new nation-states. In territories under the control of the Soviet bloc and China, the Communist governments almost eliminated the financial industry, as investment was considered an activity of the state. Elsewhere, the financial industry was often considered to be a tool of government policy. Within the hierarchy among states established by colonial and postcolonial relations, it was often understood that states should play a central role in the orientation of money—for instance, in favor of economic growth, education, health, scientific research, transport, and communication infrastructure, among other areas.

The consolidation of national financial industries and the financial relations established by the Bretton Woods agreement resulted from a new balance of power between the United States and western Europe. Outside the Soviet bloc, the U.S. dollar's position strengthened as the main currency for finance, officially backed by the gold held in the United States. This arrangement rearticulated colonial and postcolonial relations and served as a way to organize the global military confrontation with the Soviet bloc during the Cold War. The unpegging of the U.S. dollar from gold and the demise of the Bretton Woods agreement in the early 1970s, due in part to the accumulation of so-called Eurodollars by nonstate actors, again strengthened the global position of the U.S. dollar. This was further reinforced with the collapse of the Soviet bloc after 1990.

Thus, by the early 1990s, global monetary flows were centered in the previous colonial centers and in the United States and its Cold War allies like Japan. The Chinese stock exchanges were reinstated in 1990. After the mid-2000s, they started accumulating money and became a visible part of the financial industry's global monetary distribution. Their development was part of a government policy that sought to foster the state-owned financial industry on the back of the growing global role of manufacturers based in China.[17]

The current geography of monetary distribution by the financial industry, sketched here, is thus the product of this history of colonization and decolonization, world wars, the Cold War, and the rise of manufacturing in China in the last twenty years. This historical process also excluded vast parts of the world population from the increasing amounts of money collected, produced, and distributed by the financial industry. This exclusion is in part active, as it systematically forestalls the creation and orientation of money to address the lack of access to health, education, shelter, and food. At the same time, within the areas and populations where the financial industry distributes the money it manages, specific social hierarchies have developed.

Financial contracts such as bonds, stocks, and derivatives organize different social relations. Stocks establish a relation of ownership between the shareholder and the company, bonds establish a credit relation between the bondholder and the company or the state issuing the security, and the term *derivative* designates a wide variety of contracts that are usually based on other contracts—mainly foreign exchange transactions but also stocks, debts, and transactions in what the financial industry terms *commodities* (particularly mining and agricultural products).

In many jurisdictions, the last forty years have been marked by an absolute and relative increase in revenue for owners of financial assets and for organizations carrying out financial activities.[18] These inequalities often strengthen existing forms of discrimination—for instance, hierarchies established in terms of gender.[19] But the financial relations established in different financial contracts can have different effects on inequality. The increased use of stocks listed on stock exchanges has contributed to the rise in inequalities in at least two ways. In companies listed on stock exchanges, shareholder demands are used to legitimize lower salaries and more precarious working conditions.[20] And their extensive use has also had an impact on income distribution beyond listed companies; for instance, top management and the financial sector have accumulated revenue relative to the rest of society.[21]

For many states, bond issuance is a way to access foreign currency—in particular, U.S. dollars. This also gives the global financial industry a major say in these states' public policy. In the 1980s and 1990s, the International Monetary Fund (IMF) imposed structural adjustment programs on states around the world, claiming that these programs would help them access the funds of the financial industry by making their finances profitable to creditors. These programs, however, led to decreases in public expenditures for fundamental services such as education and health care, which became less accessible to the poorer members of the population. And these increases in inequality were made worse by government defaults, which were often followed by more stringent requirements by the financial industry and the IMF.[22]

The collapse of credit derivatives issued by U.S. banks in 2007–2008 was an instance where derivatives came to the fore as potential sources of increasing inequality. The banking systems in the United States and Europe were heavily affected, disrupting the organization of credit in these regions of the world. And in the United States and certain parts of Europe, the collapse of mortgage derivatives led banks to foreclose on mortgagors' homes.[23] But more frequent and widespread have been the effects of the massive investment in and divestment of derivatives of mining and agricultural products, as the resulting extreme price variations have dramatically impacted states' finances and the well-being of the people dependent on the export of these products. This played an important role, for instance, in the "food crisis" of 2007–2008.[24]

Investment management companies also purchase land, real estate, nonlisted companies, artwork, and many other objects or rights over activities. In many of these cases, this leads to drastic price changes and to reorientations of these activities or the purpose of these objects. In the case of private equity funds, they tend to impoverish workers by cutting costs in order to resell the companies they purchase.[25] In the case of land, they tend to concentrate the control over land and production in a few hands.[26]

Finally, financial methods of valuation and investment are used outside the financial industry—for example, in public administration. In these cases, the aims of these activities are sometimes drastically reoriented to correspond to the financial logics of profit making, resulting, for instance, in lower-quality public services.[27]

These inequalities do not just concern income distribution. They also concern access to health, education, shelter, and food, with the varied meanings they can have in different settings. And the companies and activities of the financial industry involved in each these cases are not always the same. Thus, to a certain extent, the inequalities produced in each instance may seem isolated, resulting from geographically contained specificities. At the same time, it is analytically limiting to avoid seeing that stocks, bonds, and derivatives are fundamentally connected by the activities of the financial industry worldwide. The ways in which they are defined, evaluated, purchased, and sold make them mutually constitutive. Inequalities observable in the relations established with stocks, bonds, and derivatives in a particular company, a particular state, or a particular region of the world must be analyzed as part of the global distribution of money by the financial industry, which is marked by the global historical processes that I described earlier.

In order to analyze part of this process, in this book I will look at the everyday practices of financial professionals as they evaluate and invest in listed stocks. This will allow us to observe how activities around the world are compared and ranked according to imaginaries of financial value that technically, morally, and politically legitimize the distributive effects of the financial industry. To do so, it is important to see that current financial industry practices share a common set of procedural rules that are intimately related to state regulation as it developed in the last forty years.

In the 1970s and 1980s, regulatory transformations started reshaping the relation between states and the financial industry and giving new meanings to the global hierarchies produced by the financial industry. In the United States[28] and certain states in Europe,[29] financial regulation has been explicitly aimed at giving the non-state-owned financial industry a bigger role in the distribution of money. This regulatory frame mobilized a particular form of expert knowledge, financial economics, itself derived from neoclassical economics. According to financial economics, this financial industry allows independent investors to meet in efficient markets where prices reflect all available information about the objects exchanged in them, thereby reflecting the true value of these objects and serving as signals for a socially optimal allocation of money.

In the 1990s, this regulatory transformation was observable, with great variations, in the jurisdictions of Japan,[30] India,[31] China,[32] Brazil,[33] and many other poor territories,[34] including some that had until then been part of the Soviet bloc that had just collapsed. The ambiguous status of so-called independence from governments that contemporary central banks have today in many jurisdictions is partly the product of these transformations.[35]

State financial regulation is established through complex social processes involving state agencies, the financial industry, and different lobbying groups. The various capacities of state supervisory or control agencies usually stop at national borders, creating a fragmented geography of jurisdictions.[36] Across these borders, the commercial network established by the companies of the financial industry is organized with shared standardized valuation and investment procedures. These procedures constitute a body of lines of reasoning and formulas that started becoming unified and standardized in the 1950s and that is now sustained by financial regulation.

The concept of investment—along with the idea that it is an activity carried out by an individual actor, the investor—is part of this history of political and institutional arrangements concerning the use of money. While the concept of investor has many meanings outside the financial industry and those meanings have varied over time, today the figure of the investor used in the financial industry exists mainly as a relation of representation.[37] An employee like a fund manager is considered an investor only because he acts on behalf of the owners of the money invested, whose interests are contractually defined as those formalized in mainstream financial methods. And these clients are considered investors only because they delegate to qualified experts the power to act with their money.

Financial regulation worldwide tends to ensure that the overwhelming majority of financial trades, by number of trades and by amount of money traded, are carried out not by the legal owners of the money but rather by employees of the financial industry acting on their behalf. These professionals correspond to the legal category of persons often termed "qualified" or "sophisticated investors," defined as those who master standardized financial methods and have the concrete means to apply them. In order to access the front-office positions, where they may have an influence on the orientation of their clients' money, employees must often prove their knowledge of financial theory by obtaining formal qualifications. And only their companies are supposed to ensure that they have the technical means to apply this knowledge.[38] In jurisdictions influenced by common law, contracts of delegation take the form of the trust and prohibit the delegator from influencing the decisions of the trustee, who is deemed to be more able to defend the interest of his clients than the clients themselves are.[39]

This theoretical figure of the investor is not embodied in a single person but is distributed in the standardized procedures of employees.[40] Investors and the efficient markets that they are supposed to constitute through their exchanges thus exist only as a relation of representation instituted by state regulation and contractual relations between companies and between employees and employers. In this relation of representation, the methods of financial valuation and investment established as the actions of investors and efficient markets constitute shared rules in the financial industry's global space of operations, crossing the boundaries of fragmented state regulatory jurisdictions. These methods are usually mandatory for all employees in their various tasks and constitute the practical rules according to which money is collected, produced, and distributed, contributing to the production and transformation of hierarchies worldwide.

Valuation and investment practices are intimately related, as all financial valuation in the financial industry is conducted explicitly with the aim of orienting investment and all investment is explicitly based on financial valuation. Yet, these two activities are also separated into professional specializations, which can even be concentrated in companies solely dedicated to one or the other. I carried out the fieldwork presented in this book at three companies between 2002 and 2004. Like most companies in the financial industry, these companies by themselves had little impact on the global distribution of resources. Brokers Inc., with twenty-five employees and $35 million in yearly revenue in 2002, was a very small company. It grew as U.S.-based investment management companies increased their investments in stocks listed on the European stock exchanges. In 2002, the traders of Brokers Inc. processed around $14 billion worth of purchases and sales of stocks listed on Euronext, a minute portion of global trades. Hedge Consulting, where I did fieldwork in 2003, was a team of three people working in the then nascent segment that was labeled in the financial industry as "alternative investment management," which comprised a vast variety of so-called hedge funds. This fieldwork allowed me to follow these consultants as they tried to sell their investment techniques to major companies in the financial industry. Finally, in 2004, I did fieldwork at Acme, which was among the smallest of the world's fifty biggest investment management companies. It managed €300 billion for other companies—in particular, insurance companies based in Europe. In the 1980s, the French government, like many others, changed regulations to open the stock exchanges to the money held by the global financial industry, especially by the investment management companies based in the United States. By the early 2000s, investment funds based outside France owned half of the stock of the largest companies previously listed on the Paris Stock Exchange, bundled in the stock index CAC 40. Acme was established during the consolidation of the investment management sector in the 1980s in France, profiting from the same trends that led to the creation of Brokers Inc.

The interest in studying these companies lies in the fact that they developed the same rules of valuation and investment in different locations and with different financial contracts, such as bonds, stocks, and derivatives. After finishing this research, in order to continue doing fieldwork in the financial industry, I completed a program to obtain certification as a certified international investment analyst (CIIA). This program was organized by a global federation of national associations of financial analysts in order to compete with the U.S.-based chartered financial analyst (CFA) program. I later pursued fieldwork as a lecturer in finance in business schools and did participant observation in a consultancy for mergers and acquisitions in Shanghai. In this way, I was able to observe the global standardization of methods of valuation and investment, which are the same in the two professional qualification programs, in any manuals used in business schools, and at all the sites where I did fieldwork.

In this book, I focus on the valuation of listed stocks, the main activity at Brokers Inc., but my main conclusions hold for the valuation of any other financial contract, since, as I will show, in the financial industry, they are all considered comparable assets. Brokers Inc., Acme, and Hedge Consulting followed professional standards shared in the financial industry at large. They are sites at which I observed the practices whereby "financial value" is defined and problematized as something that can be true, in the sense of accurate and fair, and this truth is supposed to contribute to market efficiency and a socially optimal allocation of resources that justifies the global political role of the financial industry. In order to clarify this focus, the next section explores some of the theoretical presuppositions of the political anthropology of finance that are central in this book.

POWER, MONEY AND VALUE: A POLITICAL ANTHROPOLOGY OF FINANCE

This section addresses the three sets of theoretical presuppositions that organize this book. The first one concerns the concept of power and the analysis of the financial industry as a global political institution. The other two concern how I propose to address the concepts of money and value in relation to this problematization of the financial industry.

The Financial Industry as a Global Political Institution

As we have seen, the geography of the global distribution of money by the financial industry is the result of a complex history that combines multiple logics: colonial empires, world wars, the Cold War, and the redistribution of manufacturing, among others, along with the U.S. dollar becoming the main global currency for financial transactions. At the same time, this geography of exclusion and inclusion is composed of various forms of hierarchy in different settings. These hierarchies depend not only on the place occupied by different activities and social groups in the global distribution but also, for instance, on the type of financial contracts concerned. This vast variety of social hierarchies is nevertheless produced in the everyday practices of the financial industry through the application of valuation and investment procedures that are shared across companies worldwide and within a regulatory setting that although fragmented into national jurisdictions, shares many features from one jurisdiction to another. The practices of financial valuation and investment play a significant role in the production of these global hierarchies due to the regularity of their application in the financial industry at large.

I refer to the notion of political institution to highlight three points. One is that the financial industry plays a fundamental role in organizing power relations around the access to money that happen outside its confines and that partly correspond to social processes that are not related to financial methods and lines of reasoning.[41] The multiple hierarchies established by the financial industry are indeed not equal from one institutional setting to another. In the United States, the issuance of bonds and stocks constitutes, in relative terms, a major source of money for companies and a central component of intergenerational relations through the pension system. In the states of the European Union and in China, most of the funding for companies comes from bank loans, and while states are central in western Europe for intergenerational relations through a pension system, this is much less the case in China. In many other jurisdictions, stock and bonds issuance play a very marginal role. The inclusion of activities, areas, or social groups in the monetary interdependencies established by the financial industry also changes the industry itself. For instance, the regulatory transformations of the 1980s were often accompanied by the concentration of smaller companies into bigger groups, and the importance of Chinese state-owned financial companies in global relations increased with the bankruptcies of financial companies in Europe and the United States in 2008. Thus, the application of a unified body of financial methods does not result in social life becoming a copy of the ideas that organize these methods, nor can it be understood as the deployment of a single logic that could be encompassed with concepts like financialization or neoliberalism.[42] The financial industry brings these multiple power relations together by comparing them to and putting them in competition with each other, using financial methods of valuation and investment. These power relations have thereby become mutually constitutive in a global space organized by the rules of access to the money managed by the financial industry. Any power relation organized by the financial industry in a limited geographical setting must be considered in light of the other power relations to which it is connected through the activities of the financial industry.

This description uses in part the conceptualization of assemblages and multiplicity proposed by Deleuze and Guattari.[43] The authors define a multiplicity as a series of analytically autonomous elements that enter into several relations with each other. As they come together, they form an assemblage, becoming mutually constitutive but without totally losing their specificities. Their assemblage is constantly shifting as elements transform, new elements come in, and other elements leave or disappear. In that sense, following the analytical hints of Deleuze and Guattari, we can understand the financial industry as a social space where a multiplicity of power relations is assembled in what is a constantly changing and multifarious process.

The second point I want to highlight is that this multiplicity of power relations is brought together through the use of standardized methods of valuation and investment. Sassen proposes that financial institutions are an "operational field" composed not only of these methods but also of a vast series of organizations, including financial companies, academic institutions, and state regulatory agencies.[44] This reflects the fact that there is not one center where finance decides for the rest. This corresponds to the concept of multiplicity proposed by Deleuze and Guattari,[45] who view power relations in an assemblage that does not correspond to a single logic that would be outside of it but that results instead from the actual and shifting relations that compose it at any given point.[46]

Yet, as Sassen and others remark,[47] the methods of valuation and investment used in the financial industry are extremely standardized worldwide, the result of a historical process of convergence among financial regulation across jurisdictions, professional practice across companies, and financial education across academic institutions. This standardization endows with common characteristics the multiple power relations that come together in the distribution of money by the financial industry— but without rendering them homogeneous. The rules of valuation and investment thus have an institutional character,[48] as they are compulsory within the financial industry and those who attempt to access the money managed by the industry must adapt to them. Mennicken and Miller show that accounting and financial methods like those used in the financial industry establish particular relations of power that are reproduced with variations wherever these methods are applied.[49] They show these methods thereby create a specific "territory" of power relations that is proper to them, even as they are combined and transformed by their use in different settings. I propose here to consider the financial industry as a political institution by defining it as the set of organizations that apply these financial methods in order to organize a distribution of money across a wide array of power relations worldwide.

The third feature I want to highlight is that valuation and investment methods are themselves political imaginaries. As I will show in chapter 1, the textbook definition of these methods contains explicit mention of the neoclassical imagination about a world composed of markets and individual market participants whose interactions lead to a socially optimal allocation of resources. This is not a superficial discourse disconnected from the methods. On the contrary, as I will show in particular in chapter 1, this organizes the mathematical relations and the meaning of the data used in and produced with them.

Expanding Foucault's analysis of the role of moral and political categories in the constitution of expert forms of knowledge and practices of social discipline, De Goede[50] and Langley[51] have shown how the concepts of market, investment, credit, speculation, and risk have multiple and often contradictory genealogies that coalesce around moral, political, and affective meanings in particular institutional settings. Their avowed technical aspect may itself contribute to moral and political legitimizations of particular differential distributions of capacities to act, similarly to the naturalization of moral categories described by Foucault in the institutionalization of medicine as a scientific, and hence officially not moral, endeavor.[52] Like these financial imaginaries, the methods of valuation and investment used in the financial industry must be understood both as a series of standardized techniques legitimized by professional recognition and regulatory control and as moral and political imaginaries that contribute to legitimizing, within and outside the financial industry, the global hierarchies that this industry creates by the way it produces, collects, and distributes money.

Money

The political character of the financial industry, as defined here, involves the way it produces, collects, and distributes money worldwide. This raises the questions of what is meant here by money and what role financial valuation and investment play in the process of distribution. I adopt here a pragmatist approach to money that stresses the multiplicity of its uses and meanings. In this proposition, I consider the notion of value not as an analytic concept but rather as a way people using money make sense of their practice. This results in an understanding of the power relations established by financial valuation and investment in the financial industry that departs from functionalist and idealist approaches to money and value. The rest of this section is devoted to clarifying this proposition.

What I term pragmatist understandings of money are analyses that show that money both defines and is defined by the relations in which it is used, which implies that it is always transforming and multiple.[53] For instance, gifts, debts, and expenses in part define kinship and friendship;[54] monetary policy contributes to defining and legitimizing a polity, its citizens, and social hierarchies among them;[55] conflicts around indemnities imposed by the state on polluters shape conceptions of nature;[56] money rituals define the attributes of gods;[57] and consumption practices[58] and budgetary disciplines[59] can establish the standards of religious morality. Guyer has shown how different meanings and uses of money can be combined in multiple ways, with conflicts, conversions, and hybrid or new meanings generated in the process.[60] She considers these sets of practices and meanings a multiplicity of "repertoires" constituting "ecologies" navigated differently by different actors in "performances" that are often marked by power relations.[61] The ranking of people, objects, and actions within a single order of monetary numbers must be understood as the combination, both unstable and ongoing, of multiple definitions and hierarchies, so that price is an assemblage that contributes to stabilizing the social hierarchies themselves.[62] This corresponds to more general observations about relations of credit and debt. They can be observed in relations between friends, between states and financial companies, between worshippers and gods, and between generations. These relations can become interdependent in shifting power relations, combining multiple notions of time, space, and the qualification of participants in the exchange.[63]

The concept of multiplicity evoked here is useful for analyzing monetary practices even in cases where powerful institutions extend their monetary rules violently. Anthropologists have shown that the imposition of monetary rules by colonial institutions through war and conquest did not result in the homogenization of monetary practices. On the contrary, new forms of monetary relations proliferated, with new entities defined as money and new rules established for calculation and exchange.[64]

These approaches to money are very useful for analyzing the political role of the financial industry as I have defined it. They allow us to consider how the multiple practices involving money outside the financial industry are rendered interdependent and mutually constitutive by the financial industry—but without being integrated into a single logic that would erase their specificities. This is important because, as we saw, the global distribution of money by the financial industry results from a complex history of colonial expansion, world wars, the Cold War, and its aftermath, combining multiple forms of hierarchy in terms of race, class, gender, religion, nationality, and ideology, among other factors. We need to understand how these multiple hierarchies, when they become interdependent through the practices of the financial industry, are reproduced and transformed but do not dissolve under a single logic.

This contrasts with functionalist and idealist approaches to money that give it a single meaning for all the social relations where it is used. Marxist and liberal approaches to money share the view that it is a function of the needs of market exchanges. While liberal thinkers view these exchanges as leading to a socially optimal allocation of resources, in Marxist approaches money is considered a veil that hides and renders possible exploitative relations of production.[65] Theories combining Marxism and psychoanalysis understand these confrontations in exchange and exploitation as the result of unconscious drives, of which monetary transactions are a realization.[66] In all these cases, money is considered a by-product of social confrontations that correspond to a single logic, be it market exchange, capitalist relations of production, or the realization of unconscious drives.

In different ways, Mauss and Simmel consider money the expression and realization of a universal moral ideal that is constitutive of society and humanity in general. Both highlight that money is fundamental in the creation of hierarchical social identities using multiple moral, political, and religious meanings. But for these authors, this multiplicity corresponds to the realization of a single ideal process. For Simmel, it is the realization of freedom in a dialectic between individual action and social interdependence, for which money provides the founding— most abstract and hence most universal—symbol.[67] For Mauss, exchange relations, in all their geographical and historical variety, are founded on a "morality" that is "eternal" and that obliges every person to give, receive, and give back, a hierarchical reciprocity that is differently compulsory for all members of society.[68] For both Mauss and Simmel, monetary relations, as they extend the boundaries of any one group, contribute to ever-growing interdependent groups that do not necessarily correspond to other forms of imagined communities, such as nations, and that can extend to humanity as a whole, unified by a single moral foundation.[69]

Functionalist and idealist approaches are useful for studying some crucial power relations and imaginaries observable in price negotiations, labor relations, and the establishment of imagined communities through money.[70] But because they limit the analysis to those specific logics, they tend to exclude each other, and they are not helpful in analyzing other forms of social hierarchy that may also be at play. They miss thereby the ways in which multiple power relations can intersect and be mutually constitutive.[71] Without giving up some of the important insights of these approaches, the pragmatist approach I propose here attempts to stay attentive to the multiplicity of social hierarchies produced by the financial industry through the application of standardized procedures worldwide.

Value

The notion of financial value plays a crucial role in the social processes studied in this book. In line with the pragmatist approach to money just described, I propose to analyze how the meaning of financial value varies in different practices, even within the institutional setting of the financial industry. Following Guyer's conceptualization, we can view the definitions of financial value as part of the multiple repertoires of money that are mobilized, combined, and reshaped in practice.[72] As I will show, in the practices of valuation and investment that I could observe through fieldwork, the word "value" is used in multiple ways that are sometimes contradictory and disconnected and that can be combined. There are several formal definitions of financial value that assert differently how it could be accurate, true, or fair. They all need to be understood as part of the way in which employees make sense of their everyday practices and social relations. As part of the observable practice, the definition of value can therefore not be subsumed under a single logic.[73]

In order to understand the way in which this approach to the word *value* allows us to analyze the political role of finance, it is useful to see how it contrasts with approaches in anthropology and sociology that view value as an analytic concept. In approaches that refer more or less explicitly to classical economic theory and its reinterpretation by Marx, value refers to labor and production. In the Marxist frame, the representation of value with money or financial contracts is considered a fiction, often opposed to the idea of a "real economy" related to production.[74] A different approach, close to neo-Kantian idealism, considers values, in the plural, as moral narratives that organize the meaning of action, society, and life in general. In the Weberian version, these values constitute each other through their opposition, so that the subject that carries them is shaped by their tensions.[75] Other approaches consider that these values constitute some form of structure or whole that can actually encompass dynamic contradictions.[76] Within this approach, some authors consider that the definition of value based on the sole notion of labor is totally distinct from the idealist definition of moral values, in the plural, and even opposed to it.[77] But other authors combine the Marxist and idealist approaches, thus extending the Marxian framework to highlight the importance of moral values in the articulation of relations of production and speaking of a "moral economy."[78]

Still others consider that the constitution of labor as a distinct social category, although central to what is considered a global system of capitalism, can be analyzed only as a particular activity among others, which have other values.[79] Finally, some authors view the concept of labor as the sole source of value as a capitalist constraint on the much broader activity of giving meaning to life in general, to which the concept of value would correspond more profoundly.[80]

The pragmatist approach I propose here allows us to avoid two problems that come with using value as an analytic concept. First, using value as an analytic category implies establishing a definition of it that must constantly be differentiated from the multiple and labile ways in which the word is used by the people I observed in fieldwork—with the risk of confusing them all. Second, and more importantly, the approaches that use value as an analytic category tend to focus on the instances where it seems to be at stake. This creates a particular hierarchy in the practices that matter for the social sciences. In analyses where production or labor, however defined, is considered the activity where true value lies, other social activities may be analyzed solely as addenda, or even polluters, of the former. In studies that rank practices according to their proximity to the realization of a particular moral or ideal standard, the activities that are less concerned with that value are deemed less worthy of analysis. Finally, Weber, for instance, considered the only practices worth studying were those that seemed to attempt to realize values.[81] It was not a specific value that was more important to him but rather values in general, so that practices that did not seem concerned with the realization of values were less worthy of research.

Using the concept of value as an analytic tool to observe practice implies simplifying the multiple power relations and social hierarchies into the ones that fit that analytic hierarchy, which is thus presupposed implicitly or explicitly. Instead, looking at how financial professionals use the word *value* when they evaluate financial assets in order to orient money, we can create a critical distance with their imaginaries, allowing us to analyze the way in which they produce, collect, and distribute money worldwide without subsuming the practices of the financial industry into a single logic.

In the pragmatist approach explored, for instance, by William James, the concept of meaning itself, as part of practice, does not presuppose that all practice makes clear sense for the people we observe. Meaning itself is fluid, open to change and creativity, and often vague, something that will be hinted at in this book by using the concept of imaginary.[82] Using the concept of meaning to address how people use the word *value* in the financial industry allows us to see how its meanings can remain vague, multiple, and labile. I will therefore also not draw an analytic distinction between value and other words associated to it (worth, values, valuation, evaluation, valorization, etc.), since this would hide the much broader multiplicity of meanings these words have for the people I observed.

FIELDWORK AND THE ARGUMENT OF THE BOOK

This book is based on fieldwork conducted during three periods of participant observation of four to five months each. The first was in 2002 at a brokerage firm, Brokers Inc., in New York; the second was in 2003 with a team of consultants in hedge funds, Hedge Consulting, in Paris;[83] and the third was in 2004 at a global investment management company, Acme, also in Paris.[84] I did about one hundred interviews with professionals in the financial industry, some working in the companies where I was an observer. This research was complemented by my obtaining certification as a financial analyst in 2010 and doing further fieldwork as a finance teacher in business schools in Paris and Shanghai between 2008 and 2014[85] and with professionals working in cross-border investment in Shanghai since 2010.[86] To preserve the anonymity of the people I observed, we agreed that their names and those of their companies would be changed except when I was able to refer to a few major financial companies in generic examples without compromising anonymity.

The results of fieldwork are always partly the product of random encounters, opportunities that arise and are sometimes missed. This book is mainly based on observations made at Brokers Inc. and at Acme. The work of some employees of Acme was almost identical to that of the employees of most of Brokers Inc.'s clients. This allows us to explore regularities in the practice of valuation and investment among different professions and across jurisdictions. My fieldwork at Hedge Consulting allowed me to observe activities that were considered a niche in the financial industry. These activities were also present at Acme and were part of the operations of some of Brokers Inc.'s clients. Their official niche character was an interesting entry point to analyzing how employees defined, by opposition, what they considered the mainstream.

The main activities of Brokers Inc. were selling financial valuation of listed companies to pension and mutual funds based in the United States that invested their clients' money in companies listed on stock exchanges based in Europe. The definition of the value of listed companies was the main focus of the interactions between Brokers Inc.'s employees and their customers, and around this revolved most procedures applied in the company. Acme was a global investment management company, with nearly two thousand employees in its Paris offices. Its employees invested around €300 billion in financial assets around the world on behalf of the company's clients. My observations were carried out while I was working as an assistant in financial analysis on a team investing money in credit derivatives. I was able to talk to many Acme employees responsible for valuing and investing in most financial assets around the world. Like Brokers Inc., the company was in no way exceptional, so it can be used to analyze the practices of valuation and investment in the financial industry at large.

In what follows, I will describe some of the rules of practice through which employees like Frédéric determined a financial value for the activities of listed companies. I will organize the analysis by focusing on the two main sources of the definition of value presupposed in professional procedures: the figure of an individual and independent investor and the efficient markets.[87] And I will integrate into this analysis other imaginaries that are at play in valuation—probabilities and state sovereignty, for instance. But I focus on investors and markets because of their fundamental role in the political justification of the distributive role of the financial industry, both within and outside the industry.

The focus on everyday practices as the site of relations of power allows us to understand the constitution of regularities through interaction in particular settings that change over time. Through everyday repetition, professional activities come to have very stable meanings and rules for those who carry them out, even when observation shows their contradictory and labile character. This implies that we need to pay attention to both the reproductive and the transformative potentials of repetition, to the margins, fragments, and potential new connections allowed by the multiplicity of rules.[88] The global distributive effects of the financial industry are partly the product of the activities carried out by its employees. These employees most often do not address these practices as primarily a political endeavor. When they do, it is often in a diffuse way, one that may crystallize in particular moments but that also combines these meanings with others related to diverse issues that are technical, organizational, or related to employees' personal trajectories, for instance. Yet, as I will show, moral and political meanings are fundamental for the stability of the rules of practice, even when they are erased in the name of technique.

The procedures and methods of calculation I observed were multiple, divergent, and contradictory, and they were applied by employees in complex relations, including ones of hierarchy, competition, and cooperation. However, in all cases, they articulated different combinations of the concepts of investor, market, and value. Employees had to consider that they were carrying out valuation from the point of view of an independent investor. This implied mobilizing the idea that the enunciation of value is the expression of a personal opinion. At the same time, employees had to consider that the prices they faced and that they helped to determine were the result of efficient markets. These concepts were used in various and often contradictory ways, sometimes in the same operation or within the same team or company, but always according to standardized rules. At the same time, employees showed various emotional and moral attachments to them. But in all cases, employees could consider that they had put this multiplicity into practice correctly if they benefited from the recognition of peers in this professional space, kept their jobs and continued to receive remuneration in the form of salaries and bonuses. And employees used the moral and political meanings of the concepts when they needed to justify their practices in the conflicts and contradictions that arose between methods, between people, and between companies in the changing global social space of the financial industry.

Chapter 1 introduces the methods of financial valuation and investment and their place in the organization of Brokers Inc. It shows that there are different definitions of financial value used by different professions, organized in the relations between employees and between companies. It studies in depth the main tensions in the methods of financial valuation, focusing on the concepts of investor, market, state, and risk and on three definitions of value: fundamental, relative, and speculative. It shows how different definitions and combinations of these concepts assert the existence of a true value in multiple and contradictory ways. This allows us to see the moral and political character of the financial imaginaries of value, investors, and market efficiency and the main fragmentations and contradictions that organize the practices described in the following chapters. The chapter shows how this multiplicity is assembled in valuation practices that although localized in the offices of the financial industry, are part of a global space.

Chapter 2 illustrates how different employees mobilize multiple and contradictory methods of financial valuation while sharing the understanding that the value of an asset must be the product of the individual investor's personal opinion. It shows how this personal opinion is not embodied in a single person but is disseminated in different tasks and professional specializations. The idea of an investor that determines value is thus reproduced in the relations among traders, fund managers, salespeople, and financial analysts. The figure of the investor is an effect of the application of standardized procedures in a bureaucratic commercial network. But employees are required to embody this figure with reference to ideas of sincerity, passion, and conviction that connect directly with the moral and political imaginaries of this figure present in financial methods and in financial regulation. The chapter shows how the practice of the figure of the investor connects with employees' personal trajectories and non-professional social identities as they make sense of their professional life.

Chapter 3 examines how, at the same time, financial valuation is conducted by presupposing a context where market efficiency is realized or at least is possible. It further analyzes the methods of financial valuation, showing how they all integrate this concept of market efficiency in different ways and how employees use that concept to understand the financial industry as the social space where it is realized. At the time of my observations, this occurred within a transformation of valuation and investment methods. The increasing use of market indexes, based on the idea that markets are efficient, meant a decreasing importance for the tasks of fund managers, financial analysts, and salespeople. Paradoxically, traders, who seemed the most distant from the concept of market efficiency, gained preeminence. Employees problematized these tensions with the imaginaries linking the figure of the investor, efficient markets, and value present in financial methods.

Chapter 4 brings together the findings of the previous chapters, showing how financial valuation and investment practices presuppose multiple and partly contradictory epistemologies and ontologies. This conflicts with the central idea mobilized by employees, financial regulation, and financial economics that financial assets have a true value that could be reflected in prices. The chapter illustrates how this notion of financial value that could have a truth reflected in prices rests instead on the political and moral imaginaries about independent investors meeting in efficient markets that contribute to a socially optimal allocation of resources worldwide. It examines how financial regulation and financial professionals define the notion of financial crisis within the limits of these imaginaries, which precludes a broader discussion about the role of the financial industry in the production of global hierarchies. It finds that the idea that there is such a thing as financial value is itself predicated on the idea that prices reflect its truth. The chapter concludes with a discussion of the place of the concepts of investor, market, and value in the financial industry. It proposes that we avoid using these three concepts as analytic categories and instead consider the financial industry a political institution, in line with the propositions set out in this introduction.

The conclusion summarizes the findings of the book. It shows how financial regulation and financial professionals, among other actors, framed the events of 2007–2008 as a financial crisis within the limits of the imaginaries described here. It stresses the usefulness of looking at distributive effects when observing everyday practices in the financial industry in order to highlight their role in the production of global hierarchies.

1

THE ORGANIZATIONAL SPACE
OF FINANCIAL VALUE

EVERYDAY practices in the financial industry's global space of operations are organized by the application of standardized procedures of valuation and investment. Observing the application of these procedures in the offices of two particular companies—Brokers Inc. in New York and Acme in Paris—allows us to study some of the fundamental rules of the global distribution of money established by the financial industry. In order to do this, it is important to analyze the details of these procedures and the limited variety of meanings they can have for employees. It is also crucial to study how this application occurs in an organizational setting with specific rules concerning the relations between employees, between employees and companies, and between companies. These relations are partly formalized in contracts and regulations. They are also subject to rules about how to obtain profits, salaries, and bonuses. This chapter presents the main organizational rules of everyday practice that the employees of Brokers Inc. and Acme used to define the value of listed stocks. The following chapters will then focus, within these rules, on the imaginaries of investors and efficient markets.

Arjaliès et al. provide a very detailed analysis of the contractual interlocking of companies within the financial industry.[1]

The circulation of money, from the legal owner of the money to the seller of a stock listed on a stock exchange, can involve a myriad of companies with tasks that can be different but also overlapping. Companies and employees are bound by a set of contractual relations that institutionalize procedures of valuation and investment, which are defined as the means by which to realize the money owner's interest. Arjaliès et al. show that these financial companies cannot change their investment methods even when one of their clients requests it. This is because each company has contracts with many others and any change would implicate all of them, but there is no overarching authority to do allow such change. At the global level, companies are bound by myriads of contracts across the fragmented space of state regulations. Within this organizational space, valuation and investment procedures appear to employees as fundamental requirements of their everyday practice.

Like those in other bureaucracies, employees in the financial industry may not totally understand the relation between their practices and those of companies in the rest of the industry to which they are connected.[2] Also, the ways in which employees relate to the money they contribute to distribute worldwide are multiple and often vague or ambiguous.[3] More generally, employees may consider their practices technical operations that can be repeated without concern for the distributive effects beyond the official boundaries of their organization. Part of the meaning of these practices for employees comes from peer recognition in everyday interactions. Employees may consider there is ethical worth in applying professional rules correctly.[4] They may have a wide array of emotional relations to their work, ranging from rejection to adherence and including many forms of indifference.[5] In all these cases, the way they implement valuation and investment procedures connects with their nonprofessional lives and social identities, with imaginaries of age,[6] class,[7] race,[8] nationality,[9] and gender,[10] among others.

Employees often consider valuation and investment methods important more for the ways they enable them to organize their relations of cooperation, hierarchy, and competition in the search for higher salaries, bonuses, and prestige than for their global distributive effects.[11] But the political imaginaries of investor, market, and value play fundamental roles in the stabilization of the rules of valuation and investment. Miller and Rose propose to look at how financial methods presuppose specific ontologies and epistemologies that relate to particular definitions of agency, domains of action, interests, and aims.[12] As they become self-evident in everyday practices, these financial methods contribute to establishing what is possible and what is not. The main concepts used in financial valuation and investment, like those of investor, efficient market, and financial value, are connected to specific genealogies of political thinking about the legitimate way to distribute resources in society.[13] As we will see, these methods combine multiple epistemological and ontological presuppositions. These presuppositions can be disconnected or even contradictory, giving different definitions of investors, efficient markets, and financial value. Through this variety, these concepts, and the political relations they assert, organize the possibilities and limits of the meanings of the distribution of money by the financial industry. It is therefore important to analyze the role of these concepts in the construction of mathematical formulas, in the definition of what counts as information, and in the lines of reasoning that organize how valuation and investment methods are used.

As is the case with the practices of power distributed in organizations beyond the state analyzed by Miller and Rose, it is through repetition in everyday practices that the political imaginaries of financial valuation are reproduced worldwide, connecting with multiple power relations outside the financial industry that may, in turn, transform them.[14] In this process, they are open to labile uses, contradictions, fragmented narratives, and formalization, but they are also marked by limits produced in everyday interactions that contribute to the reproduction of these rules in subsequent actions. How these standards are applied varies depending on the social relations involved. They have multiple meanings that are mobilized by employees and companies in their conflicts and negotiations. Miller and O'Leary speak of "mediating instruments" when referring to the way in which accounting and financial procedures are shared by multiple actors, who stabilize them through their use in negotiations and conflicts.[15] This process of stabilization establishes the "territory" of these mathematical formulas, modes of reasoning, and methods of calculation.[16] Studying the everyday practices of valuation and investment at Brokers Inc. and Acme allows us to see some examples of these processes.

Employees like those of Brokers Inc. make sense of these practices combining meanings that relate to the concepts and formulas they use, to personal trajectories, to organizational issues within and between companies, to regulatory issues, and to monetary relations across the world.[17] For employees, the activity of valuation has the self-evident character of standardized everyday practice, consisting, in particular, of applying procedures, with different understandings depending on the persons involved but within the limits of the salaried relationship. It is through this daily regularity that practices contribute to the constitution of the global space of financial valuation and investment.

In this chapter, I first present the main tasks and professions involved in financial valuation and investment at Brokers Inc. and Acme in order to highlight how they apply the same valuation methods differently. I then analyze these methods in order to show their political and moral meanings. I next situate the everyday practices of employees like those of Brokers Inc. within the global monetary relations to the production of which they contribute. As I show, financial methods presuppose that investors meeting in markets make these markets efficient if they apply the methods themselves, thereby leading to a socially optimal allocation of resources. In the following chapters, I will then focus on how employees mobilize the technical, moral, and political meanings of the concepts of investor and market efficiency to organize valuation and investment.

A COMMERCIAL AND SALARIED ACTIVITY

Today, financial valuation and the purchase and sale of financial contracts like stocks, bonds, and derivatives occur primarily within the financial industry. In this social space, financial valuation is carried out by employees who work for a salary and sometimes a bonus. And they do so within a series of commercial relations that links companies across multiple regulatory frames in a global space of operations. The way in which value is defined depends in large part on the place that valuation occupies in the activities of employees and companies. This section describes the professions and companies that carry out stock valuation, taking the examples of Brokers Inc. and Acme.

Companies like Brokers Inc. and Acme were established in the last quarter of the twentieth century as the result of the specialization of tasks and the consolidation of companies operating globally. From at least the nineteenth century until the end of the 1980s, in France, the United States, and many other jurisdictions, access to transactions on stock exchanges was strictly limited to an oligopoly of stockbrokers. They tended to combine the activities of buying and selling stocks and giving investment advice to their clients, the owners of the money, who were often wealthy families or businesses. This concentration was often based on the claim that brokers had better information than their clients about these stocks and the companies that issued them.

In the 1980s, in most jurisdictions of Europe and in the United States, regulatory transformations dismantled the oligopoly of brokerage houses. The specialization of professional tasks and commercial relations increased together with the amounts of money invested in stocks, bonds, and derivatives. Bigger companies, like banks and investment funds, bought the brokerage companies and established new departments or subsidiaries specializing in investment banking. New kinds of companies were created, dedicated to trading, investment management for third parties, financial valuation, and investment advice. Today, the biggest companies can sell all these services. The roles previously played by stockbrokers, which combined executing transactions and providing investment advice, were thus disseminated and transformed into a new organizational configuration.[18]

This new organization of the financial industry was designated as the rise of institutional investors, an expression signaling the bureaucratic character of these companies. It is during this process—in the 1980s, in particular—that valuation and investment in listed stocks became officially focused on the maximization of shareholder value. Listed companies were to be restructured and their management oriented toward increasing the returns for shareholders, measured in terms of increased dividends and share prices.[19] But this insistence on shareholder value was not isolated. Listed stocks are allocated less than half of the total money managed by the financial industry. The practices concerning them have been historically fundamental in shaping the financial industry—and continue to be so. But they must be situated within the broader organizational features of the financial industry that go beyond this particular type of asset.

Most of the money invested by the financial industry belongs legally to the middle classes of the rich areas of the world, to corporations, and to public institutions. The link between the legal owners of the money and the asset purchased with it is established by several components of what Arjaliès et al. call a "chain."[20] Different companies may be in charge of legally holding the money and the assets, determining the investment strategy, valuing the assets to assist investment, and providing legal and technical consultancy services, among other roles. These commercial relations are legally described as creating a principal-agent relation, where service providers have the sole duty to represent the interests of their clients. Fees and bonuses are thus established in a way that is supposed to make these interests correspond. Yet, in fact, the owners of this money often have little say in how their money is invested—and even less technical knowledge about how what are called their "interests" are defined by the financial industry.[21] Money owners have delegated the management of their money to employees of the financial industry, who then exchange it between themselves. In jurisdictions where the legal figure of the trustee is used, like in the United States, money owners are actually prevented from interfering with those to whom they have entrusted their money, who are supposed to know the interests of their clients better than the clients themselves do.[22] The activities of valuation and investment were redefined in this process. Within the regulatory frame referring to the theory of market efficiency, investment funds are expected to seek information about the assets in which they will invest their clients' money. This information must come from multiple sources in order to avoid biases or too narrow a focus. And it is expected that valuation will be carried out with the sole aim of maximizing the returns that could be obtained by the investment.

Brokers Inc. developed within this historical process. Its parent company, Brokers SA, based in Paris, started in the 1990s with a few dozen employees selling financial valuation of companies listed in France to investment management companies. The company specialized in small caps, or "small capitalizations," companies whose stock capitalization is below $2 billion.[23] These companies' stocks constitute a relatively small fraction of all financial assets. The amounts of money invested in them are much smaller than those invested in mid caps and big caps. Within the financial industry, the sale of information in which Brokers SA specialized was therefore considered a niche activity. When Brokers Inc., the company's U.S. subsidiary, was established in New York in the late 1990s, an increasing number of investment funds based in the United States were using their clients' money to buy assets in Europe, including small caps.

Employees of Brokers Inc. remarked that, due to the company's size and activities, its place in the financial industry differed from that of large brokerage firms. Financial valuation was officially the company's only commercial activity. In contrast, large companies like Goldman Sachs offer different financial services to their clients alongside financial analysis. These activities include, for instance, legal and technical services for large transactions such as mergers, acquisitions, and stock issuance and may constitute a significant part of the company's revenue, often exceeding the revenue coming from the sale of financial analysis. During a public offering of stocks, the broker is paid a fee calculated as a percentage of the total revenue collected in the sale of shares. This raises the suspicion that the broker will publish a positive financial valuation of these stocks in order to boost their purchase and collect higher fees. This would not be considered a truly independent valuation, which should focus on maximizing the value for investors whose interest the broker is supposed to represent.[24] Like many other small brokerage companies, Brokers Inc. sold only financial valuation, and this characteristic was used to market it as the product of a sincere search for true value.

Large brokerage firms often specialize in the valuation of large listed companies, the big caps. Since their capitalization is bigger, more transactions can be carried out with their stocks than with those of small caps. This means that their valuation can be sold to a larger number of customers. Conducting a detailed review is also considered relatively more complex for these companies than for small caps. Big caps are often multinationals with numerous activities and accounting and operating systems in different juridical frames. The analysis may require resources that only large brokerage companies can afford, such as a large number of analysts or access to expensive databases. Big brokers can often leave aside small caps, which attract a relatively small number of customers. Small caps are then often said to be "underanalyzed." This expression, used in the financial industry with reference to the theoretical frame of market efficiency, indicates that valuation for a company is not done thoroughly enough for its price to represent its value adequately. This line of reasoning was used to establish the professional legitimacy of companies like Brokers Inc. Investing in small caps is usually the task of specialized fund managers. Because of their size, they generally receive only a small part of the money invested by large investment management companies. At Acme SA, for example, a team of eight fund managers and six financial analysts managed €11 billion invested in big caps. In contrast, a team of two managers and three analysts managed €1 billion invested in European small caps.

André, the CEO of Brokers Inc., explained to me in an interview that in the late 1990s, Brokers SA's managers decided to change their commercial strategy. They decided to expand their valuation activities to big caps in order to profit from the increased flow of money going into stocks—in particular, due to the rising prices of the stocks of internet-related companies. As more funds from the United States were invested on European stock exchanges, the aim was to become "the French Goldman Sachs." André explained that he had opposed this move, bringing him into a conflict with the parent company's management. He expressed satisfaction that the "explosion of the internet bubble" in early 2000 had not affected the subsidiary that he managed, where all staff kept their jobs; in contrast, Brokers SA experienced massive layoffs.

Brokers Inc.'s clients were investment management companies based in the United States that purchased information about companies listed in Europe.[25] These clients could have very different official aims. Most of them were investment management companies that directly or indirectly invested the money collected by pension and mutual funds. According to the employees of Brokers Inc., hedge funds were becoming increasingly important as clients, in line with their growth at the end of the 1990s. Hedge funds sometimes worked for other investment funds, for pension and mutual funds, or for corporations and wealthy individuals. André showed me a list of more than two hundred clients with which Brokers Inc. had commercial relations. There was great variation in terms of the amounts managed by these clients and the regularity with which they interacted with Brokers Inc. But for all of them, fund management tasks were established in the clauses of the contracts linking the companies that employed the fund managers to the legal providers of funds. These clauses specified the financial assets in which the money would be invested, the methods of investment, and the temporalities of expected returns. And all these contracts were designed to comply with financial regulations.

Among other legal requirements, investment management companies must diversify their sources of information. The official reason for this is to avoid the possible biases, involuntary or not, of any individual analyst. Large investment management companies usually have in-house financial analysts, but their number is frequently considered too small to enable them to "cover" (the term used by the professionals involved) properly all the assets purchased with the clients' money. Their task is more often to control the information produced by other analysts, such as those of Brokers Inc. A client's commercial relation with Brokers Inc. was therefore explicitly established in the contractual definition of the procedures for fund management. This commercial relation had different implications for the different procedures of valuation performed by the company's traders, analysts, and salespeople.

The financial analysts at Brokers SA in Paris regularly produced documents expressing their opinions about the value of stocks listed in Europe—in particular, on Euronext. Salespeople in New York, like Frédéric, then used this analysis to sell stock valuation to clients based in the United States. Financial analysts usually specialize in a few listed companies, and all the other employees consider them the best experts on the firms they analyze. They very often sign their own name to the documents they produce. Yet, even when he is thus identified, the analyst only rarely has a direct relation with the customers—i.e., with the fund managers buying the valuation sold by the brokerage house. That relation is the specific task of salespeople like Frédéric, who sought to establish personal long-term commercial relations with each fund manager. The valuation provided in the exchange between the salesperson and the fund manager often remains close to the analysis proposed by the financial analyst. But in that exchange, the salesperson transforms the analyst's valuation and sometimes even contradicts it, adding different information or ideas. At Brokers Inc., traders executed buy or sell orders for clients, and their expertise was supposed to lie in their knowledge about short-term price movements.[26] They were often expected to use this knowledge to buy at the lowest price and sell at the highest. But their expertise could also be required for other tasks set out in the contractual requirements that bind fund managers to the clients who entrust them with their money. For instance, some transactions had to be carried out at the price listed at a predetermined hour of the day or in such a way that the price would come close to the daily average.

According to the official narrative produced by the managers of Brokers Inc., who were also partners in the company, the company's revenues, and thus the salaries and bonuses it paid, came from the sale of financial analysis. This line of reasoning articulated a hierarchy among salespeople, analysts, and traders, reflected in the different forms of valuation they produced and their significantly different salaries, bonuses, and prestige—to which money was only partly linked. Nevertheless, as with other such brokerage companies, investment management companies paid Brokers Inc. only through the activity of its traders.[27]

Usually, the fund manager is the one who decides whether to buy or sell a certain amount of shares, but he does not complete the transaction himself. Instead, he gives an order to buy or sell to the trading desk of his company, and the traders carry out the transaction through their broker. Fund managers, called the "buy side," ask their traders to make purchases and sales via their broker's traders, called the "sell side." If, for example, John, a fund manager working at Citibank, wanted to make a stock purchase that would pay for the services of Frédéric at Brokers Inc., he would give the order to his trading desk to buy a certain amount of shares through Luke, Brokers Inc.'s trader, who worked "on John's account" in tandem with Frédéric, Broker Inc.'s salesperson. This transaction would involve the payment of a fee to the broker, calculated as a fraction of the amount of money used in the purchase or sale. Typically, at Brokers Inc., the fee was 25 basis points.[28] Thus, if Luke, Brokers Inc.'s trader, bought $1 million worth of stock of the listed company Dupré for the account of John at Citibank, Citibank paid Brokers Inc. a fee of $2,500. This fee constituted the only remuneration received by Brokers Inc. for the work its employees did with John. This money paid for the activities of Frédéric, Luke, the analysts whose valuation Frédéric used, and the employees responsible for administrative tasks, usually called the "back office" in the financial industry.

Employees in the back office carry out tasks that are, of course, essential for the steady continuity of valuation activities. In order to do so, they do not need to have any knowledge of valuation methods. They are in charge of, among other things, controlling the legal and accounting registration of traders' transactions. They occupy a marginal position in terms of knowledge and revenue. As has been reported for many other workplaces, at Brokers Inc., this marginal position was highly correlated with gender and racial identities. The four back-office employees were female, whereas there were only two women among the seven salespeople and none among the traders and analysts. And while all salespeople, traders, and analysts were identified as White, in the back office two people were identified as Asian American and one as Latina.[29] The administrative secretary and the trainee in charge of the maintenance of computer equipment had even more marginal positions in relation to valuation and revenue.

The management of Brokers Inc. at the time of my observations consisted of three partners, or associates. These managers, two salespeople and a trader, launched the subsidiary in New York. They were shareholders of the company and had the highest income. In addition, a chief financial officer, who specialized in legal issues, was in charge of supervising the back office and ensuring internal procedures conformed to state regulations.

"Front-office" employees and managers differed in terms of national identities—in particular, in terms of French and American nationalities. The three partners of the company had come to the United States from France, and they established the subsidiary based on previous professional connections with financial companies based in France. They were identified as French, as were some of the other front-office employees. The French language was widely used in the company, and most front-office employees could use it, even if it was a second language for some of them. This reinforced the hierarchical distinction with back-office employees, who did not speak French. As much as I could observe, nationality and language were not actively used to create a specific hierarchy among front-office employees. But language was considered a marker of the company—not only because it had been created and was directed by three people of French nationality but also, more explicitly, because it focused on valuing companies listed on Euronext, a large share of which was French-based companies.

The commercial and labor contracts organized tensions that were explicit in the relations among fund managers, salespeople, and traders at Brokers Inc. Each fund manager was "covered" by one salesperson and one trader. The personal and professional relationship between managers and salespeople could extend beyond the duration of their employment within any one company. Sometimes it also had an important emotional aspect. However, according to the rules binding the companies, throughout the relationship the fund manager alone had the power to decide the amounts and the regularity of the fees paid to Brokers Inc. Salespeople and traders worked in tandem for each personal client. The fees paid by the fund manager officially remunerated the salesperson but were received only through the transactions made by the trader. And André, the CEO of Brokers Inc., had the legal right to decide unilaterally and without any written rule the bonus received by each employee at the end of the year. As one of the three partners and the salesperson whose customers paid the highest amount of fees, he also decided the amount of his own bonus.

At Brokers Inc., salespeople had the highest bonuses. This was supposed to reflect the fact that the company's brand was based on the quality of financial analysis, and employees remarked that it also had to do with the fact that the subsidiary had been established by two salespeople and one trader. At the time of my observations, both in the United States and in France, the salary of a midcareer fund manager, usually in his early thirties and with about $700 million under management, could reach $60,000 a year, with a yearly bonus of $10,000 to $20,000. These amounts depended to a large extent on the amount of funds under management. The official line of reasoning was that the increase of funds under management reflected the clients' satisfaction with the high returns produced by the fund manager's investment decisions. The income of fund managers was comparable to that of sell-side and buy-side financial analysts.[30] These amounts contrasted with those paid to Brokers Inc. front-office employees. Including salary and bonus, the yearly income of Céline, a salesperson in her midthirties, was about $300,000, and that of Thomas, a thirty-year-old trader, was about $200,000, an amount similar to that earned by Frédéric.

At the time of my observations, the hierarchies among professions were shifting with transformations in valuation and investment methods. Trading was gaining importance as a separate service provided by brokers to investment management companies. A growing part of the fees was decided not by the fund manager in order to remunerate the salesperson but rather by the management of the buy-side trading desk in order to pay for the work of the sell-side traders. In companies like Brokers Inc., this was accompanied by conflicts around the distribution of the revenue paid by customers. Front-office employees had forms of expertise about financial value that were at the same time competing and interdependent. The size of their remuneration was considered a confirmation of their contribution to Brokers Inc.'s revenue. The conflicts around revenue were at the same time conflicts about the relative legitimacy of the different ways to define financial value.

The definition of the value of financial assets, such as listed stocks, is impacted by the rules and procedures carried out by employees who have relations of competition, cooperation, and hierarchy. This applies to the relations among analysts, salespeople, and traders inside companies like Brokers Inc. and the relations between these employees and their customers, the fund managers and buy-side financial analysts and traders. In all these cases, the employees I observed asserted that the truth about the value of listed stocks could only be the product of their professional practice, with its specific forms of expertise. A fundamental part of this expertise was defined by knowledge of standardized methods of valuation and investment, to which I turn in the next section.

CONCEPTS OF FINANCIAL VALUATION

This section presents the methods of financial valuation and investment used by employees like those of Brokers Inc. and Acme. It focuses on the definitions of shareholder value, but the main features of valuation and investment are the same for all types of assets. These methods are systematically defined with a series of concepts that I propose to address critically in this text:

they are considered as the means by which individual "investors" seek to maximize "returns" and minimize "risks" as they exchange in "markets" problematized in terms of their "efficiency." In this process, social activities that become objects of investment are turned into "assets,"[31] and market prices are supposed to reflect their "true value." In financial methods, these concepts have multiple definitions that can sometimes be contradictory. These definitions, and the relations among them, have been established in a historical process of circulation of people and ideas among the financial industry, state regulatory bodies, and academic circles. Like many bodies of theory, they contain contradictions and a multiplicity of official interpretations and controversies. I refer to this corpus as a financial theory, but this does not presuppose any specific logical consistency. I use the term for two main reasons. As we will see, these methods are presented together as the standard rules of practice that financial professionals must follow. Also, as I show in this section, although these methods refer to various epistemologies and ontologies, they all maintain the centrality of a political narrative in which the figure of the investor and the institution of efficient markets are the source of the definition of value and hence of a socially optimal allocation of resources. Value is thereby defined as something that exists and that can be represented in a price—as long as financial theory itself is used to assess it. This, in turn, gives financial value a fundamental political legitimacy as the fair description of society's distributive priorities—thereby legitimizing financial theory as the technical tool to reveal it.

The political and moral meanings of these methods cannot be disentangled from their mathematical formulation. In financial methods, mathematical relations between numbers and concepts establish theoretical relations between social activities and actors. Vollmer remarks that mathematical functions and numbers can be connected across social settings by mathematical relations but that they are also constantly connected to moral and political imaginaries.[32] This is not because, as Beckert and Bronk suggest, financial imagination concerns that which is uncertain and cannot be grasped by mathematical reasoning.[33] Rather, it is because, as Guyer et al. highlight, numbers and mathematical relations themselves have meanings that can be moral, political, and religious.[34] These meanings can remain stable over time and organize the use of mathematical relations as they circulate in different social settings.[35] For instance, Maurer shows how the idea of an infinitely stable world, presupposed in probabilities, corresponds to a religious ontology and conception of God that was prevalent when these mathematical methods were established and how this is still fundamental for the way in which probabilities are used in financial calculation.[36] Concerning ranking in particular, Guyer[37] and Hart[38] show how using different mathematical formulas leads to establishing different forms of ranking that express different repertoires of political legitimacy.[39] The mathematical relations between numbers and concepts in financial methods are thus far from simply logically accurate or politically neutral. Doganova refers to them as "political technologies" that organize a specific distribution of resources.[40] It is therefore necessary to analyze the lines of reasoning that organize these mathematical relations in order to show the power relations they contribute to produce.

Financial theory today constitutes the foundation and almost all the content of financial education in universities, business schools, and professional training settings. According to government regulation in many jurisdictions, mastery of this theory is the expertise that distinguishes so-called "qualified," "sophisticated," or "professional" investors from the rest. This theory thus constitutes the necessary and sufficient knowledge demanded from those seeking to occupy front-office positions in the financial industry. Applying it is the official responsibility of employees like those of Brokers Inc. and Acme.

This theory, with its official controversies and more or less explicit contradictions, is standardized. For the sake of simplicity, I analyze the way in which it is presented in the official manuals given to students attempting to obtain the credentials awarded by the two biggest associations of financial analysts worldwide: the Chartered Financial Analyst Institute,[41] based in the United States, which awards the title of chartered financial analyst (CFA), and the Association of Certified International Investment Analysts, a coalition of national financial analyst associations, which awards the title of certified international investment analyst (CIIA).[42] These associations are very active in the shaping of financial regulation, and obtaining the CFA or CIIA designation may allow professionals to forego certain official accreditations to work in the financial industry. These credentials are often a means for employees to progress in their career, especially when their initial educational background is not considered very prestigious. Every year 160,000 people try to pass the CFA, which today has about 170,000 graduates, compared with 10,000 holders of the less prestigious CIIA. These manuals are particularly representative of the body of knowledge conveyed and legitimized in everyday practices in the financial industry. This is not because these associations have the power to impose their views on the industry. On the contrary, it is because, as professional associations, they are organizations where the most powerful companies of the financial industry showcase their professional norms and seek to legitimize them. The formulas and lines of reasoning presented in both manuals are almost identical, and they can be found almost without variations in most manuals of financial analysis and investment.

In what follows, I focus on seven concepts that organize the technical, moral, and political meanings of this set of methods and lines of reasoning: the "investor," the "efficient market," the "state," "risk," and three definitions of "value": "fundamental," "relative," and "speculative." As I show here, these concepts are interdependent and mutually defined but also organized around tensions and contradictions. These formulations propose different definitions of investor and market that can be partly contradictory. But in all cases, the concepts of the investor and efficient markets appear as the two sources of the definition of value, even if certain definitions of the state also play a fundamental role. The interdependent character of all these concepts means that whenever some of them are used, it is in combination with the rest. They must therefore be analyzed together.

Three Definitions of Financial Value

In the methods of financial valuation, the value of a company is defined by the value of its shares, represented by their price. The concept of "shareholder value" is identified with the profits obtained by the owners of shares. These can take two forms: the dividends paid to shareholders and the increases in share price. But prices are the main focus of the analysis because they are supposed to reflect all the information about future dividends. This reflection or representation is supposed to be most accurate in markets considered "informationally efficient"—a theoretical term that defines markets as places where participants have access to and take into account all available information about the company whose shares they buy and sell. This means that in order to achieve market efficiency, there must be individual investors who think that value is not accurately represented in the price and who look for all available information about the company. But it also means that once market efficiency is achieved, individual valuation becomes superfluous because the price already reflects all available information, and investors must accept the truth of this price and use it as a signal to orient their activities.[43] The three different methods of financial valuation define financial value in terms of fundamental value, relative value, and speculative value. These different definitions of value, both partly interdependent and partly contradictory, relate to different definitions of the theoretical sources of valuation—i.e., the figure of the investor and the market.

In financial methods, what is termed the "fundamental," "intrinsic," or "true value" of a social activity that is considered a financial asset is defined by discounting the future cash flows generated by the activity that could be received by the owner or creditor, such as dividends or interest. The fundamental value of the company is thus defined as the "present value" of these future cash flows.[44] Financial statements provide the information and conceptual frame to represent the company as a source of cash for owners.[45] The income statement represents the company as a stream of cash flows that are allocated among different components, including shareholders. From the point of view of the figure of the investor, all components are considered sources of revenue or cost, and the analysis focuses on the cash flows that can be allocated to the shareholder. Shareholder value is thus defined as a relation between the investor and the company, which is represented by accounting categories as appropriable cash.

The calculation aims to establish future monetary values for all the elements of the income statement. This should allow a determination of the "free cash flow to the firm" for each year in the midterm future, usually between five and fifteen years. This is calculated as net income plus noncash expenses (such as depreciation and amortization), plus interest payment, minus fixed capital investment and working capital investment:[46] The CFA manual explains: "That pile of remaining cash is called free cash flow to the firm (FCFF) because it's 'free' to pay out to the company's investors."[47]

These cash flows are "discounted" by dividing them by an interest rate in order to obtain their "present value." This present value corresponds mathematically to the amount that, if invested now at that same interest rate, would be equivalent to the expected income in the future.[48] For listed companies, the discount rate is calculated by considering that the company must pay two types of investors: creditors and shareholders. Payments to shareholders are referred to as the "cost of equity," defined by the "return on equity," and payments to creditors are referred to as the "cost of debt," defined by the interest rate the company pays for its debts at the time of valuation. These two components are given relative weights, measured by their capitalization at the time of valuation, and added to obtain the "weighted average cost of capital," or "WACC."[49] The present value of the firm is obtained by discounting the free cash flow to the firm using the weighted average cost of capital. All cash flows that are not costs or debts that must be repaid to creditors belong to the shareholders. The role of accounting categories is fundamental in this process. Income statements, in particular, provide the information that can be fed into an Excel file separating revenues and costs.[50] The "value of equity" is obtained by deducting the "present value of debt" from the "value of the firm." The value of equity is then divided by the number of shares in order to obtain the fundamental value of each share. The result of this method, called the "discounted cash flow (DCF)" method, is termed the company's "fundamental,"[51] "intrinsic,"[52] or "true"[53] value. This true value is thus defined as future cash owned by the shareholders.

The DCF method is considered the one that provides a value closest to the true or fundamental value of the company because it gives a conceptually accurate representation of what the value of the company should be: money available for the investor. At the same time, this accurate character is put into question by the fact that in order to calculate future cash flows, the analysis must take into account many variables that are just forecasts. This is the case not just for the future cash flows of the company but also for aspects of the environment that should affect them, such as inflation, evolution of the sector of activity of the company, future management decisions, exchange rates, and tax policy, among others. This implies that any valuation made by DCF is quite fragile in terms of how much it can pretend to reflect what is going to happen. It is mainly a series of guesses about a future that is defined as something that cannot be predicted accurately.

Fundamental valuation is carried out under the assumption that the current listed price of the company does not accurately reflect all available information about the future cash flows the company will provide to its owners but that the market will "correct" this mismatch in the future. Employees and textbooks use the term "correct" to highlight that there is a mistake, referring to the supposed capacity of the efficient market to express the true value in the price. Thus, if the price obtained with fundamental valuation is higher than the listed price, investors should buy before the market corrects itself, and sell in the opposite case. Fundamental valuation is defined by a relation between the investor and the company, mediated by the company's price given by the efficient market.

The relation among investors, efficient market, and value is different in the definition of what textbooks and the people I observed call "relative value." In relative valuation, companies are presumed to belong to an efficient market and are compared to each other, mobilizing accounting categories that are used to represent all companies as appropriable cash. In this process, companies are viewed as belonging to a unified bundle available to the investor—what professionals call the "investment universe" or also just "the market." In this case, the market is not identified with the participants that buy and sell the particular company that is being evaluated. It is defined as a universe composed of the sum of all participants and the totality of the objects they can exchange.

This relation among the investor, value, and the market is organized in mathematical calculations that mobilize partly contradictory ontologies and epistemologies. At the end of the nineteenth century, market participants started to analyze the prices of listed shares with the statistical tools in vogue at the time, and this became part of mainstream financial methods after World War II.[54] Daily prices are considered equally weighted events that occur according to what is called in statistics a "normal distribution." This gives meaning to the calculation of price averages, standard deviations in price variations, and correlations between the prices of different stocks. It combines the reasoning of probabilities with the liberal understanding of the truth of value reflected in market prices. The line of reasoning used is this: since the stock market price reflects the true value of the company, then the sum of the prices of all companies at a given moment reflects the true value of the economy as a whole. Stock market indexes were developed based on this presupposition. At the end of the nineteenth century, some of the theoreticians who developed these methods treated asset prices as a natural phenomenon, part of a vision where nature itself was defined as obeying the rules of probabilities. For some researchers of the time, this link with natural phenomena was direct, since business activity could, in turn, depend on cycles like those of agricultural seasons.

In this line of reasoning, the truth of the value reflected in the market price is based on two different ontological and epistemological assumptions. On the one hand, it is defined with the reasoning of liberal theory, considering that the price reflects all available information through the free exchange between market participants. Prices produced by efficient markets impose their truth on market participants as the result of a collective movement. On the other hand, the truth of value is defined by the positivistic use of probabilities, according to which prices obey a normal distribution. In this case, prices produced by efficient markets impose themselves on participants as a natural law. Muniesa has shown how, in the digitalization of Euronext, different actors mobilized these understandings of the representative character of price to support the adoption of different algorithms used to determine what should be considered the official daily price, itself an important reference in numerous contracts and procedures.[55]

The combination of these two ontologies and epistemologies defines the market itself as the object of investment. Because price movements are considered unpredictable and statistically "random," the standard deviation of returns, often called "volatility," is lower for a bundle of assets than for each one taken alone.[56] Therefore, according to what has been formalized as the "modern portfolio theory" (MPT), developed after World War II, the investor seeking to maximize returns and minimize risks (defined as standard deviation) should not make single bets. Instead, he should "buy-and-hold"[57] the "entire market"[58]—i.e., "all existing assets."[59]

The idea that companies belong to this bundle organizes the way in which they are ranked in relative valuation. Companies are compared to the market or to a segment of it considered relevant. This is done using the same accounting categories that are applied to all companies.[60] Thus, companies can be ranked, for instance, according to the size of their sales, their EBITDA,[61] or their earnings or according to ratios between accounting numbers, such as EBIT[62] to sales or earnings to sales.[63] But, more importantly, this ranking is done by relating these accounting numbers to listed prices. These relations take a great variety of forms, such as return on equity and the ratios of price to book, price to earnings (P/E), and price to EBIT or EBITDA, among others.[64] From time to time, these measures are reinvented, with discussions about which one is most representative of the company's value. But in all cases, stock prices are considered to reflect future cash flows according to the reasoning of fundamental valuation. The frequently used P/E ratio is an example of this. This ratio divides the capitalization of the company by the last earnings declared in financial statements. Since the capitalization is defined as the discounted sum of future earnings, the ratio is considered a multiple: it is the number by which the current earnings should be multiplied to determine what the shareholder will earn in the future. According to this line of reasoning, the manuals assert that the ratio of price to free cash flow (P/FCF) is theoretically better because it is based on all available cash, while the amount of earnings declared is often low in order to pay less tax.[65]

These relations between accounting numbers and stock prices are then used to rank companies, with the presupposition that the market is efficient for other companies but probably not for the one that is being evaluated. Thus, if the P/E ratio of the company under analysis is higher than that of companies considered comparable—for instance, competitors, companies of similar size, or companies operating in the same geographical area—investors can draw two conclusions about its value. They can conclude that the market is valuing this and all other companies efficiently because this company will provide higher earnings than comparable companies. Or they can conclude that the market is valuing all other companies efficiently but not this one, which is overvalued, so that they must sell its shares before the market corrects itself. The same reasoning applies to the use of all the other comparative indicators: other companies are the standard of valuation for the company under analysis because they are listed in the same market and therefore belong to that which should be bought in its entirety, since the market is efficient. Accounting categories provide the structure of comparability for all companies, but the value determined using the comparative indicators does not come uniquely from what these indicators allow analysts to say about each company: it comes from what they allow analysts to say about the investment universe or whole market, itself defined as the collection of all companies.

Like fundamental valuation, relative valuation is warranted, in professional practice, by the presupposition that markets will correct themselves in the future. This presupposition develops into a contradiction in the most generalized method of investment, which uses modern portfolio theory in order to designate a market that must be bought and held as a whole. This method aims to establish an investment portfolio that replicates a stock index, such as the S&P 100. Indexes are considered an acceptable representation of the whole market because, statistically, if a portfolio contains a high number of assets, usually above fifty, and if no asset has a major weight in the portfolio, then the impact of an additional asset on the portfolio's standard deviation is low. Thus, the portfolio does not even need to replicate the whole index. In practice, it is usually composed of around sixty stocks that are present in the index.

This investment method reproduces the weight of each stock in the index, with the aim of obtaining a return of 1 or 2 percent above that of the index. Thus, if the index falls by 13 percent in the year, the portfolio is expected to obtain a return of around –12 or –11 percent, and if it rises by 6 percent, the targeted performance is 7 or 8 percent. To do this, the fund manager is supposed to carry out a fundamental valuation for each company and integrate this valuation into a relative valuation, comparing each company to other companies and to the index considered to represent the market as a whole. Here the market is considered efficient; otherwise, it would not make sense to apply modern portfolio theory. But fund managers give a higher weight in the portfolio than in the index to companies they expect to perform better than the market as a whole and a lower weight to those they expect to underperform. Thus, the method also presupposes that the market is not efficient and that individual valuation can obtain a more accurate representation of the value of the company than that given by the price. This is supposed to allow the investor to "beat the market," an expression used by financial professionals to designate the capacity of the investor to do better than what he should be able to do if markets were efficient. This form of relative valuation thus considers that the market is, at the same time, efficient and not efficient. At the time of my observations, in marketing materials and everyday exchanges between financial professionals, this application of modern portfolio theory was called "classical." The label "alternative investment" was used for methods that explicitly rejected the classical investment method, which combined the "buy-and-hold" approach—i.e., buying what is designated as "the whole market" and keeping it over the long term—with the attempt to "beat the market."[66]

Fundamental and relative valuations involve the use of a concept of risk that combines many and sometimes diverging and vague definitions.[67] This labile character of the term *risk* is obscured by the analyses that presuppose risk designates what can be calculated mathematically and uncertainty encompasses all the rest.[68] In financial methods, risk partly refers to the possibility of losing the money invested. This aspect is central to the definition of the "risk-free rate of return." This notion refers to the interest paid by some European states, the United States, and a few other rich states, indicating they will never default on their bonds because they will raise taxes to give lenders priority over other members of the polity.[69] This establishes a foundational definition of financial value for all existing assets. In order to be considered part of the investment universe, any activity that is considered more likely to default than these states must pay more money than these states' bonds or than an interest rate related to them, like Libor.[70] In order to exist as an object of investment, any activity deemed riskier than the risk-free activities is expected to pay a "risk premium," which refers to a price difference that may correspond to a variety of narratives and considerations that may or may not be formalized mathematically.[71] In all the formulas of calculation and at the center of modern portfolio theory, the risk-free rate of return plays this crucial role as both the threshold of inclusion into the investment universe and the foundation of the hierarchy of financial values.[72]

The notion of risk is also defined statistically as the standard deviation of returns, usually called their "volatility." The higher the volatility, the higher the risk premium that should be demanded by the figure of the investor, even though volatility and risk premium are not related mathematically. This notion of risk is used to compare the listed company to its investment universe. The "capital asset pricing model,"[73] which is based on modern portfolio theory, values each financial asset by distinguishing a risk that is "specific" or "intrinsic" to the asset from a risk that arises because it belongs to a market, called the "market risk."[74] Both kinds of risk are calculated using past prices to obtain the standard deviation of returns that would have been obtained by investing in the stock and in the market index. The relation between these two standard deviations is measured as the *beta* of the company, a name that comes from the Greek letter β used to define that mathematical relation. The "expected return" (Er) of a listed company, used in DCF to obtain the fundamental value of the company, is defined as the sum of the "risk-free rate of return" (Rf) and the company's "intrinsic risk"—itself defined as the difference between the "market risk" (Mr) and the "risk-free rate of return"—multiplied by the company's "beta": $Er = Rf + \beta(Mr - Rf)$. In this case, the company is defined as a source of profit for the investor according to its statistical relation to two rates of return, one defined by rich states and one defined by "the market" identified with an index.

Relative valuation establishes different notions of the investor, the efficient market, and value. These definitions all refer to the market as a bundle of objects of investment, but they mobilize both liberal conceptions of the true value of assets based on individual freedom and mathematical methods that presuppose that market prices, and what they represent, follow the rules of probabilities.

The definitions of the figure of the investor, the efficient market, and value are again different in what financial professionals and textbooks call "speculative valuation." As already described by Keynes, in its more general definition, speculation usually involves assessing the future variation of prices by gauging the opinion of other market participants.[75] This is repeated, for instance, in the CFA manuals: "Technicians look for changes in supply and demand, while fundamentalists look for changes in value."[76] In the financial industry, several professional groups specialize explicitly in different forms of speculative valuation. Some methods, like those used by traders at Brokers Inc., are directly connected to fundamental and relative valuations. But in this case, fundamental and relative valuations are not considered ways to assess whether the price indeed reflects the true value of the company. They are instead considered the lines of reasoning that inform the opinions of other market participants, so it is important to use them to gauge how prices will evolve in the short term. Other methods of speculative valuation depart from fundamental and relative valuations altogether. Chartism, for instance, uses mathematics and behavioral psychology to attempt to predict market price movements based on the analysis of past prices, considered indicators of the future behavior of market participants, without direct reference to the company's fundamental value.[77] This mathematized form of speculative valuation is often included in official debates about the role and limits of the use of probabilities in financial valuation—in particular, to challenge the idea that prices follow a normal distribution. Most forms of speculative valuation thus reject the idea of market efficiency and focus on short-term price movements that would reflect just the shifting opinions of market participants rather than a fundamental value.

Fundamental, relative, and speculative valuations use different definitions of the investor, the efficient market, and value and propose different relations among these categories. This sets these three forms of valuation at odds with each other. But at the same time, the results obtained by each method are necessary for the other two, with only a few exceptions in certain forms of speculative valuation. Thus, the three definitions of financial value must be considered together.

Interdependences and Contradictions in the Definitions of Value

The definitions of fundamental, relative, and speculative value are at the same time interdependent and contradictory. It is important to analyze these relations among the three because they are mobilized in everyday professional practices as a series of official controversies, blind spots, and limitations of what is possible. These relations concern the idea that stock prices reflect the value of the company in a way that is technically accurate and politically legitimate. Thus, through these interdependences and contradictions, the possibility that the truth of value exists and is revealed in prices is reiterated as the foundation of valuation and of the financial industry's contribution to a socially optimal allocation of resources.

The three definitions of value partly imply divergent or even directly opposed understandings of what investors and the market are and do. Fundamental valuation establishes a direct relation between the investor and the object of investment, represented as appropriable cash using accounting categories and numbers. This relation is only mediated by the company's market price, presupposing that the market is not being efficient but that it will correct itself in the future. Relative valuation includes fundamental valuation in a comparison of companies, rendered possible by the fact that all companies are gauged with the same accounting categories, which homogenizes the meanings of accounting numbers such as cash flows and renders them combinable with stock prices in mathematical relations. This method of valuation establishes an indirect relation between the investor and the object of investment, mediated by the concept of the efficient market considered as a whole. This market provides the standards for valuing the company, as efficiency is supposed to be realized for the other companies composing the market or investment universe. This leads to a contradiction in the case of the classical method of investment, which presupposes that the market is at the same time efficient and not efficient. Finally, speculative valuation rejects the idea of market efficiency and establishes a relation between the investor and the object of investment that is mediated by other market participants. These are defined as holders of opinions that cannot coalesce to produce, through price, an informationally efficient representation of the asset's value. A price that reflects a speculative valuation is considered the product of exchanges between investors who are not searching for the true value—i.e., discounted future cash flows—but rather are basing their exchange behavior on information that financial professionals, would, in this line of reasoning, call "erroneous" or "disconnected from fundamentals." In this understanding, speculative valuation is, by definition, false.[78]

Through their differences, these three definitions of value reproduce a systematic problematization of the relation between the idea of the investor, defined as a free individual conducting valuation in order to maximize returns, and the idea of market efficiency. On the one hand, market efficiency presupposes the contribution of individual evaluators seeking to form a personal opinion about the financial value of any asset independently of what the current listed price is. But on the other hand, the valuation of these investors becomes useless after this market efficiency is achieved and as long as there is no new information to be analyzed. In this case, investors should adapt to the discipline of the market, accepting the price it produces as an accurate representation of value. However, if all investors thought the market was efficient, no one would do the valuation, and market efficiency would disappear because information would not be reflected in the price. And if all participants in the exchange thought the market was inefficient, they would no longer use the price as a signal leading to a socially optimal allocation of resources. Thus, according to the theory, for market efficiency to exist and ensure the optimal social allocation of money, there must be some participants who believe the market is not efficient and some who believe it is.

Fundamental value, also called the true value of the company, is always fragile from a methodological point of view because present value is conceptualized as something that originates only in the future. It is necessarily dependent on forecasts about a future that, by definition, cannot be known. In financial theory, this fragility is supposedly overcome by the process of market efficiency. The collective cognitive capacity of market participants should manage to produce the most informed assessment about the future. Yet, prices on stock exchanges vary constantly, without there always being new information that these variations would reflect. This constant variation can then be interpreted as the result of valuation that is not based on information about the company—i.e., some form of speculative valuation. At any point in time, listed prices can be considered the result of market efficiency or inefficiency, and they can never guarantee the accuracy of any particular fundamental valuation. This unsolvable uncertainty that financial theory establishes in the relation between current prices and the true value they are supposed to reflect is the conceptual space where the three forms of financial valuation become possible—and also always potentially erroneous.

The three definitions of value are not just different and partly contradictory; they are also interdependent. The results produced by each method are used in the other two. Fundamental valuation uses current listed prices as data for the analysis. But the idea that prices are meaningful data is based on the idea that the market is efficient and that prices accurately reflect the value of the assets. This can lead to contradictory presuppositions in a single procedure of valuation. For instance, the manuals generally consider that in order to calculate the weights of equity and debt in the WACC, one must use the price of equity and debt found in "the market."[79] This is so even if it entails using the company's current listed price (because the market is considered efficient and the price is considered representative of value) to find a different price through fundamental valuation (because the listed price is not considered representative of true value). Yet, the manuals consider this a matter of mathematical "circularity," not of outright contradiction.[80] Fundamental valuation also uses relative valuation, as we saw, to define the cost of equity. Relative valuation, in turn, uses the methods of fundamental valuation—but does so in order to transcend them by considering all companies as part of a broader bundle. It implies that price correctly represents the fundamental value of other companies and that it should eventually represent the fundamental value of the company under valuation—but according to the relative values of all listed companies. This can also lead to contradictory presuppositions in a single procedure. As we saw, the classical investment method presupposes both that the market is efficient and must be replicated using modern portfolio theory and that it is not efficient, so it can be "beaten" by conducting fundamental valuation. Finally, speculative valuation can be conducted by mobilizing fundamental and relative valuations as the main opinions that need to be taken into account to predict price movements. There may always be market participants using speculative valuation and affecting listed prices, so when fundamental and relative valuations use listed prices, they are constantly problematized as potentially obstructed by or benefiting from speculation.

The three definitions of value, with their interdependences and contradictions, are thus inseparable. The financial analysts I observed produced documents for each listed company they analyzed that were intended for use by professionals like fund managers in deciding whether to buy or sell the stock. Any document of financial analysis about a listed company develops an argument about how the price of the company should evolve in the future, based on how the company is expected to generate cash available for shareholders. In short financial reports of one to two pages, this fundamental value of the company is implied as the rationale linking future cash flows to the price of shares. In longer reports, analysts sometimes render explicit the hypotheses used to calculate the future cash flows, and in some reports, they may also state the value of the WACC used in the calculation. These lines of reasoning are a major tool of communication about the value of companies—and also the basis of official controversies about these values because different expectations about the future result in different present values. But in the same report, fundamental valuation is usually combined with the other two forms of valuation. The documents typically include a range of ratios, and sometimes a narrative, according to the lines of reasoning of relative valuation. Finally, the documents often have a chart showing recent price variations and a narrative about short-term trends to be taken into account in speculative valuation. As we will see in the coming chapters, these combinations are included not simply to allow for the possibility that the same document might be used by fund managers following different valuation approaches. It is the interdependence among the three definitions of value that implies they must be constantly considered together.

Power Relations in Valuation and Investment Methods

With all their multiplicity and their tensions and contradictions, these methods of valuation establish theoretical power relations in the distribution of money that appear as technical presuppositions of calculation and financial reasoning. Defining companies as something that has a "value" represents them as a source of appropriable money for the investor. The assertion that prices reveal the truth of this value in efficient markets reinforces the idea that this value indeed exists and endows its supposed reality with political legitimacy. The value that prices supposedly reflect is considered accurate in the sense that it results from the application of correct methods. And it is considered politically desirable because it is the signal produced by efficient markets that leads to a socially optimal allocation of resources. In this imaginary, the state is given the role of supporter of the figure of the investor in order to determine the bottom line of what can be valued and in order to secure a minimum revenue for him—for the sole reason that he owns money.

The manuals of financial analysis quoted earlier stress the priority that valuation must give to the figure of the investor: "Modern finance theory and practice is based on the basic principle that business managers should act so as to maximise shareholder value, i.e., the value of equity shares of the company."[81] As many studies have shown, such practices have contributed to the transformation of listed companies' wage relations and investment strategies in the last decades.[82] All the participants in the activity of the company that is evaluated—such as the company's employees, its business partners, the state as tax collector and service provider, the social spaces where the company operates, and the environment in general—are considered only potential sources of costs or of profit. The analyses produced by professionals—for instance, the reports produced by financial analysts—often come with explicit recommendations addressed to the company's management about reducing labor costs or changing suppliers in order to increase the revenue available for the investors. This understanding of shareholder value has also been used by the Chinese central government to transform state-owned enterprises in order to list them on stock exchanges and reorganize their control without privatizing them.[83] The way in which the methods of valuation and investment produce a powerful figure of the investor can create different social hierarchies, as it intersects with other power relations.

The power relation between the figure of the investor and the rest of the participants in the company's activity is also temporal. Fundamental valuation is based in the present, at the moment when cash flows and discount rates are assessed, and has the midterm future as its horizon. As a result of discounting, income that is closer in time has a higher value than income that is to be received later, so costs and income that would occur beyond ten to fifteen years in the future would have an almost inexistent "present value."[84] This creates hierarchies among the different moments in which activities in the company are expected to occur—and hence among the actors they involve—and disregards the long-term effects of valuation altogether.[85]

The notion of the risk-free rate of return establishes the power of the investor over the rest of society through the power of the state. It asserts that the investor, simply because he owns money, is entitled to revenue obtained by taxing the rest of the population. Looking much like a feudal entitlement, it breaks with the liberal definition of a free market participant. This entitlement, however, actually establishes the freedom of the investor, who can always exit a risky investment if it does not pay enough of a risk premium. The notion presupposes that this return, unlike other data used in valuation, escapes the laws of probabilities. Using an absolutist notion of state sovereignty, it endows the rights of the investor with a political and ontological status that does not apply to the rest of society. The standard of all financial value is thus founded on the sovereignty of the state at the service of the investor.

This notion of risk-free return is then used to establish a hierarchy among all social activities according to whether they appear stable and committed to prioritizing the figure of the investor over other participants, like workers, consumers, citizens in general, or the environment. This hierarchy is partly expressed and institutionalized by rating agencies and works as not only the technical justification but also the moral and political justifications for the exclusion of the most impoverished populations from the distribution of money managed by the financial industry.[86] The notion implies a certain historical myopia, since all the states included in the definition of this category today have defaulted on their debts more or less recently. This myopia erases the problematization of the historical processes whereby some particular states— marked by factors such as colonization, world wars, and the Cold War—occupy the top of the hierarchy at the service of the figure of the investor. This hierarchy often reinforces the difficulties of the poorest states and of those activities that attempt to access the money managed by the financial industry. Financial companies will demand higher returns from, and create more instability by speculating on, sovereign bonds of the states with jurisdiction in the territories where poorer populations live. This weakens the capacity of these states to provide for public services where they are most needed. Activities that are deemed too risky or not even rated by rating agencies may simply be totally excluded from investment.[87] As we will see in the following chapters, stock valuation must thus be understood in relation to the valuation of all other assets, with which each listed company is compared and put into competition.

Finally, as we have seen, the notion of market efficiency gives price political legitimacy as the socially optimal representation of a company's value. The CIIA manual thus states: "There is a substantial body of evidence to indicate that share prices in well-developed financial markets are highly correlated with the future stream of cash flows and the risk of the cash flows."[88] It justifies focusing on shareholder value by saying that, besides benefiting the company and its customers and employees,

> another rationale for using shareholder value maximisation as the primary objective for businesses is that such an objective leads to efficient allocation of capital. If the markets are efficient, those businesses which operate in the most efficient manner will experience ever-increasing share prices and therefore will be able to obtain the capital needed for growth at lower costs of funds. On the other hand, businesses, which are not successful, will see their share prices dropping, their cost of funds will be higher and consequently these businesses will not grow.[89]

In this financial imaginary, the truth of value thus obtained is a valid measure for the investor, but it is also the signal that orients economic activity toward a socially optimal allocation of resources. Once all the information has been reflected in the price, no individual investor can claim to find a better valuation than that of the market. The price can exercise its discipline, which is at the same time technical and political: it is supposed to indicate the true value of social activities, which all participants must then accept as a guide for their investment, and it is supposed to indicate the fair value of these activities; i.e., it is supposed to indicate how worthy they are of investment from the point of view of society as a whole.

According to this financial theory, valuation is the deed of independent investors, whose interests are best defined by the formulas and lines of reasoning of the theory itself. This allows for the realization of market efficiency—and therefore for the socially optimal allocation of resources. This is also, in general terms, the political aim with which financial regulation justifies the role it assigns to the financial industry and its methods. Valuation and investment methods, like the determination of a discount rate or the constitution of an investment portfolio by replicating an index, define value in three different ways that are interdependent and partly contradictory. But this multiplicity reproduces a theoretical relation of power organized by the relations among the concepts of the investor, the efficient market, and value. Navigating the professional rules of their workplace, employees with different tasks of financial valuation and investment mobilize and combine the three definitions of value differently. They enact various figures of the investor, and in different ways, they problematize their professional space, the financial industry, as the place where market efficiency occurs. It is through this everyday application of financial methods of valuation and investment that the financial industry collects, produces, and distributes money, contributing to produce social hierarchies worldwide.

EVERYDAY PRACTICES IN A GLOBAL SPACE

The employees of Brokers Inc. and Acme understood financial valuation and investment as being part of their daily professional practice and as involving the application of standardized procedures established in labor and commercial contracts. In order to show the political character of these everyday practices, it is important to situate them in the global distributive role of the financial industry. The financial relations produced by these employees extend worldwide—beyond the walls of the offices where they work and the state jurisdictions where their work is regulated.

The investment management companies that were clients of Brokers Inc. and Acme usually diversified investments according to the concept of market efficiency formalized in modern portfolio theory. The bigger the amount of money they managed, the more they tended to invest in a wide variety of assets worldwide. For example, Acme's Allocation Department was responsible for gathering statistical data on all available financial assets in the world, using modern portfolio theory to analyze them as belonging to one single efficient market. This had an impact on the amount of money allocated to each asset and therefore on the fees available for the purchase of financial valuation about it. The financial analysis produced by employees like Frédéric occurred in an organization where all social activities were evaluated, integrated into, or excluded from the investment universe, and ranked according to the multiple definitions of their financial value.

As we saw in the introduction, today the financial industry manages around $200 trillion invested in financial assets worldwide. These investments are not decided by a single company according to a single strategy of valuation and investment. They are the result of the multiple relations between companies in the financial industry across various jurisdictions. Practices like those of Frédéric, as well as the commercial strategy of Brokers Inc.'s managers, were part of this attempt to capture, produce, and distribute money worldwide. The stocks in which Brokers Inc.'s employees specialized occupied a marginal position in relation to the big caps of rich countries, but they were still considered more worthy of the money managed by the financial industry than the activities of companies and states that operated in poorer regions or that were simply excluded from the investment universe. When a salesperson evaluates a company, he establishes a power relation between the shareholders and the rest of stakeholders of the company. He also establishes a power relation between the company he favors with his analysis and those he rejects. And he contributes to establishing power relations among listed companies, other financial assets, and the social activities that are excluded by the financial industry. Each act of financial valuation and investment participates in the production of the hierarchy that both identifies, ranks, and contributes to the transformation of the activities that access the money managed by the financial industry and separates these activities from those that are excluded from the valuating gaze altogether.

The global distribution of money by the financial industry is partly shaped by states' regulatory frameworks. These are fragmented by the national logic of jurisdictions but tend to repeat the same lines of reasoning about the legitimacy of the distribution realized by the financial industry. As the Chartered Financial Analyst Institute and the Association of Certified International Investment Analyst and their manuals show, the practices of the financial industry are standardized, using a set of formulas, concepts, and lines of reasoning that I have called the financial theory. They are professional and legal requirements for all employees. As I will show in the coming chapters, the clients of Brokers Inc., based in the United States, and the fund managers of Acme, based in France, applied the same methods of valuation and investment, and they also enforced very similar organizational rules concerning relations between employees and companies. The activities of collecting money in investment funds, using this money to purchase and sell financial assets, producing these assets, and valuing them with different methods can be offered together by the same company or separately by different companies. These activities are carried out to produce profits for the companies of the financial industry and salaries and bonuses for their employees. In all cases, these activities require standardized forms of expertise, produced between academic and professional social spaces. And these forms of expertise are supposed to legitimize the delegation to the financial industry of the power to say that financial value exists and that it has a truth that is revealed by the practices of its experts.

For employees like the traders, analysts, and salespeople at Brokers Inc., the search for the truth of value in everyday practices not only seemed like a plausible series of actions but also was a necessary routine to retain their place in a global professional space. The expertise required in the financial industry is organized through specialized professions, including those of fund managers, financial analysts, traders, and salespeople. Like the companies that employ them, the employees who mobilize these different forms of expertise have relations of competition, hierarchy, and complementarity, which are crucial for the way in which they sustain their jobs and advance in their careers. As we will see, they do so by establishing a personal relation to the standardized procedures that enact the figure of the investor and presuppose the existence of efficient markets. Employees relate to these procedures with various emotional attachments—i.e., with different forms of adhesion, rejection, or indifference. And when they need to justify their work—for instance, in conflicts with other employees—or when they seem to face what they designate as a "financial crisis," they may mobilize the political and moral justifications provided by the repertoires of market efficiency and the truth of value.

From the windows of the Brokers Inc. offices, one could see a forest of glass skyscrapers with various shapes. The offices included a large room with three parallel rows of desks, with employees differentiated by professional specializations. Back-office employees and financial analysts had only one computer screen each. Salespeople and traders had three screens each. Everyone could watch and hear everyone else all the time, and the CEO, André, frequently left his personal office space to come work in the big room among his employees. Two days after my arrival at Brokers Inc., at noon, the company celebrated the birthday of Juliette, a partner of the company like André and the second-most-important salesperson by revenue after him. As was usual in such circumstances, all twenty-five employees stopped their work and scattered around the large table situated in the middle of the room. A few bottles of champagne had been already placed there and were opened when everyone arrived. All employees were more or less obliged to take part in the party, but some of them stayed there for only a few minutes, while others lingered until the half-hour break officially ended. I told myself that with twenty-five employees, the company would average one birthday party every two weeks. I would indeed find myself in this situation several times during the five months of my observations.

During the party, André, forty years old and known for his aggressive humor, made jokes about Juliette, thirty-seven years old, with whom he had worked for more than a decade. In French, the language shared by all the front-office employees of the company, including those for whom it was a second language, he remarked that she had "gained weight" and had become a "cow." This, he said, would "prevent her from satisfying her sexual desires with young men during her holidays in Jamaica." Juliette answered, with a voice as loud as his and in front of the half-smiles of several salespeople, traders, and analysts, that if he said that, it was because he was "short and bald"—his head was shaved and she was visibly taller than him. Salespeople, traders, and analysts laughed more or less loudly under the ambivalent gaze of back-office employees who did not understand French.

After several weeks at the company, I began to notice that some salespeople were less present than others at these events and that the back-office employees, who did not get along well with each other, moved the three meters from their offices to the central table in a group, remained seated together, and went back all at once under the direction of their manager. I had become used to hearing jokes and sexual or aggressive remarks. And I was learning to use them in order to create a position for myself that was livable enough in a space where social relations could make daily life painful for those identified as "weak." With time, it became more obvious to me that only some employees laughed when, for instance, André said loudly over the phone to a long-time friend that he could "go get fucked by a horde of wild boars in heat." I could observe how some employees enjoyed these jokes while others felt they worked in an atmosphere of anxiety created by the pressure to obtain income and by the contempt expressed for those who did not seem to succeed in doing so.

In this professional space, listed companies are considered investment objects with a true value that can be found by financial analysis, using a combination of personal opinions and efficient markets. Listed companies are compared and ranked according to the rate of return they must propose to access funds managed by the financial industry. This rate should always be higher than the risk-free rate, defined by the capacity of rich states to assert their sovereignty by raising taxes and honoring their debts. In this global space, the daily repetition of routine actions by analysts, salespeople, traders, and fund managers, all attempting to say the truth of value, contributes to producing the global relations around access to the money managed by the financial industry.

Valuation and investment are the products of daily practices carried out by specialized employees in different professions, including fund managers, financial analysts, traders, and salespeople. Each profession uses different ways to define value while participating in social relations that include competition, hierarchy, and collaboration. Defining financial value, problematized in terms of its potential truth, is part of the regularity of the daily practices in the professional space of the financial industry. In this global space, the application of financial theory, with its contradictions and tensions, is considered necessary for the realization of the market efficiency this theory presupposes. The study of these practices must therefore encompass their organizational aspects and the financial imaginaries they mobilize. It is then also necessary to take into account the fact that the technical tools of valuation and investment have moral and political meanings, which are part of how employees make sense of them.

As we have seen, financial valuation posits two main sources for the definition of value: the investor and the efficient market. According to the theory itself, the formulas and lines of reasoning formalized in the theory are considered the best tools for maximizing the interests of the figure of the investor. And the truth of value is supposed to be revealed in the prices of efficient markets, from which financial regulation hopes a socially optimal allocation of resources in a global space will ensue. The following chapters will explore how employees routinely put into practice these two supposed sources of the truth of financial value.

2

VALUATION AS A PERSONAL OPINION

O
UTSIDE the financial industry, the concept of the investor has many meanings that are partly disconnected
from each other. The word *investor* can be used in the
press to designate the financial industry in general. It can also be
used to talk about people who own a house or some financial contract like a stock or a bond, either directly or via an investment
fund. Its moral and political meanings vary in each case, as do the
lines of reasoning for valuation and investment attributed to it. The
definition of the investor in the procedures carried out by employees in the financial industry proposes yet other uses of the term.

The way in which financial procedures define the investor is
part of a history that has endowed this figure with specific features. Historians have shown how the meanings of the figure of
the investor changed considerably during the nineteenth century
in the United States. While it was used to designate an individual who was close to being a socially and morally irresponsible
gambler, it gradually came to designate a person, mainly male
and white, who had money and used scientific tools to invest in
order to take care of his family. Being an investor thus became a
social duty.[1] With the development of pension funds and their
institutionalization as part of the intergenerational relations in

the United States—notably with the passage of the Employee Retirement Income Security Act of 1974—the meaning of investor changed again. It was used to designate rights and duties for a segment of society that was the center of a political project, the "American middle class."[2] This group was supposed to be represented by the financial industry.[3]

It is through this process that the figure of the investor became the product of a relation of representation, as I described in the previous chapter. The theory of the principal-agent relation—in particular, in combination with the legal entity of the trust—establishes that the legal owners of money are investors because they entrust their money to experts in valuation and investment in the financial industry and that these professionals are investors because they work with their clients' money.[4] During the twentieth century, financial theory was progressively formalized and unified in academic writing. When the financial industry was given this role of representation of the interests of the middle classes qua investors, the duties of the financial industry were defined as the application of financial theory itself. It is in this circulation of people and ideas among regulatory, academic, and professional social spaces that the figure of the investor came to be stabilized as a gaze and actor of valuation and investment procedures in the financial industry.[5]

The figure of an individual investor plays a fundamental role in the definition of financial value as something that has a truth that market prices could reveal. All formulas of valuation and investment are defined from the perspective of this agent, considered free to form his own opinion about an asset's value and exclusively interested in maximizing his income. From the point of view of financial regulation, this figure is also central, since efficient markets are supposed to be composed of a multitude of investors. Regulations concerning bonus systems and legal liabilities aimed to preserve the principal-agent relation, for instance, are established to protect the interests of this figure of the investor. In this setting, this agent's investment and valuation capacities and interests are defined in the terms of financial theory.

The figure of the investor is thus defined by the methods with which it is supposed to be equipped. This echoes what Miller and Rose say about the forms of agency that are given efficacy by the reproduction of bureaucratic procedures in vast organizational settings.[6] This investor is not a particular person. It is a theoretical figure, variously defined, distributed in all the acts of valuation and investment where it is presupposed as the agent.[7] As such, it is the organizing gaze for valuation and investment procedures across jurisdictions and across types of companies in the financial industry at large. Outside the financial industry, its meanings can vary, but there is great consistency worldwide concerning its definition in valuation and investment procedures within the financial industry. This is possible only because this figure is part of the organizational rules within and across companies, where it is combined with concerns about salaries, bonuses, profit, and prestige that are formalized in labor and commercial contracts.

In financial theory, the role of the figure of the investor in the definition of value is to look for all available information on the asset. This information is then compared with the listed price in order to assess whether this price is the result of informational efficiency. The individual capacity to apply the methods of valuation is a central feature of the definitions of the different professional tasks around which valuation and investment are organized in the financial industry. In this process, financial professionals establish a direct link between the personal character of their valuation abilities and the figure of the individual investor, defined as the independent source of an opinion about value. As I show in this chapter, professionals foreground their personal capacity to apply valuation and investment methods to legitimize their position in relations and conflicts that concern bonus, salary, and prestige. What are organizationally recognized as their personal capabilities are thus made to correspond with the independent character of the figure of the investor whose gaze pervades and is defined by the formalized valuation and investment procedures that these employees must apply.

Studying traders, Zaloom shows that if they are ever able to act according to the theoretical definition of the figure of the investor, it is because there is a vast array of procedural rules and sanctions they have to follow to keep their jobs.[8] This procedural character of the individual figure of the investor is central in the everyday practices of valuation and investment. As I show in the case of Brokers Inc. and Acme, professional rules were organized so as to ensure the application of the figure of the investor—not only by mobilizing financial theory but also by showcasing the enactment of the figure in a personality. To give a reality to the gaze of the investor and to the truth of value that the investor would be able to utter, fund managers, salespeople, financial analysts, and traders at Brokers Inc. and Acme were all required to express what was officially designated as a "personal opinion" about value. Applying the methods defined as the actions of an investor had to be the product of what people termed a "personality" endowed with "convictions" and "sincerity."

The tasks of salespeople, financial analysts, traders, and fund managers imply different forms of expertise, which all mobilized the same financial theory but combined the definitions of value differently. And, in turn, each employee was expected to conduct this valuation by adding his personal analysis and interpretation, combining the lines of reasoning proposed by financial theory with other information or interpretation about what could affect the value of listed companies. Complementarities and conflicts among employees concerned the possible truth of the value uttered by each of them and the place of this truth in professional hierarchies. Professional recognition by peers that procedures have been respected was thus the confirmation that the valuation achieved was indeed the act of a maximizing investor. Sanctions imposed for the breach of these rules were aimed at asserting that the sole aim of establishing a personal opinion is to determine the truth of value. This directly connected the moral and political meanings of the figure of the investor established in financial theory with its application. Enacted sincerity was the marker that valuation was indeed done with the freedom and independence that market efficiency needs for prices to serve as signals for a socially optimal allocation of resources.

Personal opinion was considered the legitimate starting point in establishing a hierarchy in the access to monetary resources, between investors and other stakeholders within companies and among financial assets. However, the employees I observed did this with different forms of commitment that depended on their relation to their work and to its place in their lives in general. As I show, for employees at Brokers Inc., the personal character of the search for the truth of value was connected to the way in which they understood their own social identities, within and outside their professional lives.

This chapter describes how all these elements are at play in the definition of listed companies as things that have a value, which, if correctly represented in market prices, can contribute to a socially optimal allocation of resources. It first shows that the figure of the investor is multiple and disseminated in the everyday practices of employees, who have to showcase the morality of sincerity and conviction. It then examines how this multiplicity is understood as the enactment of this figure of the investor through the repetition of procedures that reassert this figure's existence. Finally, the chapter explores how employees use this figure differently, giving it meanings that connect with their professional and nonprofessional lives.

THE MULTIPLE AND DISTRIBUTED INVESTOR

As we saw in the previous chapter, in financial valuation there are three ways to define value that are interdependent but also contradictory. Thus, any definition of value, whether fundamental, relative, or speculative, depends on the other two. This means that in any form of valuation, the figure of the investor is always multiple, since each definition of value implies combining different definitions of the investor, the efficient market, and their relation. The tasks of the salespeople, financial analysts, traders, and fund managers I observed were partly distinguished by the way in which they stressed different ways to combine the three definitions of value. In doing so, they also foregrounded the definition of the investor that was closest to the particular definition of value most associated with their professional tasks. Professional differentiation in the ways to define value was organized in relations of hierarchy, cooperation, and competition among employees concerning their salary, bonus, prestige, and career prospects. In these relations, employees had to stress their personal contribution to the search for true value. They did so by putting forward their personal valuation capacities, thus mobilizing the imaginaries of an independent investor expressing his personal convictions.

In this process, the multiple figure of the investor is distributed in the practices of all employees. The conflicts among employees and among professions are thus organized as tensions among the different definitions of value, investors, and markets. The figure of the investor is thereby constantly reproduced as the foundation of the truth of the value. These practices thus constantly reassert the legitimacy of the hierarchies in the access to money that financial valuation establishes within a company and between listed companies and other social activities worldwide. This section describes this process, looking at how financial analysts, salespeople, traders, and fund managers stress the superiority of their form of valuation and how this organizes their relations within and between companies.

The fund managers, salespeople, traders, and analysts I interviewed shared the opinion that the analysts were the ones who "best knew" the listed companies they evaluated. This meant they were the most able to assess a company's fundamental value based on its capacity to procure income for shareholders in the mid-term. Brokers SA employees based in Paris produced financial analyses of companies that were mainly listed on Euronext, and Brokers Inc. sold this information to U.S.-based fund managers. Financial analysts studied each listed company's accounts, history, and management strategy. They met with the top management of each company in official meetings where they discussed their strategy and accounts. Following the requirements of financial regulation to ensure market efficiency by making information equally accessible to all market participants, these meetings were supposed to be public. In practice, this meant that they were attended by financial analysts working for several companies and that the meetings or their syntheses were broadcast and made accessible to the financial press. Analysts attended such meetings only for specific companies on which they focused. Each financial analyst specialized in a particular group of companies, often defined by business category, industry sector, size, and geographical location—i.e., those factors that made these companies comparable according to relative valuation.

Analysts presented their research mainly in the form of the written reports that I referred to in chapter 1. These reports came in different lengths, usually between one and ten pages, and mainly focused on a single company. They included some accounting numbers, elements used to compare the company with other companies, a text about the company's commercial situation, and a proposed stock price, which was usually different from the current listed price. The reports produced by the analysts at Brokers SA all had the same formatting and were presented in a way that was very similar to that of reports produced by other brokerage companies, which were also available to fund managers. One of the differences between brokerage companies was that some reports visibly included a recommendation—such as "buy," "sell," or "neutral"—along with the proposed stock price. This was not the case for the reports produced at Brokers SA, but the difference between the proposed price and the current price in the stock exchange made the recommendation obvious. These documents bore the name of the analyst who had produced them. Occasionally, they also mentioned the names of other analysts or assistants in an explicit hierarchical order. Thus, they indicated who was the leading expert on the company, responsible for the most important assertions of the report, and therefore the one who most carried out the gaze of the investor. These teams often also produced longer reports on a particular sector, which tended to synthesize and update the analyses produced in single-company reports.

Salespeople were responsible for offering this financial analysis to each fund manager. They made the first contact with their potential commercial partner and initiated the relation between their respective employing companies. Many salespeople had first been analysts, and in general, these employees knew in detail the valuation procedures applied by financial analysts. Financial analysts' reports were distributed by email to all customers and were available exclusively for them on Brokers SA's website. As all employees told me in interviews, the fund managers and buy-side analysts rarely read these reports in their entirety due to what everyone termed "lack of time." Salespeople used these documents as the basis for the customized analysis they sold to fund managers, supplemented with other information produced by specialized or mainstream media. While analysts' reports did not change once published, salespeople developed arguments and synthesized information differently for each of their clients. From time to time, fund managers or buy-side analysts contacted sell-side analysts for detailed information about a particular listed company. But most of the time, fund managers accessed what was considered the most thorough analysis, that carried out by sell-side analysts, through its customization by salespeople.

Buy-side and sell-side analysts usually applied the same procedures of valuation. But sell-side analysts specialized exclusively in one particular group of companies, according to the categories described previously. Buy-side analysts, on the other hand, mainly focused on the companies in which their employer, through the work of fund managers, invested its clients' money. Most Brokers Inc. clients were fund managers specializing in companies based in European jurisdictions. European small caps were a small part of their total portfolio, although a few hedge funds sometimes focused on this category. In the majority of cases, fund managers applied the classical investment method, described in chapter 1. For pension and mutual funds, this was typical and often mandated by regulation. It meant that each fund manager invested the money under his management in the stocks of between fifty and sixty companies. Salespeople were required to alert buy-side analysts and fund managers about daily changes in information concerning these companies. But salespeople, fund managers, and the few buy-side analysts working with them did not have time to constantly study each listed company thoroughly. The most thorough analysis was thus the specialization of sell-side analysts, each of whom focused on a limited number of companies. In the case of big caps—i.e., vast companies with operations in several countries—each sell-side analyst could specialize in only a dozen companies or fewer.

Employees generally presented valuation produced by sell-side analysts as the most informed about the listed company's operations. At the same time, fund managers were described by other employees, and presented themselves, as those who were most connected to the investment based on personal opinion about the company's value. Each fund manager was expected to elaborate this opinion based on different sources. These included discussions with different salespeople, analyses produced by sell-side and buy-side analysts, and other information provided, for example, by the specialized and nonspecialized press. Nevertheless, the fund manager remained officially at the center of the valuation process because he was supposed to bear personal responsibility for the decision to buy or sell shares depending on how he evaluated them.

Several studies have shown how emphasizing the role of personal opinion and conviction is part of the official rhetoric defining the tasks of fund managers and financial analysts.[9] As we saw in chapter 1, this assertion corresponds to one of the cognitive, moral, and political components of the figure of the investor in financial theory. Conviction is the moral ground on which valuation, based on standardized cognitive tools, is supposed to lead to market efficiency and a socially optimal allocation of resources. In the financial industry, this moral aspect of the definition of the figure of the investor is part of the rules for employee interactions within and between companies. Thus, the production and confirmation of this conviction or sincerity in the opinion about value are performed relationally as the application of standardized procedures.

Salespeople I observed and interviewed eagerly said that they could influence their customers with ideas about which stock to buy or sell but that this influence was rarely recognized when it led to good results. Fund managers' insistence on the centrality of their personal opinion was part of an explicit conflict among employees concerning the importance of their respective contributions to the discovery of true value. The fund managers I met all insisted that they were the independent source of the decision to buy or sell—in particular, in opposition to financial analysts and salespeople. Carla, for example, was a former fund manager with whom I conducted an interview in 2003. She had been a fund manager, had then headed a team of fund managers at the Compagnie Universelle (a major French bank), and had retired a year before I met her. Talking about her experience as fund manager and director of a team, she said: "Fund managers are very individualistic people, with a strong personality. So if someone comes saying 'You must do that!' it does not work! [. . .] A manager is interested in his fund, he does not care at all about . . . besides, he is self-sufficient. He can listen, but . . . yes, he can listen, discuss, etc., but probably, in fine, he only cares about his own opinion."

Jérôme, a fund manager who was close to fifty years old, was based in Paris, and had extensive experience in various financial professions, described the relation with salespeople in a way that was very similar to the way Brokers Inc. employees described their relations with their customers based in the United States. He stated: "In general, I am rather the motor, I have always been the motor, it means I do not wait for him [the salesperson] to tell me to buy. In fact, I check, I confirm my information with him, I discuss with his analyst to see if, maybe, there is something I did not see because the analyst is pretty much closer to the company than me, but I'm still the motor . . ." When I asked him to clarify his meaning, he said, "The idea comes from me, it never comes from him. [. . .] I stand on the principle that I'm the [fund] manager, so . . . so it's me who presses the button. When I say 'I buy,' it is my decision. The guy, he can say what he wants, it's me who presses the button. So he is discharged of all responsibility."

Some employees used terms referring to emotion and affect to describe the personal connection between the fund manager and the money he managed. Paul, a thirty-year-old fund manager, was part of the Acme team responsible for investing €11 billion in European big caps. He said: "I buy something, it first starts going down, it goes down so much that you end up saying to yourself: 'Ah, I can't take it anymore, I can't bear it anymore,' that is to say that we feel physically, especially when we are passionate, in the flesh, that it hurts, and that's often the moment when one must not crack." This bond between the money invested and the body of the fund manager could be used to stress the legitimacy of the fund manager in relation to other professions. Thus, a fund manager explained to me that when a salesperson's recommendation did not correspond to what happened later, he could be aggressive with him in order to make him "feel, like [him], the pain in the body when the price drops." This staging of self and passion was one of the possible ways to comply with the official description of the professional tasks of the fund manager. The bond it portrayed combined the repertoire of personal conviction about a company's value with the idea that the money invested was an intrinsic part of the figure of the investor enacted by the fund manager, in line with the idea of the principal-agent relation. Financial analysts and salespeople could then be ranked second to fund managers in the definition of true value because they could not claim this intimate bond with the money of their clients.

At Brokers Inc., salespeople were officially considered to be main source of fees for the company. From this position, they criticized almost daily the valuation produced by the financial analysts working for Brokers SA in Paris. Salespeople were unanimous in their assertion that in their relation with clients, it was their duty to carry out valuation independently from the valuation produced Brokers SA's analysts. This could mean expressing opinions that were different from or even opposed to those of analysts. But this demanded particular care because, as I have explained, fund managers and buy-side analysts received the analyses produced by Brokers SA by email and could find them on the company's website. Salespeople were therefore required to know the arguments and reasoning of the analyst that they criticized. To do so, they explained, personal experience in valuation was crucial. Frédéric, twenty-seven years old, was the youngest salesperson at Brokers Inc. He explained that because he had little experience, he rarely opposed the views of financial analysts. Rather, he considered that his work was to synthesize and complement the analysis produced by financial analysts in order to respond to personal characteristics of each of his clients.

Juliette and André, on the other hand, had an explicitly contemptuous attitude toward the analysts of Brokers SA. In everyday exchanges in the office, they often pointed out that they had over ten years of experience valuing companies listed on the European exchanges, especially in France. This, they asserted, was much more than the experience of the average analyst at Brokers SA. Admittedly, these analysts had more knowledge of the accounting details of companies they evaluated, they met more often with these companies' managers, and they followed their companies' business context more closely. But for these two salespeople, this was not enough. Valuation had to be based on a conviction that relied on their personal experience, which resulted from the consolidation over time of lines of reasoning about listed companies and about the customers who paid the fees.

In an interview with me at the end of my observations at Brokers Inc., Juliette said:

> The idea is that, once again, we, what we must do, it's the filter, you see, I have enough experience and it's my role. It's not because a little young analyst has just started, just finds a stock and will tell me that one must buy it, that I'm going to say one has to buy it. First: It's me who must go . . . I want the analyst to convince me first. So already I provide a big filter . . .

In response, I asked, "And you can tell your client 'My analyst says that, but I do not agree'?" Juliette answered:

> Yes, absolutely! First, I am not obliged to tell him, I am not obliged to tell him everything the analyst thinks. I will do it if he asks me, "What does your analyst think of such stock?" I will tell him, "He says this, but I think that," and that's my job, that's what doing my job well means. In the morning when I read my emails, I am the one who has to interpret; when I read what analysts are saying, I am the one who has to interpret what the analyst says, and to say if it is worth something or not. So I eliminate already many things. And then the way that I work is that, when I tell someone, "You have to buy, you have to sell," it's because I am convinced myself. Which means that I have a reasoning to back it.

Fund managers tended to assert their independence in relation to financial analysts and salespeople as a way to stress their own centrality in the process of valuation. Within Brokers Inc., the stress employees put on the quality and the personal character of their personal valuation was in part a way to position themselves

in the power relations among employees. André often said he
found that, outside of a few exceptional individuals, financial analysts at Brokers SA generally produced valuation of poor quality.
This was due to the fact that the management of the company
had hired "clones from the *grandes écoles*"[10] who knew valuation
methods but did not have any "originality." As I have described,
Brokers SA had grown quickly in the late 1990s, hiring new
employees with the money coming from increasing fees during
what André and the other employees referred to as the "internet
bubble." This had changed the product offered by the company,
increasingly favoring the analysis of big caps for large investment
management companies, with the aim of becoming a big global
brokerage company. In this period, Brokers SA hired students
who graduated from elite institutions, like Frédéric.

André's criticism of Brokers SA analysts was partly a way to
legitimize his position as manager of the subsidiary in relation
to the management of the parent company. In the negotiations
between André and Brokers SA management when Brokers Inc.
was established, André had argued that he would be bringing an
important and steady stream of fees to the company from the
start. As was customary for senior salespeople, the fund managers to whom he had sold information for years as a salesperson at
a major French bank would follow him to his new position and
keep paying fees for the information he sold them. This would
provide basic revenue to Brokers Inc. from its launch. The loyalty
of fund managers to André could therefore be considered independent of the analysis produced by the analysts of Brokers SA.
André thus told me that, according to him, Brokers Inc. could be
considered a franchise of Brokers SA. The parent company provided its infrastructure of analysts and its name, which was well
known in France, in exchange for fees that came from the analysis provided by people like André, Juliette, and Frédéric, which

did not necessarily depend on the quality of the financial analysis produced at Brokers SA. By emphasizing the weakness of this financial analysis, André mobilized an argument that was considered legitimate in the profession—the importance of the personal opinion of the salesperson in the relation with clients—in a negotiation aimed at lowering the price of the franchise and, more generally, the right of Brokers SA's management to monitor the subsidiary in New York.

Using me as a unpaid intern was partly related to this tension. My official task was to conduct financial analysis of small listed companies that were not covered by Brokers SA analysts. These companies were chosen by Brokers Inc.'s salespeople based on their curiosity or the explicit requests of some of their clients. Due to regulations, my analysis could not be presented to clients directly and was given only to the salespeople themselves. When my analyses began to look professional enough, André asked that they be sent to some salespeople based in Paris. Then, referring to the fact that I was an anthropologist and visibly omitting the fact that I had graduated from one of these French elitist institutions, something André had taken into account when assessing my resume, he declared, in the big open room and in the presence of all the other employees, that he was going to "show these assholes in Paris that with an intern that I don't even pay, I can do better than them with their analysts who graduated from the *grandes écoles*."

At Brokers Inc., income depended officially on the personalized relation of each salesperson with the fund managers assigned to him. Financial analysts did not establish or maintain this relation and were thus considered more easily replaceable than a salesperson. Their role in the production of valuation sold by the company was therefore considered less important. This tension was particularly strong for the three analysts who worked at Brokers Inc.: a thirty-year-old senior analyst, a twenty-six-year-old junior analyst, and a twenty-one-year-old intern. They worked on a team with a trader and two salespeople who sold information about companies listed in the United States to fund managers based in Europe. At the time of my observations, the only income produced by this team of six people came from fees paid by fund managers who were clients of Hervé, the head of the team and the senior salesperson, who was around forty years old. To a large extent, these fund managers were people with whom he had established long-term relations in his previous position as a salesperson at a large French bank and who had followed him when he had joined Brokers Inc. four years before my observations. The second salesperson, Julien, twenty-eight years old, was starting in the profession and had just begun to solicit clients who did not pay him any fee yet.

The financial analysis sold by Hervé was not based on fundamental valuation produced by Brokers SA because its analysts did not evaluate companies listed in the United States. But his financial analysis was also not necessarily based on what was produced by his team of analysts in New York. In an interview with me, Hervé said:

> There are many ways to proceed, right? I am not a systematic person so, hum, I adapt also a little to the interests of the clients. So what I do can be very different. I can call a client only to talk to him about stocks he has in his portfolio. If there have been new developments on the stocks he has, I will tell him, "Look, there is a risk of strike at Boeing," hum, it's an example. I have other clients that are eager to find new ideas, so I will call a client and tell him, "Oh! You should buy Wendy's today, because they will announce" hum . . . I don't know "a new product today" or "because its valuation is interesting."[11] I have other clients who like to have

an overview, so, for instance, what the research [teams] of other brokerage houses have published, so I will call him and tell him, "Well, today, what matters is to see that Merrill Lynch has turned negative on a sector and that Goldman has turned positive on oil companies because, hum, because of these reasons" and so in a certain way to be the filter between the clients and Wall Street. It is really very different, in sum, hum . . .

In that interview, conducted toward the end of my observations at Brokers Inc., Hervé explained that the analysts on his team were mainly an "alibi." It was clear to anyone that just three people could not cover all the companies listed in the United States. His customers, he explained, were primarily interested in his own experience valuing these companies. The reports produced by his team's analysts were not published on Brokers SA's website, and according to the analysts themselves, fund managers rarely commented on them. Hervé noted, however, that sending these documents regularly ensured a "presence." Also, it fulfilled a crucial requirement concerning the contractual obligation of investment management companies: according to their internal procedures, to justify why they were paying Hervé brokerage fees, fund managers had to "check the box" corresponding to their assessment of the quality of the valuation produced by sell-side analysts.

The other employees of Brokers Inc. acknowledged this situation more or less explicitly, although in interviews, the team's analysts did not describe it in the same terms. They decried their weakness by flipping the arguments put forward by salespeople like André and Juliette. These salespeople tried to distance themselves from Broker SA's analysts, who were recognized as much more necessary than those of Brokers Inc., by insisting that standardized financial analysis was inadequate to meet the requirements of individual customers. According to the analysts at Brokers Inc., fundamental valuation and in-depth knowledge of companies were indeed sidelined in these exchanges. But this was because fund managers worked with a horizon that was too short-term and did not take the time to consider all the calculations and hypotheses about the future that were necessary to evaluate a company. Repeating the idea that financial analysts were those who best knew the companies they evaluated, these employees attempted to claim a fundamental position in the process of valuation that was denied by their colleagues—something that was visible not only in everyday comments but also in the distribution of salaries and bonuses. Nicolas, the senior analyst on the team, had passed the level 1 exam of the chartered financial analyst (CFA) program, and at the time of my observations, he was preparing to take the level 2 exam. The CFA has three levels: the first is the most accessible, and analysts who reach levels 2 and 3 are less common. Often employees try to obtain this certification to strengthen their resume, and this was Nicolas's goal, one that he and his colleagues considered typical. In an interview with me, he explained that he intended to enhance his resume in order to find a job in another brokerage or in an investment management company where he would be "taken seriously."

Employees articulated the tensions among them concerning the importance of their various professions in the search for the true value of companies by asserting their individual capacity to develop a personal opinion that referred to the cognitive, moral, and political meanings of the figure of the investor. These tensions also concerned the methods that were most associated with each profession. The way salespeople and analysts at Brokers Inc. viewed the discounted cash flow (DCF) method of valuation provides a good example of this.

As we saw in chapter 1, the DCF method is considered the one that best approximates the theoretical definition of the fundamental value of a company. However, its application implies personal interpretations about the future that can vary widely from one person to another and that can thus result in theoretical prices that can be very different from each other and from the listed price at any given moment. Because this method implies studying the listed company's accounts and conducting several calculations to test different hypothesis about the future, it is associated with the kind of work produced by financial analysts. The reasoning organized in the DCF method was usually an important part of the analysts' reports. Yet, salespeople at Brokers Inc. generally said that the DCF was not a useful tool for selling financial analysis because it could not be synthesized in a few lines. Indeed, in order to justify the theoretical price, it would be necessary to explain all the hypotheses about the future made to carry out the calculations. Frédéric criticized what he considered the overextended character of the DCF explanation: "I will never say to a client, 'I think that it is necessary to buy because the analyst tells me that his DCF shows that the theoretical price of the company is this much.'" But, more fundamentally, these salespeople emphasized that modifying hypotheses about the future would lead to big changes in the results of a DCF analysis, so that it was too "easy" to obtain any kind of result. In the words of Frédéric, this meant that the theoretical price could not have "a truly scientific character."

Nicolas, the senior analyst working on the team directed by Hervé, said that, on the contrary, the DCF method was much better for finding the "true value" of a company than the kind of analysis carried out by salespeople and traders:

There are valuation elements that cannot be taken into account, that are not . . . that cannot be sold. So, then, it depends on the sophistication of the client. [. . .] DCF is a complicated model, [. . .] you cannot say "The DCF gives a target price of 30," you must say "With a DCF that takes into account these hypotheses, these hypotheses, these hypotheses, we reach thirty. If you do not agree with certain hypotheses, we can recalculate it." But then the client is going to say "What is he talking about?!" It breaks the discourse, it becomes boring, it's a catastrophe. No salesperson in the profession ever talks about the DCF. The DCF is there only because everybody knows that it is the only way to evaluate a company, so it must be in the analysis report.

In this case, the defense of the representative character of the DCF was also an attack on relative and speculative valuation, which the financial analyst associated with salespeople, fund managers, and traders. Nicolas said:

Well, there are a lot of problems with relative valuation [. . .] there are enormous problems with relative valuation [. . .] the huge problem with relative [valuation] is that when you have a strong variation of a sector upwards or downwards, maybe the relative [valuation] is not going to change, and that is a huge problem. [. . .] Relative valuation is to say, when Amazon is worth 200, is to say "Well, it's not expensive, Amazon is paying fifty times its sales while Yahoo! is paying two hundred times its sales." Yeah right, but in DCF [valuation], it is not worth two hundred times its sales, it is not worth one hundred times its sales, it is not worth ten times its sales, it is worth two or three! So it's, in fact, saying "such a sheep is whiter than another," but we don't know if the sheep are going toward catastrophe or toward pasture, we do not know where the sheep go, and that's the problem with relative [valuation].

Nicolas presented himself as an analyst specializing in fundamental valuation who was forced to deal with short-term price changes and customer demands:

> So the DCF protects you from bubbles, it protects you from crashes . . . so sometimes the problem is that the DCF puts you completely out of phase. And that's the problem of Wall Street analysts [. . .] the problem of the DCF is that it is a long-term instrument. [. . .] When I do my DCF and my DCF works, it's going to convince me that I should do the analysis. But I can't call the client . . . , I can't put on the first page: "the DCF says that it's worth twenty dollars" when in fact it's worth five,[12] it does not work, people do not buy that. People buy a story, a change in management, they buy matrixes that improve, they buy hope . . . a dynamic that is on, you see . . . [. . .] Me, I don't know what can happen in the short-term [. . .] there is no theoretical foundation for that. [. . .] People use relative [valuation] on companies that are not comparable, some kind of historical P/E,[13] and when it does not go in the direction they want, they take the historical price/sales, and if the historical price/sales is not interesting, they take the historical book to value, there will surely be one of the three that is going to work, right?! So that's the problem, it's that we're going back to the same debate about comparing historical P/E. The historical P/E . . . who gives a damn about the historical P/E! All these measurements [. . .] you need a lot of adjustments for these measurements! All those measurements thrown out like that, it's just to go in the direction one wants to go, and very often, unfortunately, in the direction of the clients . . . [. . .] The customer wants to know what to do now [. . .] people have very short-term perspectives [. . .] the DCF says what it's worth today for the next five years.

In this long argument, Nicolas put forward his most specific expertise, the in-depth analysis of listed companies aimed
at determining their fundamental value. In doing so, he openly
opposed relative valuation and what he termed the "short-
termism" of speculative valuation. Salespeople used all the methods of valuation in their relations with fund managers. As I have
described, this was also the case for the documents produced by
financial analysts. And, more fundamentally, as we have seen, the
three definitions of value are interdependent. The reports produced by Nicolas were actually not different from those produced
by other analysts in this respect. His defense of fundamental valuation was concerned more with protecting his own position at
Brokers Inc. and in the financial industry in general than with
denying the other constitutive components of valuation.

It was within this same opposition to analysts that Juliette, the
salesperson and partner of Brokers Inc., rejected the DCF:

> I don't like the DCF unless it's done by someone who is very good
> at it, but in general analysts can say anything and everything about
> growth, the same for margins[14] . . . Nobody has any idea about the
> margins for a cyclical company over ten years, whereas a growth
> company, if you think it's a growth company, you do a market
> analysis and all that, maybe you can get to be a little bit more
> specific. In general, what I like is to value a company by the sum of
> the parts, saying "this is worth this," "this is worth that," and "that
> is worth that." Mh . . . stocks . . . what I really like is a demonstra-
> tion that the company, today, is cheap, but not with models over
> twenty-five or thirty years. It's today, in relation to the industry, in
> relation to the market, in relation to what the market is expecting,
> it's not expensive. It's more a vision . . . mh . . . today, a picture of
> the company today, in comparison with the rest.

Unlike Nicolas, Juliette rejected the importance of the central method of fundamental valuation. She put forward the importance of relative and speculative valuation with an analysis based on a view of comparable companies but also of the market as a whole, explicitly diminishing the utility of focusing on just a few companies, which is the task of financial analysts.

Salespeople were supposed to be capable of personalizing and reinterpreting long-term and short-term data to satisfy the personal requirements of each client, building a story that would give them "hope." The junior analyst on the team directed by Hervé lashed out at this, saying that the analysts were "the intellectuals of valuation" and opining that this capacity of salespeople to change their discourse according to each customer was "prostitution," a word that for the employee mainly indicated female sex work and that was considered a major insult, thereby reproducing repertoires about gender and sex that were widespread in the financial industry.[15]

The conflict described previously among fund managers, salespeople, and analysts concerned mainly fundamental and relative valuations, oriented at discovering the true value of the company. In contrast, Brokers Inc. traders were in part outside this problematization. Their expertise on the value of listed companies concerned mainly short-term price movements, variations that occurred usually within the same day. This expertise was supposed to allow them to find the best price for purchase or sale but also to respond to other kinds of requests made by clients, which, as traders remarked, could be very different. According to the contracts signed with their clients, some fund managers had to report that transactions were done at a price that supposedly reflected price changes during the whole day. Thus, fund managers could request, for example, that traders fragment a single transaction into equally weighted transactions carried out at different moments in the day. For instance, for an order to sell €1 million worth of shares of Dupré, the trader would sell ten tranches worth €100,000 each at regular intervals during the day. Other fund managers could request that the transaction take place at a specific time of the day or that it be capped—i.e., that the shares not be bought (or sold) at a price higher (or lower) than some limit indicated in advance. This request presupposed that the trader could predict future price changes during the day in order to do the transaction at the best price but within the limits demanded by the client.

Thus, the expertise of traders at Brokers Inc. was not directly based on fundamental or relative valuation. These forms of valuation were taken into account only as information about opinions that could influence short-term price movements. The working day of traders at Brokers Inc. began around 1:00 A.M. in New York, two hours before the opening of stock exchanges in continental Europe. Traders read news for about an hour and then sent short emails to clients. In the largest investment management companies, buy-side traders were also working at that time, sending orders for particular amounts of shares to be bought or sold as soon as the stock exchange opened. Yet, most orders were sent at around 6 or 7 A.M. Then, and for another two or three hours, traders at Brokers Inc., in a frantic agitation, answered the phone, passed orders to buy and sell to traders based in Europe, and followed price movements that they considered would mark trends for the rest of the day.

Traders, analysts, and salespeople at Brokers Inc. openly shared the idea that trading was radically different from fundamental valuation and long-term analysis. However, the points of view of these employees varied when it came to assessing whether traders' professional tasks contributed to the production of a truth of value and to the flow of fees paid by customers, which had an impact on everyone's bonus. Luke, one of the two junior traders on the team working for fund managers based in the United States, often remarked that salespeople were overpaid in relation to the importance of their work for the stabilization of commercial relations with clients. In an interview with me, he stated that "everyone wants to complicate this shit, everyone wants to be intellectual in this shit, but it's basic, it's really basic, it's not complicated." He was thus attempting to undermine the idea that there was a specific knowledge required to retain clients. Thomas, the other junior trader on the team, took the opposite stance, saying that he did not have enough knowledge about accounting to do the work of salespeople. He had obtained an MBA and had probably studied more accounting than Hervé, who had learned the job by doing it. In a conversation with me, he said, however, that knowledge was what distinguished traders from salespeople: "[To become a salesperson, you] must know the companies way more in depth, you need have much better knowledge in accounting. I think really I have the intellect to do it, if I really made the effort. But practically, it's completely different customers, you see, it's different interlocutors, so I would have to start from scratch."

Pascal, in his late thirties, was one of the three partners of Brokers Inc. He was also the trader who obtained the highest fees from clients and the head of the team of traders composed of Thomas and Luke. He had started the company with Juliette and André, with whom he had worked before at a bank. He often made self-deprecating jokes about himself and the industry at large. Thus, when I was first introduced to him, he said: "You're an anthropologist? We don't need an anthropologist here, what we need is a zoologist!" He agreed to do an interview with me but requested that we do it at the central table in the big room, which meant that we talked in the presence of several analysts and salespeople, as well as Thomas, whom he invited to listen. During this interview, he insisted on the different kinds of expertise required for trading compared to fundamental and relative valuation in these terms:

> There's nothing technical. Thomas, when he started, he had never done that, he learned in three months. There are exceptional cases where it's important to have experience, but there are not many parameters, and there are parameters that you can't control. You need experience, not theory, and you get it quite quickly, you don't need to be Einstein, you could not have a school, it's experience, like love [everybody laughs]. There are more technical markets, derivatives, where it is better to have graduated from Central[16] than from the Business School of Nancy.[17] I would have more trouble, but I could nevertheless do those things. But in these markets, you have more parameters, a sophisticated theory, Black & Scholes,[18] you are assisted by software. Me, in the morning, I listen to the news, to what analysts say, it gives me an idea of how it will vary at the beginning. Then you always have parameters that are added during the day. If I don't have an idea, I'm blind. And then I call my customers to sell them my soup, to bring added value. [. . .] To trade a stock, you do not need to know the research,[19] it is affected by news about the stock and by news about the market. But there are no constant variables from one day to the next, no really accumulated knowledge that you could retain, to treat a stock. If one day there is a big seller, a takeover, shitty numbers, it can influence prices for a couple of weeks, that's all.

In other companies in the financial industry, traders often have extensive mathematical expertise and develop trading software and methods the ownership of which they can negotiate with their employers.[20] But even in other settings, the argument that the definition of value cannot be the result of knowledge is nevertheless closer to the valuation practices of traders.[21] In the preceding passage, Pascal was explicitly undermining the legitimacy of the other two professions that constituted the core business of Brokers Inc.—i.e., the production of financial valuation. Yet, he accepted the idea that in order to be a good trader, one needed to form a personal opinion on stock price variations. Repeating the critique of the concept of market efficiency present in speculative valuation, Pascal considered that the arguments used in fundamental and relative valuations were factors that would influence these short-term variations but not tools that would enable one to find the true value of the company. The truth about the stock prices that he was after was that of short-term movements, for which these theories had nothing to propose, as analysts and salespeople themselves would acknowledge. Pascal's position was thus articulated according to the tensions present in financial theory concerning the relation between fundamental valuation and the constant variation of stock prices. The way he used it to assert his position at Brokers Inc. reiterated, within the official controversy among professions, the centrality of the figure of the investor as the source of the definition of value.

Salespeople, financial analysts, traders, and fund managers have to assert that they have produced a personal opinion about value based on specific expertise. This valuation could be based, for instance, on short-term price movements for traders, long-term forecasts for financial analysts, or a combination of different forms of valuation for salespeople and fund managers. In all these cases, the procedures of valuation necessarily include the three definitions of value: fundamental, relative, and speculative. Employees thus mobilized the multiple gazes of the figure of the investor and assembled them in different ways.

The figure of the investor, multiple and contradictory, is distributed in employees' practices, as the personal character of valuation is part of the relations of hierarchy, competition, and collaboration that they have to develop in their professional lives. The investor's gaze does not just define the meaning of calculations and procedures. It is also central to how employees justify the application of the procedures in terms of conviction, pleasure, and sincerity. In the conflicts among professions and valuation methods, the personal opinion of the investor that each employee must express is constantly reaffirmed as a necessary condition for a truth of value to be possible. The everyday application of valuation practices thereby contributes to the legitimization of the social hierarchies effected by the financial industry worldwide within listed companies and among all the social activities that are included in or excluded from the investment universe. The application of the gaze of the investor in everyday practices is not just dependent on how employees appropriate it in their attempts to assert their positions. It is also stabilized by a series of rules and penalties. Respect for these rules and penalties, the next section argues, serves then as a further confirmation that the price of listed companies indeed reflects a value that is determined by independent investors. At Brokers Inc., this was particularly noticeable in the relation between salespeople and fund managers.

THE VALUATING PERSONALITY AS THE EFFECT OF PROCEDURAL RULES

The relation between fund managers and salespeople was central in the operations of Brokers Inc. This relation followed procedures and rules of practice that I could observe and hear about in interviews outside of the company with fund managers and salespeople working in the United States, France, and the United

Kingdom. All the professionals I interacted with referred to them as clear professional standards. These rules concerned the temporality of exchanges between fund managers and salespeople, the way in which fee payment was decided and carried out, and the content of what these employees were asked and allowed to exchange.

Fund managers and salespeople had to assert that their relation was developed in order to produce an independent opinion about the value of listed companies. To do so, they had to combine the valuation produced by financial analysts with other information and interpretations. This resulted from a dialogue between fund managers and salespeople. While the content of this dialogue varied from one person to another, it never departed from the framework of financial theory. The application of these procedures was standardized and controlled so that its outcome would indeed be considered the result of a personal opinion, itself a necessary condition for the truth of value. At Brokers Inc., I was able to follow an event where these rules were breached, which allows us to explore what is asserted when the rules are respected.

Direct exchanges between salespeople and fund managers during working hours were usually very short. They were most often done by telephone and rarely happened more than a few times every week or every month. According to most fund managers' descriptions in interviews and to what I could observe at Acme, in a working day of nearly ten hours, the fund managers' direct contacts with salespeople rarely exceeded one hour. The rest of the time was used to read financial analyst reports, to decide on transactions with stocks, and to exchange views within the fund management team, among other tasks. At Brokers Inc., salespeople often arrived at the office around 7 A.M. For an hour or two, they read the documents published by Brokers SA's analysts, the specialized press, and other sources of information, which could vary depending on the subject. They then contacted their regular or potential customers and spent between one and three hours sending short emails and leaving short voice messages on answering machines. The atmosphere at this time in the office was frantic. Salespeople also received phone calls, which they answered quickly. Contacts with clients rarely lasted more than a few minutes. It was not unusual for a salesperson to give exactly the same information several times to different people, even if they tried to change their presentation for each client.

From noon onward, after European stock exchanges closed, contacts with customers occurred less often. Salespeople would quickly leave the office to buy food, which they brought back and ate in front of their computers or at the central table of the big room. In either case, the priority was to remain available in case there was a phone call for them. One of the rules I learned at the beginning of my observations was that no phone should be left ringing more than a few seconds. The rest of the day was devoted to reading financial analyses and to discussing the daily news with colleagues. Salespeople remained available the whole afternoon for fund managers to call them. When they did, it could result in longer conversations. Direct relations between fund managers and salespeople were thus usually intense and short, marked by a "lack of time" and the need to be "concise"—expressions they used in interviews with me and in everyday interactions. Most of the working day of salespeople was thus devoted to preparation for these minutes of exchange, for which fund managers could pay substantial fees.

The relation between fund manager and salesperson developed over the long term according to a chronology that was described to me in very similar terms by employees in Paris and in New York. It started, for the salesperson, when he searched professional listings for contact information about the fund manager.

The salesperson then needed to learn about the category of listed companies in which the fund manager specialized. For the first six months, the relation was mainly limited to the regular messages the salesperson left on the fund manager's answering machine. These were usually thirty-second messages that synthesized information and reasoning about the value of a company or sector. The salesperson would also send the fund manager short emails with similar content. In general, during this initial period, the fund manager did not answer. Salespeople and fund managers in New York and Paris all justified this silence as a way to test the valuation abilities of the salesperson.

After this first phase, if the manager judged the analysis convincing, he answered emails, talked to the salesperson over the phone, and met with him a few times. If the relation moved on, for the first one or two years, the fund manager would pay for the salesperson's services, but the regularity and the amount of payment could vary considerably. They remained explicitly at the sole discretion of the fund manager, so the salesperson would not know whether the payment would continue or how much he would obtain for his services. Throughout their relation, the fund manager always retained the option to end it at any time and without further explanation or penalty.

At the end of this period, if the relation was to continue, it was considered that the two people had found what employees called a "fit," a shared "way of thinking." The fund manager would pay fees more regularly and in more regular amounts. The relation could last for many years and could continue when one or both employees changed employers but continued working in the same profession, so the fees paid by the same fund manager for the services of the same salesperson would be part of the commercial exchange between new companies, as had happened when André and Juliette launched Brokers Inc. Framed by the temporalities and the commercial concerns of their employers, the dialogue between salesperson and fund manager, explicitly aiming to affect the opinion of the latter, could thus continue with a certain degree of autonomy from employers as long as it remained within the financial industry, i.e. as long as the two employees remained officially employed to carry it out.

Over time, salespeople would almost completely stop soliciting new fund managers and focus on a stable clientele that provided them with more or less constant income. As I described in the case of André, this clientele represented an argument when negotiating a salesperson's place within the hierarchy of the company, a process that Godechot has analyzed in the case of certain types of traders.[22] At the time of my observations, André's clients paid Brokers Inc. around $6 million. This amount can be compared with the company's yearly revenue of around $35 million. According to André, most of these fees, and therefore his own bonus, were the result of commercial relations with less than ten clients, ones he had started establishing at the beginning of his career as a salesperson when he arrived in New York at the age of twenty-five. At the time of my observations, fifteen years later, dealing with fund managers took less than two hours of his twelve-hour working day. The other ten hours were mainly devoted to managing employees and the relation with the parent company. In his career as a salesperson, he had worked for four employers. Each move involved the kind of negotiations that led to his position as manager and partner of the New York subsidiary of Brokers SA that I described earlier.

At the time of the creation of Brokers Inc., the revenue of the company came from fees paid by customers who had followed the salespeople—in particular, Juliette and André—to their new company. This possibility for a salesperson to leave an employer and carry with him his customers, on which basis Brokers Inc.

was founded, was also a constant threat to the stability of the company. At any time, Brokers Inc.'s salespeople could leave to work for another employer, thus depriving the company of a part of its revenue. A year after my observations Frédéric left Brokers Inc. to become partner in a company created by one of his professional acquaintances. Two years later Frédéric hired two salespeople from Brokers Inc., offering them a higher income and the prospect of a more attractive career. This happened at a time when a major investment bank was in the process of acquiring Brokers Inc. itself. Brokers Inc.'s employees expected that this acquisition would result in the arrival of a new management team and a number of new salespeople, limiting the career prospects of those who were already there.

According to the people I observed, the long-term relation between salesperson and fund manager was supposed to allow each employee to develop a personal style. These styles could vary, however, from one professional relation to another and could not be categorized. The only official confirmation that they led to valuation of good quality was given by the continuity of the commercial relations and of the job that depended on them. In interviews and comments in everyday interactions, salespeople and fund managers explained that establishing a relation of "trust" required a "correspondence," a "fit" between salesperson and fund manager, that was possible only as the personal relation extended over time. This would make it possible to judge the quality of the valuation provided by the salesperson, which fund managers and salespeople generally qualified using expressions like "having a good idea," "a story that attracts his attention," or "to be synthetic, sharp and accurate." These expressions, drawn from interviews or informal conversations with fund managers and salespeople, all conveyed the idea that financial analyses could be ranked according to their quality but that the criteria for making distinctions remained vague. The definition of the quality of financial analysis was supposed to depend on the personality of each participant and was partly defined by the way in which the different definitions of value were combined.

Employees also stated that a fund manager's choice of one salesperson over another did not depend solely on the technical content of the analysis. In interviews and conversations with me, they expressed, sometimes without further elaboration, that the rhythms of the dialogue and other implicit rules mobilized during the exchange were part of the quality of the salesperson's service: not to sound "too matey," to have a "story ready" before the manager can define the situation as a "waste of time," not to get "discouraged." In conversations with me, salespeople insisted that part of their job was to identify the "styles" or "personalities" of the fund managers, who could be very different. What was "too matey" for one fund manager would be "really friendly" for another; the story a salesperson left on an answering machine could be proof of the "commitment" of someone "searching for ideas" or a mere "peroration." What for one fund manager was "banal information" was called a "discovery" by another. The salesperson who repeated the same public information to two different fund managers could be considered a "parrot" by one of them and an "effective filter" by the other. What was a "stupid" analysis for one fund manager was "smart" for another.

According to the explicit definitions of the professional tasks of fund managers and salespeople, good analyses were the reason they established and maintained relations over time. Jérôme, the fund manager based in Paris, presented this situation as follows:

> You don't choose your interlocutors, by working you know who's talking nonsense and who's saying serious stuff, so you always work with the guys that seem the most serious [. . .]. There are

some people . . . there are very intelligent guys with whom you can have very interesting discussions. And, over the years, it's these people that you call back, because the others, little by little, you take a distance. The personal relation is important, after all, it's a people job, it's really a people job: if the guy starts to get on my nerves, after two or three months, I'll tell him: "Listen, you're nice, but don't call me anymore."

The styles and ways of evaluating companies were determined in each relation, based on the exchange of opinions about financial value. Conviction was also supposed to be a central component of the way in which salespeople and fund managers discussed value. Senior salespeople, like Juliette, stressed that generally when dealing with long-term customers, they could develop a style of analysis that they "liked" or that seemed to "make sense" the most. As we have seen, while Frédéric, twenty-seven years old and with less than two years of experience, tended to repeat the explanations of the analysts and those suggested by his colleagues when he spoke to clients, Juliette, thirty-seven years old and a partner at Brokers Inc., affirmed her independence by emphasizing the importance of speculative and relative valuations compared to the DCF and fundamental valuation. But she could do this only with fund managers who shared her appreciation for this approach. These were the relations that had the most chance to develop in the long term. Jeremy, a thirty-five-year-old salesperson hired at the time of my observations, had relatively extensive experience with clients managing personal or family fortunes, but he was confronted for the first time with fund managers working for pension and mutual funds. He had a tendency to go into long explanations about the economic and political situation concerning companies and their environment. He did this with a loud voice, energetically pacing up and down in the reduced space between his chair and those of his neighbors, something his colleagues said was quite unusual. Eventually, these styles, which could not be categorized in standardized terms, would stabilize as pleasures, certainties, and advantages in the dialogical production of financial valuation. Over time and through interpretive dialogues, salespeople and fund managers thus constituted valuating personalities that varied from one relation to the other and that assembled differently the multiple ways to define value.

As we have seen, the personal character of valuation is supposed to be at the basis of its quality. The good quality of valuation is confirmed by the consistent payment of fees by the fund manager and by the absence of disciplinary sanctions. Sanctions were nevertheless imposed in certain cases. They could involve a conversation with the head of the team for which the employee worked. They could also take the harsher form of a cut in the employee's bonus or in his capacity to expand business—for instance, by assigning new clients to another salesperson. In the worst case, the employees could be fired. In the dialogue between salesperson and fund manager about the quality of valuation, the salesperson is supposed to avoid the temptation to express an opinion for the sole purpose of generating fees—for example, by encouraging the fund manager to sell or buy shares immediately. He might also be tempted to express only what he considers to be the fund manager's own opinion in order to flatter his ego and avoid conflicts, something that is considered to diminish the richness of the thinking they carry out together. In interviews, fund managers regularly denounced this risk. Salespeople often evoked it in everyday exchanges, sometimes using the language of a confession. In order to avoid this, some fund managers said that they did not give the order to buy or sell shares of companies to the trading desk of the salesperson who had advised them in order to avoid giving him an immediate benefit from the opinion he had expressed. Instead, they would conduct that transaction through a second broker and pay the first one with transactions in stocks on which the salesperson had not immediately expressed an opinion. This was supposed to encourage salespeople to speak freely, without calculating how much they could obtain from each of the opinions they expressed.

However, the power relation between fund managers and salespeople was clearly shaped so that salespeople had to adapt as much as possible to serve their clients. Hervé remarked that in the job of the salesperson "what one must do, hum . . . it is quite sad to say! But you must manifest your presence. So, obviously, since you cannot call to say 'howdy!' You must call to say something . . ." The sadness evoked by Hervé confirmed, by opposition, that conviction was the legitimate basis of valuation. He had been a professional musician before becoming a salesperson, and unlike his subordinates, he did not have a formal financial education. His colleagues often said he had a poor knowledge of accounting and therefore of the basic tools of fundamental evaluation. Surprised at first glance by what seemed to me a contradiction between what gave salespeople their legitimacy and this description of Hervé, I asked Frédéric what he thought about the quality of the analysis sold by Hervé. Frédéric replied laconically: "I think that if this guy is capable of bringing two and a half million dollars to Brokers Inc., he must not be bad." A steady and considerable amount of fees would confirm, in case of doubt, the correct application of procedures and the good quality of valuation.

But the uncertainty about the sincerity of valuation was enhanced by a more fundamental part of the procedures organizing the relation between salespeople and fund managers. These relations included outings financed by the brokerage company during which salespeople and fund managers were expected to get to know each other better by sharing personal characteristics that were unrelated to valuation. These outings could consist, for instance, of going out to dinner, spending an evening at the opera or at a striptease show, or going hunting for a weekend. Just like in the case of financial valuation, during these outings each sales-person tried to mobilize his aptitudes and personal tastes and adapt them to those of the client. Some of these activities were of little interest to salespeople, who were more or less resigned to having to participate for the pleasure of their customers. Frédéric told me, for example, about attending a wrestling match with a fund manager close to him in age, although he was barely inter-ested in this type of activity. Juliette and Céline could go to fancy restaurants and manage a few hours of friendly conversation with customers for whom they had little appreciation. The legitimacy of these outings was similar to that of analyses done in a personal way but without deep conviction. They were considered part of performing professional tasks correctly but they lacked the moral component that defined the enactment of the figure of the inves-tor, which implied an intimate connection between the person and his practice.

The outings that employees designated as the most "success-ful" were those that salespeople could say they performed with pleasure, sharing personal affinities with their commercial coun-terparts. Thus, when Juliette invited her customers to the opera, this was a successful outing because they appreciated the show and she was able to understand it and to talk about it with them partly because she also enjoyed it. Frédéric, at the beginning of his career as a salesperson, had discovered striptease bars and went there often with clients because he had started to like them. The way these outings were discussed referred to the personalities of the salespeople and their customers. Frédéric would spend many minutes describing the striptease shows he went to, claiming to be at once amazed and amused to find himself in such situations. Céline, thirty-five and in an emotionally difficult situation at the company, spoke much less willingly about her outings at the opera or her dinners at trendy New York restaurants. Jeremy, used to the activities of his previous wealthy clientele, invited his new customers to a very selective sports club of which he was a member. Since he was developing a new clientele, he was often establishing connections with fund managers who were starting in the profession and were younger than him. He sometimes took them on outings together with Frédéric and his clients—for example, to striptease bars—but he did not mention these with the same enthusiasm that he expressed when he talked about his squash games at the club.

According to the principle justifying the outings, the good quality of valuation depended in part on social identities that were unrelated to the techniques for defining value. Frédéric, for example, put forward his youth and his liking for nightlife as assets, but they were also limits in terms of improving his relations with fund managers. He was able to attract fund managers of his generation who shared his interests, but he had more difficulty finding interesting outings for older fund managers. Gender identities were also important for the choice of the outing and the persona the salesperson would adopt during it. Céline was in the process of consolidating her clientele and explained that it was harder to contact fund managers who were her age because they usually already had enough salespeople with which to work. She said that some of the fund managers, who were mostly male, did not take her analytical abilities seriously because she was a woman but that sometimes her gender could be an asset, since she would take on a "maternal" role with some of her younger male or female clients. She contrasted this gendered role with that mobilized by Juliette, who, according to Céline, was more oriented to "flirting."

Juliette, like Céline, expressed that in the "macho atmosphere" in which she worked, her gender was more often than not a negative marker with which she had to cope. This gender identity was the sole reason why some male and female fund managers would not want to work with her.

In interviews and exchanges with me, salespeople said that the hours spent together during outings were a very rich source of information about the personality of the fund manager. For an outing to be successful, salespeople were expected to mobilize not only ways of thinking but also practical knowledge acquired and mastered during their professional and nonprofessional lives. During these outings, the salesperson and the fund manager shared not only a moment of entertainment but also the more or less compatible parts of their nonprofessional social identities, presented with more or less success, and this was supposed to strengthen the personal aspect of valuation produced through their dialogue.

The outings also presented two official dangers for the logic according to which personalization was the basis of a good financial analysis. Presented as a way for salespeople and fund managers to get to know each other better, outings were nevertheless marked by the constant suspicion that the quality of the analysis would take a back seat and that salespeople would receive higher fees, and hence higher bonuses, solely because of the quality of the outings they offered to their clients. Also, sharing their lives and building personal relations meant that salespeople and fund managers could develop friendships that would exceed their professional focus and take priority over the loyalty they were expected to have for their employer and thereby for the people whose money was going to be invested on the basis of their valuation. During interviews, fund managers almost routinely stated their disapproval of outings, considering them an attempt by salespeople to get paid for something other than their financial analysis. Yet, this statement always came with the admission that they did participate in outings—but only with the aim of enhancing the quality of valuation. Paul, the young fund manager working at Acme, considered outings illegitimate because they put into question the ethics of respect required for professional relations. When I asked him whether salespeople invited him to nightclubs and, if so, how he responded to those invitations, he said:

> In this case it also depends on who we choose. Me, it's people who invite me, but I am not going to hang out with people who take me to places I do not appreciate. To have a good meal is good, but if it is to do it with someone I don't like, I'm not interested. I prefer to have dinner with friends . . . So again, that's one of the criteria, not to be bought, not to ask, there is some ethics to have, in order to be respected . . . Me, I don't go to a nightclub with brokers, except . . . except, if, after a conference, all guests are invited, it's an evening to celebrate the end of a two-day seminar somewhere. I will not just go like that, invited . . .

When I noted that it allowed Paul to meet people, he responded: "Yes, but well, in terms of invitations, entertainment, there are a lot of possibilities. It can be a football match, it can be playing tennis, it can be to have a drink, it can be a meal . . ." And when I mentioned that he appeared to discriminate among activities, he said:

> Yes, for example, I quite like opera, it's rather unusual, so I know that not all brokers will invite me to the opera, so . . . it's rather people who are more educated than the average . . . me, I have rather intellectual brokers because I am intellectual . . . that does not mean that I believe that one has to be intellectual, rather the

opposite, but that, if these people get along well with me, it's also because, in a way, they find in me a part of themselves . . .

In this conversation, Paul said the content of the outing was a filter that rendered the relation between salesperson and fund manager similar to the ones between him and his friends. Just like with financial valuation, he made sense of outings as a matter of personal choice involving the ethics of sincerity in the relation between the salesperson and the fund manager. In an interview with me, Frédéric raised the same concern:

> I wonder, how to use marketing well? Because, if you do too much, you look like a clown. So for example right now, I have a new prospect,[23] I met him once, he's young, he loves to party, I know he likes girls, he likes going out. I know because he sent me two, three emails, in one of them he was telling me: "Yeah, I'm hoping to get laid tonight, blah blah blah." At the same time, he has a job . . . so I wonder, do I go directly at it: "OK, buddy, let's hang out"? He is super Russophile like me, so I wonder, do I propose to him a big outing, Russian baths, Russian restaurant, Russian massage, he's going to dream! But if I do that, I look like a clown. It means that I prioritize marketing and show over fundamental research, or sending serious emails, all that. I think there is a balance.

Like in the first exchanges where he offered financial valuation, Frédéric had to try to find, among his own possibilities, those that would lead to a "fit" with his client and that would be the basis for deepening a relation based on personal characteristics shared by both of them.

The relation between fund managers and salespeople developed in the long term by sharing what they called "ways of thinking" that concern valuation directly, by exchanging opinions and information, and, indirectly, by going on outings. The relation could become emotional, and André and Juliette remarked that some of their long-time customers were also among their best friends. However, they explained, this friendship had to be controlled so as not to tarnish the image of the company by suggesting that the fees were no longer payment based on the quality of financial valuation.

Shortly after I left the company, Juliette went on vacation for two weeks. Frédéric told me a few months later that she had previously distributed her customers among the salespeople at Brokers Inc. so that they would be "covered" during her absence, a practice that was usual in the office and in the profession at large. On this occasion, Frédéric had to work with a fund manager of his same age, with whom he eventually had a romantic relation. This was discovered by chance, Frédéric said, one day when he and the fund manager were walking hand in hand in downtown Manhattan and they came across Juliette, who had returned from vacation earlier than expected. It was a scandal at the office, and André told Frédéric that he was very disappointed. Frédéric started looking for another job, knowing that his bonus for that year would be heavily compromised and that the everyday tension at the office would not be tolerable in the long run. Frédéric had committed two misdeeds. First, the existence of too close a link with a customer covered by Juliette could be described as the theft of one of her sources of income. Second, and more fundamentally, this intimate bond risked taking priority over the sincerity of the financial analysis he was supposed to sell to the fund manager.

The issue was important partly in terms of the company's image. The top management of Brokers Inc. wanted to make it known to the company's employees and, through them, to business partners that this kind of relation was not acceptable. After a few months, Frédéric indeed left Brokers Inc. As I mentioned previously, he became a partner in a brokerage company established by one of his acquaintances, a move that he was planning to make at one point or another anyway. When I met him occasionally in the following years, Frédéric explained to me that his relation with André had remained very tense and they had no direct contact for two years. Then, at Frédéric's initiative, they met to have a coffee, as Frédéric wanted to ease tensions in order to keep a good professional contact—"because you never know"— and also to thank André, who had "after all taught [him] everything." He said: "You know how he is, André, he pretended to be tough for a little while, and then in the end it started all over again, he started messing around, telling dirty jokes . . ." Frédéric had been sanctioned because he had crossed the official boundary of acceptable behavior in the relation between salesperson and fund manager. He had gone beyond the series of practices considered specific to the figure of the investor, defined exclusively by the search for a truth of value with the purpose of maximizing returns. But once the issue concerning image was over for his employer, the scandal was over too. The two salespeople, now with no hierarchical relation, could restore a cordial connection, in which it was difficult to distinguish the part intended as personal pleasure and that aimed at maintaining good relations with someone who, as a member of the same professional group, was also potentially a future commercial partner.

The details of the procedures established to create what the people I observed called a "fit" between salespeople and fund managers were officially aimed at helping the latter produce an informed personal opinion about financial value. With the uncertainty that marks concepts like that of inner conviction, the continuity of the payment of fees by fund managers could be considered a confirmation of the good quality of the financial analysis proposed by the salesperson. In this professional space, Frédéric's success after his departure from Brokers Inc. and Hervé's ability to maintain a strong clientele without using a standard team of financial analysts appeared to be reasons to respect their contribution to the search for the true value of listed companies. The respect for procedures and the continuity of the commercial relation over time constituted the confirmation that their valuations were the product of the investor's gaze.

As we have seen, this figure of the investor is multiple and distributed across all investment and valuation procedures. Employees have to use it in order to assert the legitimacy of their professional tasks in the relations of competition, collaboration, and hierarchy within and between companies. The rules organizing the relation between salespeople and fund managers are explicitly aimed at producing valuation as an independent personal opinion through the dialogue of valuating personalities. The practices of employees thus combine their professional and nonprofessional social identities within the spaces of play and the limits and the sanctions aimed at producing the figure of the investor as the source of value. The nonprofessional lives of employees are thus part of their professional tasks. These professional tasks are possible, however, only when employees make sense of them in their nonprofessional lives. This is the topic of the following section.

ACTING LIKE AN INVESTOR IN EVERYDAY LIFE

For the people I observed at Brokers Inc., Acme, and elsewhere in the financial industry, applying valuation and investment procedures was a job they did for a salary, a bonus, and eventually a dividend if they were partners in their company, like André and Juliette. These standardized procedures were explicitly aimed at enacting the figure of the investor, with its technical, moral, and political meanings. To do so, as I have showed, employees were expected to express a conviction about the value of companies that was supposed to connect with their cognitive abilities and with their nonprofessional identities. But in order for these jobs to be possible, they also had to make sense for employees as part of their nonprofessional lives.

Ho has highlighted how front-office employees in the financial industry justify their high income by referring to their elite education and long work hours.[24] In the same vein, Godechot shows how traders put forward their highly qualified expert knowledge when they claim their mastery, and even ownership, of trading methods in negotiations to demand higher salaries and bonuses.[25] Most employees I observed and interviewed at Brokers Inc., Acme, and Hedge Consulting and in the rest of the financial industry had indeed graduated from such schools and universities. The high remunerations of the financial industry made available by these degrees had actually been one of the major reasons for them to look for a job there. But employees still had to make sense of their income, the hours spent at the office or on outings, and their valuation and investment procedures as part of their everyday lives. Zaloom shows how some of the traders she observed could develop diverging personas, enacting ruthless impersonations of the investor at work and experiencing vulnerability and despair in their family lives.[26] In this section, I explore the relation between the professional and nonprofessional lives of salespeople of Brokers Inc. in order to show the multiplicity of ways in which they made sense of their practices of valuation in relation to their nonprofessional lives, including social identities like gender and age.

Salespeople spent most of the day at the office, trying to contact their customers or preparing to meet with them. A part of their free time was, as we have seen, devoted to outings. In all these cases, they were expected to develop a personal opinion about the value of listed companies and about the activities they shared with their customers. The personal character of valuation was thus not totally separable from the rest of their lives. In interviews and everyday interactions with me, their considerations about wages were often accompanied by reflections about the pleasures of work, especially about the intellectual and emotional content of the relation with customers. Finally, these expresions were usually inscribed in multiple temporalities concerning careers and ways of living. It is in this assemblage that employees could consider it possible to express a personal opinion about the true value of listed companies.

In the context of interviews, my interlocutors articulated all these elements in order to make them intelligible for themselves, for the researcher, and in relation to their situation in the company. Without trying to determine the sincerity of their expression, my analysis here aims to understand the possibilities and limits of the meanings that valuation had for them. Of the seven salespeople who worked at Brokers Inc., Céline was the only one who said that her main motivation for getting up every morning and going to the office was the money she was paid. She said that her relations with fund managers were otherwise irrelevant to her because they were empty of any emotional content, something she found all the more frustrating because they absorbed most of her leisure time. Frédéric, on the other hand, considered the conflictive relation with customers one of the pleasures justifying his work because it had a playful aspect, which he considered close to "sport," "flirting," and "competition." He said that this was more important for him than his remuneration because, coming from a rather wealthy family, as I reported at the beginning of the book, he was not very impressed by sums that allowed him to "earn a good living but not to become rich." André and Juliette, in turn, did not mobilize these kinds of arguments. They said that they liked their jobs because of the pleasure of thinking and interacting with interesting people who could become friends. According to André, it was crucial that income did not become the most important reason for his employees to work. He explained that he had been "getting up at 5 A.M. for the last seventeen years" and spending nearly twelve hours a day at the office, which is "more than with [his] family." He said that he kept doing this even though he no longer needed "to work in order to live," given the revenues he had earned for several years and his wealth as one of the company's partners. If he continued working, he said, it was because he "loved" his job as a salesperson and as CEO of Brokers Inc.

André's discourse was consistent with his hierarchical position in the company. This prevented him from questioning the viability of realizing the valuating personality, in which the representation of customers' interests is supposed to be fundamental. The arguments of Frédéric and Céline were, in part, ways to respond critically to the view defended by their boss. André's remarks indeed incorporated these resistances, situating them within the two extremes of not caring for remuneration and focusing solely on it. He said that he expected employees to enjoy their jobs—but still live with a "healthy" pressure to make sure that "the level of remuneration is there." The comments of Céline, Frédéric, and Juliette concerning the difficulties or pleasures of their everyday lives were also ways to take positions with respect to André. In particular, their remuneration and their professional legitimacy depended on how he valued their work through bonuses and in everyday remarks at the office. The distance exhibited by Frédéric concerning the very definition of the quality of the work and the importance of its translation into monetary revenue could be understood as a way to assert his independence from the power André had to define the correspondence between his work and his bonus. Similarly, Céline considered as a whole the difficult relation she had with some of her clients and the optimism displayed by André, who did not leave her any room to express her discomfort in the office—i.e., the place where she spent most of her time. By stressing the difficulties of her work, she was responding to the official discourse concerning the intellectual interest and the pleasures it was supposed to provide. Thus, Céline rejected the pleasure of flirting or playing in the commercial relation, which both Frédéric and Juliette put forward, although in different ways. Juliette, close to André and more able to negotiate her bonus with him because of their long-term friendship and her status as a partner, took his side most of the time when there were tensions with employees.

I will focus on how employees related to the distributive role of the financial industry in the following chapters, after discussing the role of market efficiency in everyday practices. Here I explore the relation between employees' lives beyond work and the application of the figure of the investor. The pressure to obtain fees from clients is organized as an opposition, a collaboration, and a hierarchy involving ways to define value and each employee's personal capacity to express a convinced, and convincing, opinion. When employees consider their professional lives in relation to their nonprofessional lives, they may distance themselves from the moral meaning of the figure of the investor that they are supposed to apply. This figure thus appears as the product of the application of standardized procedures. Their job can then have meaning of a source of income to which they must devote time and from which they can try to find pleasure. They may continue the job only as long as it is bearable in their personal trajectories.

Conflicts among employees are thus organized by the opposition between forms of valuation and the place their jobs have in their lives more generally.

When employees accepted or embraced the pressure to obtain fees, they attributed a certain legitimacy to the link between the quality of their valuation and the bonus, based on the fees paid by clients and its evaluation by Brokers Inc. managers—in particular, André, the CEO. Employees were thus situated in a hierarchy defined by the fees paid by clients, which served as recurrent assertions of their respective, potentially shifting positions. Every month back-office employees would put at everyone's disposal on the large central table a document detailing the fees provided by each customer to each salesperson. Thus, traders, salespeople, analysts, and any other employee could assess the fees earned by each salesperson and the trader with whom he or she worked in tandem. This invariably gave rise to group discussions and comments among front-office employees that were more or less ironic, enthusiastic, or worried. In addition, when they took coffee breaks or left the office to buy lunch, salespeople and traders often commented on the styles of their colleagues and the quality of their valuation. For instance, Jeremy's long tirades were sometimes the object of ironic remarks about the loud volume of his voice and the fact that he was providing arguments that seemed too distant from each particular listed company. But these remarks were often accompanied with admiration for what was considered his originality and argumentative coherence. On other occasions, these forms of hierarchy and assessment led to conflicts that could be more or less open.

One day at lunch time we were sitting around the central table. Most of the employees present there were talking about the list of fees paid by customers. André mentioned a potential client, floating the idea that a trader would be needed to take care of him. Luke, visibly excited and enthusiastic, asked him if the client "like[d] to party." This question suggested that if the answer was positive, it would be up to him to take care of this client, since he was the trader most able to take his clients to nightclubs and striptease bars. Being a trader for this client would increase the transactions managed by Luke and hence his bonus. André replied with a smile: "He is married with two children." Luke threw himself against the back of his chair and said: "No! No!" Luke then mentioned a customer who was "a really good trader, really smart, a really good guy," and André replied that "what matters is not whether he is intelligent, but that he has kids to feed, money and wants to buy . . . there is no need that he be intelligent!" He then started speaking about himself, remarking that now that he was married and his wife was pregnant, he was going to "need even more money, with these two new mouths to feed." This hinted jokingly at the idea that he might decide to increase his own bonus at the expense of the bonuses of the rest of employees. Luke then said to him: "Come on, with the bonus you have already!" and André replied: "Alright, next time, I'll take the whole bonus for myself, so that it will create a good spirit of desire." Luke then said: "Yeah right, you are the one with the biggest bonus!"

André then raised his voice, as though he could at last express what had been on his mind since the beginning of the conversation: "No, but what is the question you have to ask yourself, the real question, huh?" Luke said nothing and made a grimace, impersonating a little child who did not know the answer, under the attentive and amused eyes of the audience. André then said: "The real question is: How many Lukes does it take to make an André? That's the question!" Luke defended himself, still with a joking tone: "No, it's OK, I know you're the best!" and André insisted: "No, but it's not a question of being the best, it's a question of how many Lukes for an André, you see? You put us in a car, we die in an accident, the question is: How many Lukes does it take to replace an André? The bonus, it's based on that!" Looking at the others, Luke said: "Yeah! I swear to you! I should have stayed in my old job!" André went on: "Go! Go back with your other boss!" and Luke said, "Well, I swear he paid me more!" Julien, the junior salesperson on Hervé's team, had followed the conversation in silence and then said to Luke, laughing: "Come on, on top of it, here you go all the time on trips, hunting, it's the Club Med! You're on paid holidays!" Luke, in his early thirties, had been a soldier for the U.S. Army for six years. In a long interview with me, he explained that everybody in his family liked hunting, something that was "normal in Texas" where he grew up. He was usually in charge of the outings for clients who also liked hunting. Luke said nothing in response to these remarks and laughed sneakily as André approached him and began to give him small slaps on the head and on the cheeks. As Luke acted like a little child who was being punished, André said: "You see, he always tries to make me cry, but it never works!"

When André left the room, Luke looked at us with a grin of resignation and, with a slightly ironic tone in the voice, said, "He is hard," to which Julien immediately added, "He's really hard," and Luke replied, "Well, he's good." We all laughed in chorus, and Julien concluded by saying aloud what Luke was hinting at: "Yes, especially, he's a good boss!"

In these exchanges, in a friendly atmosphere and with a joking tone, André reminded Luke and all the other employees present at the table that he had the right to decide on their bonuses arbitrarily. He had also justified the fact that he gave himself the highest bonus in the company, within limits, because of his ability to obtain fees from fund managers. When Luke tried to compare traders and salespeople in terms of their intellectual abilities, which would have justified his lower place in the bonus hierarchy and condemned him to it, André rejected the argument in order to keep up the pressure to get more fees, something the employees stressed by saying that he was a "good boss." André's reply was reminding everyone that the legitimacy of salespeople in the company was not directly based on their capacity for reflection and that the hierarchy of bonuses could be different if it turned out that traders were playing a greater role in commercial relations. This possibility was actually foreshadowed by transformations in the organization of investment at the time, as I will explain in the next chapter. André recalled this fact just when Luke's outings were openly described as a way for him to have fun that was unrelated to any valuation capabilities. By leaving open the possibility of reconfigurations in the relation of power between traders and salespeople, André was recreating widespread pressure on all of them.

The tension staged by André on that occasion could also be silent, as in the case of Céline. She had little interaction with the other employees of Brokers Inc., many of whom said, when she was not present, that they thought she was going through depression. While most employees had close links with at least some of their colleagues, with whom they went out to buy lunch or even for drinks after office hours, Céline had a cordial but distant relation with all of them. She often had lunch alone and rarely shared this break with others. The other employees said the amount of fees paid by her customers was "not bad." But they sometimes said that it seemed difficult for her to "take off" in order to come closer to the levels reached by Juliette and André, to whom she was close in age and professional experience. Always without addressing her openly on this, some predicted that she would soon resign—not because she did not meet André's criteria but because she would not be able to stand her work for much longer.

The conflicts could also be open. One day, at noon, most salespeople and traders and some analysts were sitting at the central table and made comments, once again, about the list of fees paid by customers in the last month. Some people made ironic remarks about Frédéric, noting that he obtained less in fees than his colleagues. Frédéric had cordial relations with all employees and friendly ones with some of them. He was particularly close to Luke, the trader with whom he worked as a team. In the exchanges around the table, Luke pointed out that the smallest amount paid by a customer since the beginning of the year—$36—had indeed been paid to Frédéric, and then he added: "Once again, thank you for coming!" Frédéric responded to the comments with jokes, making fun of himself, and the conversation remained serene. A little later in the afternoon, while the atmosphere was calm, Juliette raised the topic again, and Luke, used to making aggressive jokes, joined her, announcing that if Frédéric kept that level of fees, he had better change jobs at the company and just "take care of the coffee machine." Frédéric then got up from his desk, went to the center of the room, and shouted that he had "had enough," that he was young but had "still managed to generate enough of fees in one year," and that if they continued to put pressure on him in these terms, he was going to resign. When Luke got up to try to calm him down, Frédéric began shaking his arms as though he was using a broom and said swiftly: "And you! You! Where were you sweeping when you were twenty-seven years old?!"—hinting at Luke's time in the army when he was Frédéric's age. He then left the office, slamming the door on his way out, and did not come back for several hours. Right after he left, Juliette said to André, who had silently observed the scene, "This kid is full-blooded! I did not think he would take it like that!" as if to justify her comments by stressing that she had not wanted to push him that far. André replied that it was "not serious" and that he was rather "positively impressed" by the intensity of the reaction. Thereafter, Frédéric apologized, as he said to me, "for form's sake," but no one joked about the amount of his fees anymore—in particular, because they were increasing steadily.

Frédéric's remark to Luke was partly addressed to André and Juliette. He stressed that he had just recently started in his job and had already established several relations with new customers. Frédéric was also targeting Luke, whose bonus also came partly from the fees paid by these new clients. Luke had been a trader at Brokers Inc. for four years. He worked in tandem with Frédéric and with other salespeople in the company. His income was higher than Frédéric's, although Frédéric could hope to earn more than him in the future. These two employees had developed a friendship and went on vacations together at the time of my observations. However, this did not erase the tension that existed between them, which was linked to the hierarchy of professions and definitions of value, a hierarchy expressed and justified by the fees paid by customers.

The procedures for developing a personal opinion, with their obligations, their limits, and the margin of play they allowed for, make sense for employees only as they accept and problematize them as a relation between their professional and nonprofessional lives. Salespeople, like fund managers and others employees, can apply valuation procedures with more or less pleasure, sincerity, or indifference and with varying emotional and moral attachments. However, they always have to justify their practice as though it is the product of their individual point of view, combining valuation methods with social identities like gender, age, race and class, which are not directly connected to financial valuation. It is in this process that the true value of listed companies, presupposed in financial theory and regulation, made sense for them as something that was possible.

The figure of a free investor seeking information to assess the value of assets he buys and sells in order to maximize return and minimize risks is fundamental in all valuation procedures. It is also central in the political legitimization of the distributive role of the financial industry, as investors' interactions are supposed to lead to market efficiency and a socially optimal allocation of resources. In the case of listed stocks, the activities of a company are analyzed as appropriable money for the investor, and the value of that company is determined by the money that the investor can obtain from it—in particular as a shareholder exchanging stocks in a market problematized in terms of efficiency. This is the figure that employees like André, Juliette, Frédéric, Céline, Paul, and Jérôme, among others, are supposed to put into practice in their everyday professional activities.

Salespeople, traders, and analysts are considered investors because they manage the money of their clients. And their clients are considered investors because they entrust their money to these experts. The investor is not embodied in a person who is the free subject of financial exchanges presupposed in financial theory but instead is established as the result of a relation of representation of the interests of the clients of the financial industry. The figure of the investor is thus distributed in all the practices of front-office employees, who must presuppose it as the source of the value that is expressed in the application of standardized methods. The figure that is thus put into practice is also multiple and contradictory. Fundamental, relative, and speculative valuations are mutually constitutive, but they also assert different definitions of value, the figure of the investor, and the efficient market. Depending on the employees' specializations, they combine these methods of valuation in different ways in relations of hierarchy, competition, and collaboration within and between companies. The mutually exclusive presuppositions about the role of investors and efficient markets implied in these different definitions of value partly organize the relations between employees and companies. And it is through these relations that financial value, in its multiple and contradictory definitions, is asserted as something that says a technical and political truth about listed companies.

The fund managers, salespeople, traders, and financial analysts I observed had to present a personal conviction about the value they defined, which corresponded to the moral component of the definition of the figure of the investor in financial theory. Conviction was supposed to refer to the intimate opinion of the investor has about his private property. The procedures that employees followed to present this conviction implied that they had to combine the methods of valuation with their social identities. This was the case both when they were calculating financial value and when they were participating in outings and interactions where they shared each other's fits and personal styles in order to get to know each other better and supposedly produce better valuation. The procedures aimed both at allowing this personal aspect of valuation to be realized and at limiting the potential dangers that personal involvement by employees could imply for the independence of valuation that defined the moral character of the figure of the investor. Brokers Inc. employees carried out these procedures with various forms of emotional attachment. They could relate their work to pleasure, like Juliette and André; express indifference to their work, like Hervé and partly Frédéric; or reject their work, like Céline. The moral component of the figure of the investor could be mobilized in conflicts among employees who could identify with the figure of the investor in particular situations, as we saw in the cases of Paul and Nicolas. In this multiplicity of positions, the figure of the investor was constantly asserted to be the source of an independent opinion about value, aimed at maximizing returns and minimizing risk according to the standardized methods of valuation and investment. The controls and penalties relating to compliance with professional procedures, as well as the consistency and the amounts of revenue obtained by employees, indicated that this figure was indeed realized in everyday practices and that what it uttered was a financial value that, once reflected in price in efficient markets, was technically accurate and socially fair.

Employees' repetitive assertions of the gaze of the investor reiterate power relations in the access to the money managed by the financial industry. This concerns the power relation between shareholders and creditors in opposition to all other participants in the social activities that make up a listed company, as well the power relations between the social activities that can access the money managed by the financial industry and those that are excluded. The distribution of the figure of the investor in the procedures of the financial industry worldwide thus contributes to legitimizing these social hierarchies in the global space of the industry's operations. According to financial theory and financial regulation, the efficient markets are the other source of the truth of value. The existence of a personal valuation is a necessary condition for the financial industry to be considered the place where independent investors meet—i.e., the social space where efficient markets can be realized. This chapter examined how the figure of the investor organizes all practices of valuation; the next chapter will show how this is also the case for the concept of the efficient market.

3

THE TRUTH OF VALUE AS THE
RESULT OF EFFICIENT MARKETS

As we saw in chapter 1, according to financial theory, the figure of the investor can be considered a source for the definition of true value only in relation to efficient markets. Probably even more than the word *investor*, the word *market* has multiple meanings outside the financial industry, including in the social sciences. This is also the case when it is used to refer to the financial industry as *financial markets*. Just as I did for *investor* and *value*, I propose not to use the word *market* as an analytic category but rather to analyze how the employees I observed used it in order to make sense of their professional practice. As I show, they used the word as part of the procedures of valuation and investment but also as a way to denote the financial industry at large. In both cases, the different problematizations of market efficiency in financial theory remained a fundamental reference.

As we saw in the previous chapters, according to financial theory, financial markets are composed of investors who seek all available information about the assets they buy and sell in order to maximize their returns. Market prices are then considered the most adequate representation of assets' value and serve as signals for other investors seeking to maximize returns, resulting in a socially optimal allocation of resources. This is a temporal relation. According to the theory, independent valuation is necessary to achieve market efficiency, but once the latter is attained, it renders the former superfluous, since prices already reflect all available information. Moreover, if markets are efficient, there must be at the same time investors who believe in the truth reflected by prices and use them as signals and investors who do not believe in this truth and therefore carry out valuations likely to incorporate new information in prices. The concept of market efficiency thus refers to a dynamic process where the ongoing search for information is followed by changes in prices that reflect it.

In this understanding of what a market is, there are two important tensions that it is useful to review before seeing how employees mobilize financial theory. The first is the tension between fundamental and speculative values. In classical economics—for instance, in the work of Adam Smith—the idea of a true value reflected in free market prices is connected to the idea that competition reduces prices to the point where transactions ensure compensation only for the labor involved in producing the objects of exchange.[1] The ontological connection among value, labor, and price makes market prices politically indisputable. After World War II, neoliberal thinkers disconnected labor and value. For them, in free markets, prices are accurate and fair not because they have an ontological connection to labor but because they are the best representation of participants' informed opinions in their quest to maximize utility.[2] In financial theory, fundamental value is not defined in relation to labor; yet, its moral and political legitimacy refers to a substance that prices can represent if it is assessed properly. This substance can be represented only in market prices—and even then only if investors' opinions treat correct information with the tools of financial theory. Prices may otherwise reflect speculative valuation. In everyday practice, these distinctions organize a constant uncertainty about whether prices reflect true or speculative value.

The second tension concerns relative value, which in financial theory is defined through a combination of the liberal and neoliberal imaginaries about markets referred to above with the development of probabilities in the nineteenth century.[3] With stock prices considered to reflect the true value of companies, stock exchanges came to be considered of as representative of the whole economy, and stock indexes became proxies of stock exchanges. Prices and indexes were deemed to move according to natural laws that can be represented by probabilities, thus defining the market as a social institution that works according to natural laws, which thereby impose a discipline beyond human control. As I show here, indexes play a fundamental role in valuation and investment today.[4] The tension between these two ways of defining a market present in relative valuation is very important in everyday practice. For employees, the word *market* can refer to the group of investors that is more or less identified with the financial industry, to the laws of probability that are supposedly observable in price and index movements, or to a combination of both.

The concept of efficient market formalized in financial theory has different meanings. They imply different authorities and legitimacies for fundamental, relative, and speculative valuations, which, as we have seen, are interdependent. And in everyday practice, these meanings are combined with the way in which employees understand themselves as enacting the figure of the investor and the financial industry as being the place where market efficiency is realized. As with the concepts of investor and value, using the concept of market as an analytic category may render the analysis all the more confusing in that the people I observed use the word *market* in different ways.

But there is a broader problem with using a concept of market as an analytic category through which to study the financial industry. Using a concept of market that is close to that of neoclassical economics to describe the financial industry risks erasing this multiplicity of meanings and legitimizing the way this industry is presented in financial theory and financial regulation. Callon's study of the performativity of economics[5] has influenced many analyses of the use of financial theories in practice, the findings of which have been very useful in conducting the research presented in this book. Yet, Callon considers that the performativity of markets that function "correctly" implies that "politics" occurs "outside of markets."[6] As several authors have highlighted, this runs the risk of "rationali[zing] the reliance on orthodox conceptions of the economy."[7] It eschews the point that market itself is a concept long conceived within theories in political philosophy. And, more fundamentally, it obviates the analytical proposition that performance, as an act of shaping, must be considered part of the power relations that contribute to producing and designating social relations and identities as economic or as markets.[8]

Fourcade has shown how, in economic sociology, the definitions of market vary according to the definitions of social relations proposed in different sociological theories.[9] Following Zelizer, we can say that when social scientists use the concept of market as an analytic category, they need to determine moral and political boundaries between what is a market and what is not.[10] This is also the case for the analytic status given to the concept of *price* that the concept of *market* is related to. As Guyer has shown in her studies of western Africa, prices may result from various social relations that imply moral, religious, and political imaginaries. Negotiation to obtain a monetary gain with a higher or lower price may be a marginal part of the transaction.[11] In the financial industry, the operations of buying and selling, in spite of the misleading simplicity of the words *buy* and *sell*, are actually just moments in a broader set of relations whereby the value that prices are supposed to reflect is defined and money is distributed in a way that creates social hierarchies. Focusing on actions of purchase and sale as the main activities of the financial industry foregrounds the problematizations of market close to neoclassical economics and erases the bureaucratic processes whereby social hierarchies are defined and legitimized with the political imaginaries that connect different notions of investor, market efficiency, and value.

The approach I propose here is concerned with the distributive effects of the financial industry. Just as with the concepts of *investor* and *value*, it is therefore important to analyze how the concept of *market*, with its multiple definitions, is used in this distributive process. Mennicken and Miller consider the concept of "market" to be an "abstract" space established by financial methods.[12] They highlight how people who use these methods consider they must act like abstractly defined investors in abstractly defined financial markets.[13] At the same time, it is important to see how, in everyday practice, employees used the word "market" with different, albeit related, meanings. For the employees I observed, these meanings reflected the way in which employees understood their role in enacting the figure of the investor. They considered the financial industry as the site of market efficiency because all the participants transacting in it were enacting this figure. They used the word "market" to refer to the concrete social spaces and interactions occurring within the financial industry in a way that is much more labile than the definitions formalized in financial theory but that still refers to the authority of market efficiency and the truth represented in prices. And they also used the word to designate the whole world, defined as an "investment universe" and considered an efficient market, i.e. a place where the inequalities to which the financial industry contributes would be socially just.

In what follows, I first analyze how the concept of market efficiency, with its multiple definitions and lines of reasoning, is fundamental for all the definitions of value. I then show how the definition of markets as the source of value played an important role in the way employees understood the social space where they worked as the site of market efficiency. Finally, I show how the moral and political meanings of the concept of market efficiency organized conflicts among employees, companies, and professions as they tried to legitimize their activities—in particular, with the increased use of indexes in valuation and investment.

A FUNDAMENTAL CONCEPT IN VALUATION AND INVESTMENT PROCEDURES

As we have seen, when fundamental and relative valuations are carried out from the point of view of an individual investor, procedures presuppose that the listed price may not adequately reflect the true value of the listed company but that it will do so when the market corrects itself. In this case, the concept of market efficiency justifies conducting valuation in order to anticipate corrective price movements—and therefore justifies the act of personal valuation itself. But this concept is also crucial in valuation and investment procedures in a much more direct way: it is used to determine the list of assets that are part of what is called the "investment universe" and to organize that list into a hierarchy—thus establishing the domain of what is valuable. The concept of market efficiency is the basis of the classical investment method and therefore a central reference for the definition of value. Valuation and investment methods that do not use this concept—for example, those of certain traders or hedge funds— are themselves problematized in relation to how they deviate from it. In summary, the concept of market efficiency is quite ubiquitous in valuation and investment procedures.

As we saw in chapter 1, modern portfolio theory postulates that an investor in a situation of market efficiency who aims to maximize profit and minimize risk must diversify investment to the maximum—i.e., "buy the whole market." Valuation and investment procedures are designed to apply this approach to indexes, considered reliable proxies of "the whole market." These indexes play a fundamental role in valuation and investment today. In particular, the indexes produced by three major financial companies are used as a general benchmark in the financial industry. As we saw above, at the end of 2017, the financial industry managed around $200 trillion invested mainly in bonds and stocks. According to Petry, Fichtner, and Heemskerk, "US$14.8 trillion, US$16 trillion and US$8.9 trillion of assets (equities and bonds) was benchmarked against the indices of MSCI, FTSE Rusell and S&P DJI in 2017/18 respectively."[14] And, as they remark, beyond this benchmarking, these indexes are used as a general guide for the definition of the investment universe and the investment strategy for a much larger proportion of stocks and bonds.

There may be many reasons why companies use these indexes, among which is the fact that they have become part of the standard professional procedures. But as part of these procedures, these indexes make sense according to the notion of market efficiency. Conceptually, their use is supposed to be justified by the idea that they are a good proxy for the "market" and that this market is "efficient" in the sense that the prices it produces are reliable representations of the value of listed companies. In the investment and valuation practices I observed at Acme and Brokers

Inc., indexes were problematized by the tension between the concepts of the investor and the efficient market: i.e., in order to be efficient, markets need individual valuations, but once this goal is achieved and there is no new information to consider, these individual valuations become superfluous. I first present how this understanding was used to organize valuation and investment at Acme, which was a relatively large global investment management company and, in that sense, aligned itself with the professional standards that it helped to legitimize. This allows us then to better understand how employees at Brokers Inc. integrated the notion of market efficiency into the valuation they sold to investment management companies in the United States that organized valuation and investment like Acme in Paris did.

Acme managed around €300 billion entrusted to it by a large number of companies such as banks and insurance companies. This money was invested in assets around the world, in great part based on calculations carried out by employees in the Allocation Department. In a practice that was typical for a company of this size, the employees carried out these calculations using the conceptual framework of modern portfolio theory as their general guideline. They analyzed averages, standard deviations, correlations, and other mathematical relations between prices of all financial assets considered available for investment around the world. They thus conceptualized the whole world as a single efficient market to be replicated in Acme's portfolio. In practice, the decision on which assets to integrate into the portfolio depended on several factors, among which were their presence on indexes and their availability for purchase, and the company developed its own rationales to determine what the "whole" market was. Also, as I have noted, this served only as a general guideline because many of Acme's clients wanted to use the company's services to invest only in a particular category of assets; as a result, the total amount of money Acme invested in each asset did not replicate their weight in what the employees of the Allocation Department identified as "the whole market." Nevertheless, the overall distribution of money among assets, as detailed by the company in its annual reports, reflected the capitalization of these assets worldwide. Two-thirds of the money managed by the company was distributed equally between stocks and bonds of rich countries. About 10 percent was invested in stocks and bonds of "emerging markets." The rest was invested in other financial assets considered "exotic" or "too risky" to make up a large part of the portfolio, such as real estate and credit derivatives, generally based in rich countries.

At Acme, these methods largely determined the list of companies that its fund managers and analysts should evaluate and invest in. The company was organized in departments that specialized in each type of asset. Thus, the Equity Department was in charge of investing about a third of the money managed by the company. Within each department, further sections, subsections, and teams specialized in particular assets. The simplest unit in this organization was the individual fund manager, who usually worked on a team, where, together with his colleagues, he was in charge of a portfolio in which the money of many clients was invested. Most fund managers managed the money in the portfolios under their responsibility using the classical investment method, which replicates an index according to modern portfolio theory but tries to "beat the market" by changing the weights of the assets. At Acme, this was the general investment strategy designed in the Allocation Department and used by each department, section, team, and individual fund manager. At all these levels, investment was thus organized by the conflict between the ideas that investment and valuation were the acts of an independent investor whose personal valuation was absolutely necessary and that they took place in markets that were efficient so that it made sense to replicate them according to the general guidelines of modern portfolio theory.

The notion of efficient market was thereby distributed at each of these organizational levels, and its application tended to reproduce in portfolios the list of available assets around the world, especially those that were included in indexes. Most of the time the company bought assets that were already listed from other investment companies and the money did not flow directly to the activities to which these financial contracts referred. But these monetary flows influenced the capacity of listed companies, states, banks issuing credit derivatives, or other social activities to eventually obtain more money from the financial industry. Thus, all these assets were compared to each other and put in competition to access the money managed by the company. This brought together and rendered interdependent a myriad of power relations occurring outside the financial industry.

For instance, sovereign bond issuance tends to create a hierarchy in the distribution of money by the state where public services become secondary to debt repayment. But this hierarchy can be combined with imaginaries of republicanism in the French state,[15] imaginaries of Hinduism and modernization in the Indian state,[16] or imaginaries of elite corruption in the Chad basin.[17] Similarly, bank credit for poor populations often enmeshes them in further forms of dependence on the financial industry, but these hierarchies can be coconstituted with imaginaries of political integration that combine with imaginaries of Catholicism and Peronism in Argentina[18] and of postapartheid racial discrimination in South Africa.[19] In all these cases, the meanings and the social relations constitutive of states, companies, and families are partly shaped by the specific financial relations that connect them in multiple and shifting ways. At the same time, the meanings of financial methods of calculation, financial companies, and financial contracts are transformed as they are combined with these social relations. How employees of the financial industry apply valuation and investment methods for one type of asset must therefore be viewed in relation to how all these assets are brought together in the financial industry, but this does not erase the specificity of the social relations concerned with this particular asset. In what follows, I examine how Acme and Brokers Inc. used these methods for listed stocks, but we should keep in mind that they were interdependent with all other assets because of the way in which indexes and the concept of market efficiency are used throughout the financial industry.

Yves directed an Acme team of eight fund managers and six analysts that invested €11 billion in big caps listed in Europe. In an interview with me, he explained that the distribution of the money to each fund manager was designed to find a "balance" between investment based on replication of an index, which was the main guideline for the whole team, and rules that would respect the "need" each manager had to express his "personality." This reasoning was used to justify a "core-satellite" organization of investment, which Yves considered standard in the industry, something that I was told by many other professionals during my observations and in interviews.

This European big-cap team divided its investment over sixty funds for an even larger number of customers. The "core" was defined in relation to MSCI Europe, an index produced by Morgan Stanley, one the three most influential index producers in the industry worldwide, as noted earlier. The official goal and the marketing narrative proposed to potential customers accorded with the rules of the classical investment method. Investment performance should exceed the benchmark by 1 or 2 percent a year. For example, if the price of the companies composing the index varied 15 percent up or down, the goal was to obtain a performance of +16 or –14 percent, respectively. To achieve this, the team members did not replicate the index exactly. They gave less weight in the portfolio than in the index to companies whose price was expected to fall and more weight to those whose price was expected to increase. Thus, the fall in the price of under-weighted shares would detract less from the performance of the portfolio than it would from that of the index, and, conversely, the rise in overweighted stocks would benefit it more. Once the price of the targeted share moved as expected and the gain was realized (or the loss avoided), the portfolio would "return to the index"—i.e., stocks would be bought or sold in order to replicate in the portfolio the exact weight that the listed company had in the index.

Yves explained that a small group of senior fund managers would meet regularly to set the weights for each listed company. Their discussions were based on previous exchanges with the other fund managers on the team and with the team's financial analysts, who each had a specific expertise on certain stocks and sectors. This was supposed to create "synergy" between the different specializations. Invoking as a matter of fact the reasoning of modern portfolio theory and its statistical approach to investment, Yves said that the principle followed in investment decisions was not to make "big bets" on a small number of companies but rather to make "a lot of small bets" on many companies in order to minimize the volatility of the fund's performance. Each fund manager oversaw several funds that replicated this "core" portfolio. In these funds, they could actually change the weights of the stocks so they differed from the core—but only very marginally. According to Yves, the goal was to avoid big differences in the returns of the portfolios managed by each fund manager. He considered that otherwise, if fund managers were given more leeway, they would be tempted to deviate from the core to out-perform their colleagues. The small margin of play they were allowed was there in order not to "kill their creativity."

In addition, Yves explained that each fund manager had a "personality" and a particular "expertise" that he needed to respect and put to good use. Thus, besides managing the core fund repli-cating the index with slight variations, Yves explained that each fund manager had a "satellite" fund that he could manage more "freely." This freedom concerned the choice and the weight of the listed companies to be included in the fund. Several basic com-ponents of modern portfolio theory and the capital asset pricing model were still mandatory, including the principle of diversifica-tion, as well as the calculation of the volatility of the fund based on historical data about the selected companies and their sectors of reference. But strategies not allowed for the core portfolio, such as the use of derivatives, were permissible. These satellite funds accounted for around 20 percent of the €11 billion invested by the team. Their sizes varied from one fund manager to another according to their investment strategies, seniority, and clientele.

Paul, the junior fund manager, was in charge of nearly €700 million, of which €90 million was invested in his satellite fund. For this fund, he could freely choose the listed companies whose stock he purchased as long as they were already included in the index, and he could use financial derivatives to make bets that were different from those permitted by adjusting the weight of each company in the portfolio. He did this by investing in futures contracts on the index itself.[20] This allowed Paul to make bets both on certain companies and on the benchmark as a whole. Paul thus applied two investment methods that were considered different and even partly contradictory with each other.

The first method, which, as we have seen, is called "classi-cal" in everyday conversations, financial manuals, and marketing materials, is also termed "indexed" and "buy and hold." Like the rest of the team, Paul explained he bought shares to replicate the benchmark but gave more or less weight in the portfolio to certain stocks in order to "beat" the index by a few basis points. In the second method, Paul could say he was "freed" from the "constraint" that required him to replicate the index. He remarked that the two approaches could be contradictory. The listed companies chosen for the core fund could sometimes be different from those he chose for his personalized fund. In addition, the core strategy was aimed at doing slightly better than the index, which implied following it even in its downfall. But if Paul made the right bets in his satellite fund, the use of derivatives could provide him with strongly positive results despite a fall in prices.

According to Yves, Paul's expertise in index futures was an asset for the team, since it was useful to look at the prices of these contracts in order to forecast the evolution of stock prices in general. But as Paul's example showed, Yves considered that other fund managers also experienced this "synergy" as a contradiction. He insisted at length during the interview that, to prevent this contradiction from becoming too salient in relations between employees, the bonuses of the fund managers did not depend on the performance of their personalized funds but were mainly linked to the performance of their core funds. This rule was explicitly aimed at preventing fund managers from focusing more on the performances of "their" fund than on that of the team as a whole.

As we have seen before, there is a constitutive contradiction in how modern portfolio theory is used in the classical investment method. Valuation and investment are based on the idea that the market is efficient, so the only strategy must be to "buy the whole market" in order to diversify investment to the maximum, something that is done by replicating the index in the portfolio. But at the same time, the classical method presupposes the market is not efficient, so it makes sense to try to "beat" the index using personal valuation. This tension organizes the global distribution of money by what Petry, Fichtner and Heemskerk show is a major part of the financial industry.[21]

I could observe this tension at Acme and in the way Brokers Inc. employees described most of their clients. In these cases, this tension organized the way in which fund managers themselves were evaluated at the companies where they worked. The difference between the "performance"—i.e., the gains or losses—of the index and that of an investment portfolio was called the "track record." This track record was used to compare employees, teams, and companies. At Acme, this assessment happened every three months, with emphasis on the assessment at the end of the year. Yves described it in these terms:

> What counts is the quarters and full years, how you finish your year. It's a one-year business. [. . .] Well, let's say that [clients] give you a warning if you have a bad year. If you have a second bad year, they leave during the second year. And if you have a good year, they do not necessarily buy your fund, they will arrive in the second year. You see what I mean? It's the second year that is critical.

Once a customer—for instance, an insurance company or a pension fund—had a contract with the team led by Yves, the first quarterly results of the second year could mean the gradual withdrawal or arrival of hundreds of millions of euros for the team to manage. This flow had a direct impact on the income of fund managers, a part of which depended explicitly on the amount of money they had supposedly attracted with their results. More crucially, a mass withdrawal of customers, and therefore a smaller amount of funds under management, could result in the dismissal of the fund managers or analysts considered to have the worst performances—and eventually even the dismissal of the whole team.

This organization of time in trimesters within a one-year time span organized the contradiction between personal valuation and market efficiency created by the classical investment method. As we have seen, fundamental valuation implies that the fund manager expects the actual price of the share to increase (or decrease) as other investors realize that the business activity is more (or less) profitable than what its current price reflects. This price change will happen only when the results of the listed company's activity prove to be better (or worse) than what was expected in the forecasts reflected in the stock price—a process that depends on the temporality of the activity of the company and of its income statements, which are published quarterly and annually. As we saw in chapter 1, with the discounted cash flows (DCF) method, these changes in the listed company's activities must be considered within a temporal horizon of several years. Classical investment, assessed by the clients of investment management companies every quarter of a year, however, relies on much shorter time horizons. Thus, the most mainstream investment and valuation method based on modern portfolio theory implies a temporality that is different than that of fundamental valuation defined in the DCF method. In the application of these methods by employees, the tension between personal valuation and market efficiency is thus in part organized by this difference in the temporal horizons.

In interviews, most of the employees who expressed attachment to fundamental valuation—in particular, fund managers and financial analysts—considered that fund managers faced somewhat contradictory demands. They were supposed to invest with a long-term perspective, according to fundamental valuation, but had to obtain visible results in the short term—i.e., quarterly. In both cases, the method justified the time horizon by invoking market efficiency—but in contradictory ways. In fundamental evaluation, efficiency comes in the future, even though, as we saw in chapter 1, the discount rate is calculated using current prices, implying in a contradictory way that market efficiency is already the case. In the classical investment method, index replication presupposes market efficiency, while at the same time adjusting the weights implies that the market is not totally efficient and will "correct" itself in the future. According to the way in which fund managers are assessed, that "correction" should happen within a period of three months.

Employees did not usually pinpoint all these contradictions at once, but they referred to them when explaining disappointing performances and expressing difficulty with everyday practices. They often said that following a benchmark allowed fund managers, teams, and companies to avoid veering too far away from their competitors. Paul noted that the core-satellite organization of investment, giving priority to index replication, was the only means of responding to customers' short-term demands. Yet, he considered that this led to a situation he described as "frustrating" because he could not apply all his expertise and was obliged to act in contradictory ways. This discourse was repeated to me often in interviews and comments during participant observation. As we saw in the case of Nicolas in chapter 2, with this discourse, employees attempted to assert their expertise without challenging the conceptual framework of their methods, instead attributing its constitutive contradictions, for instance, to the "greed" and "ignorance" of supposedly nonexpert clients.

The tension between personality and market efficiency experienced by fund managers using the classical investment approach was reinforced by the fact that these two concepts could in practice be separated into distinct investment methods. At the time of my observations, these methods had a marginal status in the financial industry, but employees presented them as being conceptually more consistent. On the one hand, a purely index-based method of investment could be implemented with software that issued daily buy and sell orders in order to replicate the content of the index. On the other hand, a purely personal approach was often put forward, for example, in the marketing materials of certain hedge funds, where the investment strategy explicitly rejected following any index or diversification rule. In the manuals mentioned in chapter 1, like in the profession at large, the replication of the index is described as a "passive" approach, and the method supposed to demand personal involvement is, in contrast, called "active."[22] These adjectives qualify the valuation and investment attitude of the figure of the investor, differentiated according to whether he submits to or challenges market efficiency.

In an interview with me, Sébastien, responsible for developing Acme's software to replicate indexes, explained that the software was supposed to reduce fund management costs for customers by reducing the involvement of fund managers, analysts, and salespeople. Although the software's copy of the index could never be perfect, since stock prices vary constantly and the software replicates them only at predetermined moments, this difference would be smaller than those caused by the transactions of fund managers trying to beat the index by changing the weights of stocks. Transactions would be made less often and in smaller amounts, reducing transaction fees below those paid by a fund manager who would make bets and then sometimes need to correct them, thus doing a transaction twice for no results.

Investment funds using this method, called trackers or exchange traded funds (ETFs), exist on most major world stock exchanges. As Petry, Fichtner, and Heemskerk show, after being marginal for a long time, they grew by over $3 trillion since 2006.[23] Some of the major investment management companies—in particular, the three biggest investment funds that tend to invest in most assets around the world—have specialized in this approach.[24] Because ETFs are listed on stock exchanges, anyone with access to the exchange can buy shares of the fund and therefore invest in the index. Sébastien considered that in the long run, the development of these investment tools posed a very strong threat to professions that specialized in personal valuation and investment. Thanks to these instruments, people who have no professional connection with finance and who accept, implicitly or explicitly, the presupposition of market efficiency can invest in indexes without receiving the personalized valuation of managers, salespeople, and analysts except for the work of analysts who determine the composition of the index. This was expressed, for instance, in the *Course Manual* of the Association of Certified International Investment Analyst: "Defenders of the efficient markets hypothesis will adopt a passive strategy, i.e. they won't try to beat the market. They will simply adopt a buy-and-hold strategy, holding the market (or a mix of the market and the riskless security depending on their risk tolerance) since the market is supposed to be fairly evaluated."[25]

Some fund managers, salespeople, and analysts, using terms similar to those found in the manuals, said that if the software-based index replication investment method seemed a logical implication, it was also an impossible limit for the very notion of market efficiency. In a tension already described in chapter 1, the notion of market efficiency requires investors to do valuation because they do not think that efficiency has been reached. At Acme, employees who felt threatened by the growth of software-based index replication often stressed that if this became the only form of investment, market efficiency would be impossible: no one would be doing valuation, so prices would not reflect all available information, thus negating the foundation of software-based index replication itself. These remarks were often made in passing because this form of investment was still considered marginal.

In contrast, employees who used valuation and investment methods that challenged market efficiency explicitly denied the legitimacy of the classical investment method. This was the official position of some hedge funds, which I could observe in interviews with hedge fund managers, in their commercial brochures, and in the academic analyses developed to support their practices.[26] They asserted that the classical investment method was a copy of software-based investment replication but with higher fees.

The term *hedge fund* designates investment management companies that use a wide variety of techniques that may sometimes not have much connection with each other beyond their explicit rejection of the classical method. In marketing materials, hedge funds often presented themselves as small independent companies that first started operating after World War II. As I described earlier, they developed as a distinct category of investment methods inside large financial companies during the 1990s. In the late 1990s and early 2000s, they came to be defined as opposed to the classic investment method and were presented as a separate financial service labeled "alternative investment." For instance, in 2004, at the time of my observations, Acme employed a small group of hedge fund managers. The people I interviewed described this situation as common for companies of this size. At Acme, investment in hedge funds was clearly mentioned in marketing materials but did not exceed 2 or 3 percent of the total funds managed by the company. These hedge funds invested in all sorts of financial assets and were partly in-house hedge funds owned by Acme and managed by its employees, and partly companies owned by competitors outside of Acme, in which Acme invested the money of its clients.

Hedge funds bring together a wide variety of forms of expertise that are applied to all kinds of financial assets. For example, they can be investment funds that buy stock only in companies undergoing restructuring or likely to be acquired by another company. They can also be investment funds that invest in pairs of companies whose stocks are supposed to move in opposite ways, so that one stock is purchased and the other is sold "short."[27] Hedge funds may also make massive use of derivatives, and they can conduct many intraday transactions or, in contrast, be based on very long-term investment. In all these cases, the hedge funds' investment strategies are officially based on the personal, and sometimes even exclusive, know-how of the professionals involved, something often stressed by employees of these companies in marketing materials and in interviews with me.

In classical investment, fund managers cannot modify or avoid the index they must replicate, the investment method, and the time horizon for the calculation of their performance. In interviews, employees often presented the alternative investment methods as "free" from these rules, which they sometimes associated with the idea that these methods were therefore "speculative" and "riskier" than the classical approach. Hedge funds were thereby defined in relation to market efficiency. Because they did not follow indexes and were dependent on the know-how of managers, they were expected to have a potentially larger standard deviation of returns than the indexes themselves, resulting in higher returns or losses for investors than those from the classical method. This argument was used to justify the much higher remuneration of hedge fund managers compared to classical fund managers, a difference that was observable at Acme and expressed in interviews with professionals.

The idea that know-how can "beat the market" presupposes that the market is not efficient and that the fund manager may do better than his colleagues who are investing in the same assets. This understanding was expressed by some fund managers using the classical method who, in interviews, referred to hedge funds either as scarecrows or as more or less acknowledged objects of desire. These two poles organized the tension that Yves managed as head of his team, where fund managers could be tempted to focus more on what he referred to as "their" satellite fund than on the one using the classical investment method. The same tension can be found in financial regulation and in academic production about hedge funds. They are characterized both as increasing efficiency because speculation leads to arbitrage that contributes to eliminating market inefficiencies and as causing excessive, unjustified volatility that distorts the signal function prices are supposed to play by conveying the truth of value.[28]

The people I observed designated software-based index replication and hedge funds as two extreme positions in valuation and investment. These methods were problematized in terms of the discipline that is expected from market efficiency and the independence that is supposed to characterize the figure of the investor. In relation to the classical valuation and investment approach, these two extremes were presented either as a "logical implication" or as "liberation." Together, these three approaches—software-based index replication, valuation and investment rejecting market efficiency, and the classical investment method—organized the possibilities for valuation and investment. Although the classical investment method was the most widely used and was presented as the mainstream approach, the other two approaches were officially legitimate as marginal approaches. Software-based index replication asserted market efficiency, while methods based on personal valuation and investment rejected it and claimed they could "beat the market." The marketing materials of some hedge funds, for instance, openly presented the two extremes as complementary: rather than invest in an entire team of fund managers following the classical approach, like the team headed by Yves at Acme, it would be better to use cheap index trackers and to spend more money on hedge fund managers, who have a really personal and hence unique expertise. The valuation and investment practices of fund managers were thus all situated somewhere between these two poles in a tension organized in commercial relations where they must produce results that would be compared to indexes quarterly and annually. The conceptual formalization of market efficiency and the valuation and investment methods associated with it constituted the fundamental set of references in relation to which all these positions and tensions made sense for employees themselves.

This omnipresence of the concept of market efficiency as the source for the definition of the true value of companies was also observable in the practices of the employees of Brokers Inc., who sold their services to fund managers who used investment methods like those I observed at Acme and Hedge Consulting. As we saw in previous chapters, personal valuation is carried out in relation to the concept of market efficiency in several ways. The idea that prices reflect the true value of listed companies is the basis of fundamental and relative valuations, since they are conducted with the expectation that markets will "correct" their temporary inefficiency. But the concept is also present in the detail of procedures themselves. The use of listed prices as meaningful information is premised on the idea that they adequately reflect the value of companies. This organizes the production of all the comparative ratios in relative valuation, which takes the prices of companies as representative of their true value except in the case of the company being evaluated. This also occurs in contradictory ways, as we saw in the determination of the discount rate in the DCF method. More generally, the contradiction between personal valuation, which denies market efficiency, and the use of prices as data, which presupposes that markets are efficient, organizes the general presentation of valuation in the documents of financial analysts, where they make arguments based on fundamental, relative, and speculative valuations. As we saw in the previous chapter, although Nicolas would stress in an interview the superiority of the DCF for determining a company's value and would use this argument to try to legitimize his position at Brokers Inc., he produced documents that combined these methods, which was the standard in the financial industry. This combination was thus organized as much by the idea of personal valuation as by the concept of market efficiency.

The valuation sold by salespeople also followed this combination, organized around the same tensions described earlier for the valuation and investment methods of fund managers. Frédéric, the salesperson at Brokers Inc., explained a financial analysis proposed to a client as follows:

> I have a client, he has Hallo [in his portfolio], Hallo is a company that does . . . collective catering, for big companies, you know, canteens, for big companies, right. It has a big brother, called Satata, which is just like Hallo, the same business model, but four times bigger, OK? I have a client, he has Hallo, obviously the benchmark is Satata. He's not, I'm not even sure that he knows that, because the guy, he spends 4 percent of his time on France. Because the people I talk to, they [invest] in the world, so one must not get it wrong, you see, I mean, France, if you look in relation to global benchmarks, it can only be 4 percent of his time, if time is proportional to the value of the portfolio, OK? So what I mean by this, is that he does not know France, and I know France,

so that's my added value . . . well, no matter. The guy has Hallo, Satata publishes its numbers. Satata is the benchmark in the sector: Satata makes Hallo move, the reverse is probably not true. I call him and I tell him: "Satata this and that, Satata publishes shitty numbers, here you have the probable impact it will have on Hallo, they publish shitty numbers on the activity . . . on the highway restaurants, which is the core business of Hallo, so probably Hallo's numbers next week will be shitty." It's not a great idea, but the guy is happy, you see. It means I remembered that he had Hallo and that I told him some stuff that maybe not everybody told him, and that opens his mind: next time he knows that Satata is the benchmark of the sector.

In this argument, Frédéric combined fundamental, relative, and speculative valuations. He did fundamental valuation when he considered how well the business was faring in highway catering. He thereby activated the line of reasoning according to which costs and sources of profits in the company had to be appropriated by the figure of the investor. He did relative valuation when he compared the two companies and asserted that one was a benchmark for the other and when he considered that France constituted 4 percent of a unified global market that should be bought as a whole. In that act, he included Hallo in a hierarchy within its sector of comparison and the two companies, as part of France and within the totality of available assets, in a global hierarchy of returns that the investor could appropriate. Finally, he did speculative valuation, expecting to gain from a short-term investment either because the numbers published by Hallo would be bad or because it would just move according to the benchmark, irrespective of what the company's activity would be in the longer term. The concept of market efficiency organized the aim of valuation, which was to attempt to anticipate a price correction that should occur when other market participants integrated the information in the price. It also organized the relative position of these two companies and of France as investment objects within the global distribution of money by the financial industry. And it organized the way in which Frédéric understood his own position as contributing to the evaluation of the place of a single company or of its economic and geographic sectors within the global portfolio. In this analysis, he took into account the time horizon over which fund managers were evaluated, hoping that his valuation could lead to short-term gains, benefiting from a soon-to-come change in prices. Thus, Frédéric also assessed the legitimacy of his role in this general contribution to the definition of value organized by market efficiency, what he called his "added value." This connected with his aim to obtain fees, and a bonus, for his work.

The idea that value is defined by prices found in efficient markets is fundamental in valuation and investment in the financial industry. Through its formulation in modern portfolio theory, the concept is central in the definition and use of indexes and in the determination of the investment universe. Diversifying among available assets and representing them in an index are thus defined as ways to engage with an efficient market in order to maximize returns and minimize risk. Fund managers combine this idea with the idea that valuation and investment are the actions of an individual investor. They do so, however, in contradictory ways, situated within the two extremes of software-based index replication and the rejection of market efficiency in the name of personal know-how. In the financial industry, these extremes are defined in relation to the concept of market efficiency. The three investment methods establish the limited possibilities of what financial value can be and how money should be distributed. They are organized by contradictions that are also mobilized by employees like those of Brokers Inc. when they do valuation. In all these cases, the concept of market efficiency plays a fundamental constitutive role. As it is present in all these procedures, it reiterates the designation of the totality of financial assets as a single market whose efficiency is attained when all investors implement standardized financial methods to assess value. The concrete social space where these investors are supposed to meet—i.e., the financial industry—is thus designated as the space where market efficiency can be realized. The next section analyzes how employees used the word *market*, with its multiple meanings, to designate the financial industry, problematizing it in terms of its efficiency in the sense of its capacity to express the true value of financial assets.

THE FINANCIAL INDUSTRY AS THE SOCIAL SPACE OF MARKET EFFICIENCY

In chapter 1, we saw that financial methods presuppose the existence of individual investors transacting in markets that will be efficient if investors apply these methods themselves. In chapter 2, I described how employees position themselves in everyday interactions as individual investors whose opinions are a crucial source for the definition of the true value of financial assets. And as we saw in the previous section, the concept of market efficiency plays a fundamental role in the procedures of valuation and investment. In this section, I show how employees consider that efficient markets correspond to the social space of the financial industry, where they are recognized as enacting the figure of the investor. This is what state regulation presupposes when it takes up the circularity of financial theory and requires that efficient markets be composed of qualified investors whose actions are defined by the application of standardized financial theory itself. The market is defined as efficient in different ways, as we have seen. It is some-times considered already efficient, sometimes the consideration is that it will be so in the future, and sometimes these two views are combined in a contradictory way. The word *market* can be used with different meanings in everyday practice outside the finan-cial industry. Within it, it is also used to designate the financial industry in different ways. Here I want to explore those meanings that connect with the concept of market efficiency because they are important for the way in which the distributive effects of the financial industry are legitimized. In particular, I want to high-light two sets of practices where employees recognize their pro-fessional space as the efficient market. First, they do so when they consider the information that circulates in the financial industry to be reliable in the sense that it can contribute to the definition of the true value of financial assets. Second, they do so when they designate other colleagues or part of their professional space as the market in the context of the definition of value.

The presupposition that the social space of the financial indus-try is the efficient market organizes the use of data for valuation, as well as the circulation of concrete tools used in valuation and investment. Some specialized media like Reuters and Bloomberg and some newspapers like the *Financial Times* and the *Wall Street Journal* are often seen as mandatory references for employees when forming a personal opinion. At Brokers Inc., the first task of salespeople and traders when they arrived at the office in the morning was to analyze the news available in these media. They explained that it was a way to know "what the market is saying" and "what the market knows." These media were thus considered a voice of "the market" that it was important to listen to—in par-ticular, because it summarized the news concerning, for instance, a listed company, an economic sector, or a geographical region that had to be integrated into valuation and investment. But these media were also a way to know what news was going to be used by rest of the financial industry, designated as "the market." The word *market* is thus used to designate the social space of the financial industry, considered a source of reliable knowledge and the totality of participants who are using this knowledge.

The idea that data is reliable because it is produced by the market also depends on the idea that it is obtained with expert methods officially recognized within the financial industry. As we saw in chapter 1, using the DCF method to determine fundamental value requires analysts to forecast the activity of listed companies and their economic context. Large brokerage firms, rating agencies, and large investment management companies usually have a department of economists who formulate these opinions. The employees of Acme, for instance, received a monthly internal letter announcing the forecasts of the company's economists concerning GDP growth, inflation, and other macroeconomic data. Employees were expected to use these predictions in their own valuations because they constituted the official opinion of the company. But as the reports themselves noted, this data often came in large part from other, more legitimate organizations, such as the Bank of International Settlements (BIS), the Organization for Economic Cooperation and Development (OECD), the International Monetary Fund (IMF), or the "big four" major auditing companies.[29] Acme's economists appropriated and eventually modified it slightly.

In the case of Brokers Inc., analysts used reports published by organizations like the OECD or the IMF, among other sources recognized as legitimate within the financial industry. Among these sources, certain financial media played a central role. This was particularly the case with what is called the "analysts' consensus" published by Bloomberg. This company, owned by the former mayor of New York City, provides a closed network of computer terminals that links tens of thousands of finance employees around the world and allows them to communicate by email. This was the means used, for example, by Brokers Inc. salespeople to send information to the fund managers and by their traders to send and confirm transaction orders. The Bloomberg network is also a source of economic and financial information, including the prices of financial assets, and offers its own statistical treatment of this data. For example, it provides a calculation of what is called the "beta" of listed companies—i.e., the relationship between the stock and its index of reference, following the calculations formalized in the capital asset pricing model, described in chapter 1. In addition, Bloomberg collects forecasts from financial employees on many issues and establishes what is called the "analysts' consensus" or "market consensus" by averaging the numbers thus collected. These forecasts can concern, for instance, inflation for different time horizons in the United States, unemployment in Spain, or GDP growth in China.

Most financial analysts do not have the time or even the expertise to produce these numbers themselves. At Brokers Inc., the "analysts' consensus" produced by Bloomberg were thus used systematically. While these forecasts were not endowed with the kind of truth that prices produced by an efficient market were supposed to have, they were considered much more accurate than data produced by a single employee or even by a small team. Indeed, this data was supposed to be much closer to "the market" and thus a reliable source of information because it was understood to result from the accumulation of the opinions of a large number of maximizing investors—i.e., a source similar to that which is supposed to lead to market efficiency.

The idea that the social space of financial professionals is the space of market efficiency could also apply to the tools used to conduct valuation and investment. In order to do valuation using the DCF, Nicolas, the senior analyst at Brokers Inc., systematically used an Excel file produced by a professor at New York University and freely available on his website. In order to use this file, the analyst just needed to fill in the available accounting data for the company he was evaluating and the forecasts about its future and that of the economy. The file directly provided a result in the form of a theoretical price. Nicolas explained, as it seemed quite obvious, that he could have created this file himself, since it simply reproduced the mathematical relations between numbers that were indicated in any manual of financial analysis. However, using this file saved him time, and the fact that it was posted by an NYU professor guaranteed that it was well designed—and most likely better than what he could have done by himself. The quality of the file's author and of the institution that employed him gave the tool, and therefore the standard reasoning that it contained, additional legitimacy in establishing the true value of listed companies.

In all these cases, the concept of "the market" is defined as a source of reliable information that can be used to determine the true value of listed companies because that information is produced by organizations and methods that are recognized as legitimate within the financial industry. Employees also used the word "market" to designate employees of the financial industry themselves. They did this in ways that varied but that all referred to the capacity of this market to be efficient in the senses given to this word in financial methods.

The academic background of front-office employees in the financial industry often includes studying at a business school and obtaining a master's degree in finance or certification as a financial analyst. The sense of belonging to the professional space of finance is reinforced by these educational institutions, which offer their students access to a restricted social group of experts.

Yet, although all employees are supposed to share the same methods, they can also rank or gauge each other according to the prestige of their diplomas.[30] Ho showed the importance of U.S. elite academic institutions in the formation of a professional feeling of superiority defined by "smartness" on Wall Street.[31] More generally, business schools, as the institutional space where financial theory gained its scientific status and professional legitimacy, are a fundamental channel that enables financial employees to recognize each other as part of the social group constituting the investors that make up the efficient market.[32]

As I have discussed, for employees, obtaining the chartered financial analyst (CFA) credential is often a way to reinforce their academic legitimacy when they do not hold a degree from a prestigious institution. This was the case for Nicolas, the senior analyst at Brokers Inc. The Chartered Financial Analyst Institute, which bestows the CFA designation, reinforces this sense of belonging by claiming to speak for the whole profession of financial experts (cf. chapter 1). Its *2011 Annual Report* includes this testimony of a graduate:

> I never thought I'd want to be part of a "club." That's not what I had in mind, but I like how it's turned out. We go to society gatherings and conferences, and it does bring people together. You look at each other and know you've all studied the same CFA exams; you've done that hard slog, and it's this thing you have in common [. . .]. Being part of this community makes me feel like it is my responsibility—it is our responsibility—not to just blame the market. We are the market.[33]

For Nicolas, obtaining the CFA credential was a way to be further accepted as a legitimate member of this market. Upon my arrival at Brokers Inc., Nicolas gave me a financial analysis manual that he had used as a student. I discovered later that this manual repeated the same formulas and reasoning as all the others. As an object that repeated the standard methods, the manual was supposed to start opening the doors for me to enter the same group to which Nicolas belonged.

As we saw in chapter 2, employees explained that the procedures organizing the relation between salespeople and fund managers were aimed at making them think together through dialogue. They also said that these relations aimed at something beyond the personal relation between two employees. They were a way for each of them to "feel the market." Each fund manager had regular exchanges with a dozen salespeople, each of these salespeople worked in companies that often had several financial analysts, and each salesperson could have dozens of other more or less regular customers. The dialogue between salespeople and fund managers was thus seen as an opportunity for both to get an idea of what other salespeople, fund managers, and financial analysts were thinking. Céline, a salesperson at Brokers Inc., said she sometimes felt that her clients wanted her to tell them "gossip." She explained that in this case, what mattered was not the originality of her personal opinion but the fact that she could convey to them opinions considered dominant in the profession at a given moment.

Outings with salespeople and fund managers could also facilitate this connection. Sometimes salespeople proposed collective outings to their clients—for instance, sharing a secluded space to watch a tennis match, playing golf together or spending an evening at the opera or at a nightclub. These events allowed salespeople to reduce the cost per fund manager of the outing. But also they might convince reticent fund managers to participate in an outing with the salesperson. As explained by Paul in the interview quoted earlier, this was because the event would then be an opportunity for these fund managers not only to get to know the salesperson better but also, and above all, to meet competing fund managers and discuss listed companies. This was all the more interesting because these other fund managers, as clients of the same salesperson, most likely specialized in the same kinds of listed companies. The capacity to enhance knowledge for valuation blended with the occasion provided by these events to interact with colleagues working in the same field, expanding the list of contacts that could be helpful for the next professional move. This reinforced the sense of belonging produced by these events and its connection with the supposed capacity of all participants to look for the true value of listed companies with the appropriate methods.

In these examples, the expression "the market" is used to designate the social space of the financial industry, either in its totality or as a segment of professionals—for instance, those specializing in a particular kind of financial asset. But in all these cases, this market to be felt or listened to is considered the source of information that will lead to the reflection of the true value of the listed company in a price. Yet, as we saw above, not all employees conduct valuation and investment with the presupposition that they do so in an efficient market. Some traders, hedge fund managers, and some salespeople and financial analysts that work with them explicitly reject this. In this case, the social space of the financial industry is presented with the same terms that problematize the rejection of market efficiency in speculative valuation: a series of opinions that are "disconnected" from fundamental value but that can be evaluated according to their own logics.

At Brokers Inc., the conflict between traders and salespeople was often articulated around this tension between the efficient market and a market composed of psychologies with no relation to efficiency. Salespeople needed to mobilize fundamental valuation and all the data produced under the presupposition of market efficiency in their relations with fund managers. Traders, on the other hand, could challenge this analysis by denying the existence of any truth about listed companies that could be reflected in prices. The relationship between salesperson and fund manager was limited, as we have seen, by the idea that it should focus on the quality of the analysis and not, for example, on an exchange of fees for outings. This barrier could be broken in the case of trading if there was no truth of value to be found. The relation between employees was thus marked not by the concept of market efficiency but by that of speculative valuation. This was not the case in the official marketing discourse of Brokers Inc., but it did happen in open conversations within its walls. As I have described, it was the kind of argument proposed by Pascal, a senior trader and partner of the company, whose interview with me was done, at his request, at the central table in the big room and in the presence of other analysts, traders, and salespeople. In front of them, he described the relations between traders:

> We, we're at their mercy! We pull down our pants and say thank you every time, huh! The guy, he gives me small orders, instead of giving me one big order he gives me small orders from time to time,[34] I don't care, what matters is that he pays! [. . .] The buy-side trader, he has a list of brokers, he has twenty brokers in his list, and on each trade, he can choose his broker. He still has an annual target to respect, more or less, but he has a margin. So he does what he wants. That means he's going to help his buddies. [My clients] I go see them, I do restaurants. Luke[35] does golf, striptease shows, that's it, he does strips, restaurants, I only do restaurants. [. . .] When you look at it, you say: "Look, Luke, he took the other bugger to hunt buffaloes, it cost ten thousand dollars for four days, to kill two buffaloes, hum, shit, say what, that's

expensive!" Then, you tell yourself, you realize that the guy, he just gave 500,000 bucks of business, and that, even though he was already a big client, very clearly, if we did not have that relation,[36] we wouldn't have made that much. You tell yourself: "Well, those were some well spent ten thousand dollars." And sometimes, you spend twenty thousand dollars on a guy and nothing comes after that, you can't know, but overall, yeah!

During the same interview, quoted in chapter 2, Pascal asserted that fundamental valuation cannot predict prices, while speculative valuation does. In the excerpt just quoted, he then says that each trader's income derives not from his valuation capacities but from his personal relation with clients. Pascal's status as a partner of Brokers Inc. allowed him to contradict, during an interview in front of many other employees, the official narrative about the core business of Brokers Inc. As we saw in the previous chapter, this was part of the tension between professions—in particular, salespeople and traders—concerning their respective importance in obtaining fees for the company. But in this excerpt, the way in which Pascal challenged the legitimacy of valuation methods based on the idea of market efficiency concerned the description of the relations between the people who composed the financial industry. He designated the social space of the financial industry as a group of people where relations were driven by friendship and the exchange of personal services. This, as we saw in the previous chapter, was exactly the kind of relations that were supposed to endanger the possibility of obtaining the true value of listed companies.

In many important ways, employees of the financial industry who conducted valuation and investment recognized their professional space as the place where market efficiency would be realized. This recognition played a fundamental role in the legitimization of certain information and methods of analysis. It was also a way to make sense of, or at least justify, important forms of exchange between employees. This reference to the financial industry as the place that realized the idea of market efficiency could have several meanings. It was adopted and transformed in a multiplicity of practices that were partly disconnected or contradictory. These tensions were themselves organized in the conflict between personal valuation and market efficiency and in the concern about whether the true value of assets can be attained. These tensions were present in the details of procedures, in the lines of reasoning available to justify their application, and in the relations between employees. The next section explores the dynamic character of these tensions, showing how they were part of transformations of the financial industry at the time of my observations.

THE RESULT OF SHIFTING ORGANIZATIONAL RELATIONS

The notion of market efficiency is fundamental in procedures, and employees also use it to make sense of the social space in which they work. Present in all the types of expertise, it is used in divergent and contradictory ways by the same employee, the same team, or the same company. But in order to understand these practices, it is important to situate them in particular temporal transformations. As Petry. Fichtner, and Heemskerk remark, the fact that investors use indexes as benchmarks is a crucial element in understanding how the financial industry distributes money around the world.[37] At the time of my observations, the classical investment method was considered a general professional standard—but one whose history was still relatively new. The way in which employees problematized market efficiency had to do with this recent transformation and with the memories of what it was replacing. This was all the more the case because this extension of market efficiency came with a change in the hierarchy among specializations. All the employees I observed and interviewed, in the United States and in Europe, problematized the change as a conflict between personal valuation and market efficiency. In this process, they highlighted that in a somewhat paradoxical way, the activity of traders was gaining importance in relation to that of financial analysts, salespeople, and fund managers. In this transformation, the concept of market efficiency, with its labile character and multiplicity of uses, remained the horizon of investment and valuation. Employees thus reproduced, in these conflicts, the understanding of the financial industry as the social space where this efficiency could be realized. In what follows, I first give an example of how this problematization was shaped by the way in which employees experienced their work in the financial industry over the span of their careers. I then show how classical investment transformed the relations between the different specializations at the time of my observations and how this happened in a way that strengthened the centrality of the understanding that the financial industry was the social space of market efficiency.

Some of the people I interviewed in the first half of the 2000s had been working in the financial industry for decades. They compared their situation at the time of our meeting to what they had done in the 1970s, 1980s, and 1990s. In doing so, they shared a general description of the changes, which they presented as a change from personal to classical investment. Carla, the fund manager I quoted above, had grown up in Italy before going to work in France as a fund manager investing in "Italian equities." She then moved up in the hierarchy, initially managing a fund with a broader scope, "European equities," and she finished her career as the head of the team of fund managers who specialized in this sector at the Compagnie Universelle, a major French investment management company. She retired in her midsixties, just before I met her in 2003. In the interview, she told me a story that I had heard in almost the same terms from other fund managers and salespeople I interviewed in New York, Paris, and London concerning the decreasing importance of the personality of the fund manager. Like many of these professionals, she lamented a transformation that challenged the expertise she had acquired in the 1970s and 1980s and with which she had built her career:

> Management, before, I mean about ten years ago,[38] was very personalized. Which means that someone, each manager, was responsible for a fund, which he managed as he wished. [. . .] There were no shared guidelines coming from the director of management. So that, at the same time, in the same management company, a manager could sell a security and another one buy it, because their opinion was different and there was no coordination between the different funds.

According to Carla, increasingly important institutional investors from the United States imposed a certain consistency in their demands:

> And that's where we realized we had to have some kind of organizational policy within a same company. [. . .] The investment process became extremely important. [. . .] Logically, logically, there was a top-down scenario, which was given by economists, and normally one followed that. [. . .] And then, for each stock, the bottom-up, you have to choose according to analysts. Because if we have a team of analysts who works for the managers, it is obvious that we will follow the analysts, we are not going to tell them:

"No, no, you are completely wrong, I will buy this stock." [. . .] We could do it, but in general we tried to follow them unless we had a very strong opinion. But normally, if we had a very strong opinion, opposite, we would speak with the analysts. You could keep your own opinion, but after having discussed with the analyst. It is a power relation, who convinces the other.

Carla problematized the compulsory adoption of diversification with a fixed list of companies as a loss of fund managers' personal contribution:

And that, I would say that, this investment process, to the extent that it involved people, especially in "Europe" management, for which I was responsible, it involved all the managers who had "country" funds, so we had big meetings, and we asked . . . well, big formal meetings, where we asked for the opinion of the analyst, and the opinion of the manager for the country, and with that we were trying to make a kind of mayonnaise, which worked or didn't. But that means what? When you manage a fund, to succeed, to have performance, you have to take risks. Risk means that you are going against the market, you have strong convictions that are not in the consensus and that are sometimes a little . . . sometimes a little, unreasoned decisions, see? It's by taking big risks that one has strong performances. The result of this whole process is that we had a flabby consensus, and that we never took risks. And when one does not take risks, it means that one . . . , one deviates a little bit from the index, upwards or downwards.

Concerning this situation in which fund managers could not go "against the market" any more, the former manager described a "new" method that had become the standard at the time of my observations and that Yves described with the same terms when he explained what they did on the team he directed at Acme:

> It lasted from 1998 to 2002. In 2002 they realized that this may not be the right solution. And so little by little, we went back to the manager, to the personality of the manager. So now, for what I know [. . .] now it's a mix. [. . .] We always follow the index, because in the end a manager always tries to beat the index, to do better than the index. And that's why it's very hard, to do better than the index. So the ideal is to make +1 compared to the index, that's it. [. . .] We followed a little the market. We stick a little bit to the index and we overweighted or underweighted the index. [. . .] For us, when you look at it, we have followed this process, but when you look at it, all the French banks followed it. [. . .] We did it from 1998 onwards, there are other banks that did it before.

The way Carla described the expansion of the classical investment method was shaped by her professional trajectory. She stressed, in particular, that which seemed to challenge the expertise that she had acquired and about which she expressed professional pride. The terms she used to describe this transformation—as a conflict between the personality of the fund manager and the legitimacy of the index—made sense as part of the relations between employees and their respective expertise and legitimacy. The relation between the concepts of the individual investor and the efficient market, with all its tensions and contradictions, is organized by the negotiations among employees, companies, and professions in a shifting process over time. For the people I encountered in fieldwork, this meant that professions whose legitimacy was based on the idea of an individual investor seeking the true value of financial assets were losing part of their power, while the use of indexes based on the idea of market efficiency and short-term trading both gained prominence.

At Brokers Inc., salespeople were at the top of the hierarchy based on remuneration and prestige, in line with the idea that their capacity to personalize valuation was the most important and most legitimate source of income for the company. As we saw in the previous chapters, the fees customers paid were perceived primarily as the result of the work of salespeople. The company's financial analysts and traders tried to challenge this in different ways—in particular, by emphasizing the legitimacy of valuation practices on which they were supposed to be the main experts. Financial analysts were, in turn, considered to be in an even weaker position than traders. The employees I observed considered that the development of the investment method described by Carla, which also corresponded to Yves's description of his own practice, was weakening the role of salespeople because a growing share of investment choices was already made in the construction of indexes. This gave increasing power to the financial analysts who worked at the companies producing the indexes to determine the list of available assets and their weights in the portfolio.[39] But beyond these few central companies, this transformation actually meant that financial analysts and fund managers were less necessary, whereas traders saw their legitimacy as a source of revenue increase. This was accompanied by discussions about their personal remuneration and the hierarchy among professions—in particular, because the decision about these amounts, as I could observe at Brokers Inc. and Acme, was explicitly unclear. These debates about the legitimacy of professions and their expertise were all organized around the conflict between the importance of personal valuation and the growing role played by indexes understood to replicate markets that were already efficient.

The expansion of classical investment meant a decrease in the influence of personalized valuation, something that relegated analysts to a lower position in the professional hierarchy than the one they already had. Thierry, a buy-side analyst working for the team of fund managers investing in European small caps at Acme, could have been a customer of Brokers SA. He would have then used exactly the same analyst reports that Brokers Inc. salespeople used to sell valuation to their clients in the United States. This was not the case, however, because his team's directors had chosen to use other brokers instead. In his interview with me, Thierry explained that the team was composed of two managers and three analysts, with €1 billion under management, to be invested in a potential "investment universe" of three thousand companies. Small listed companies often had only a few shareholders who might own a large percentage of shares, which were therefore not available for purchase by investment funds. The amounts available, called "the float," could be relatively small compared to the amounts invested by companies like Acme. Employees said that the market was "not very liquid" because the amounts exchanged and the number of participants were lower than for larger caps. Like the team managed by Yves, the team on which Thierry worked used the index produced by Morgan Stanley. But the team members concentrated on the specialized index containing only small caps and could invest only in companies that were included in it. Thierry proudly declared that he was interested in the "life" of companies and in the kind of analysis carried out with the DCF method. But he said that although it was regrettable, he did not have the time to do fundamental valuation in order to choose the companies that he would recommend to fund managers for investment.

Thierry explained that although the team invested only in companies belonging to the index, they actually used a shorter list of companies than the totality of those composing the index. This list was established by brokerage companies. His job was to corroborate the information given by salespeople and sell-side analysts by meeting personally with the managers of these listed companies at public presentations. These meetings were usually organized by brokerage companies and attended by several buy-side analysts like him, who worked for other investment management companies. Nevertheless, the index itself remained the reference used to evaluate the performance of Thierry's team. In order to "beat" the index, the team sought to replicate the weight of economic sectors in the index—but without investing in all the companies of each sector. Thierry explained that as a buy-side analyst, he had to follow fundamental valuation more closely than the fund managers on his team. Yet, he said that because of the large number of companies included in the funds managed by his team, he did not have the time to do a DCF for each company in which they invested. Instead, he "work[ed] based on the P/E" of the companies. In order to choose among the large number of companies included in the list that was established by stockbrokers, he looked at each company's price/earnings ratio according to relative valuation, He spent most of his time in meetings with the managers of the listed companies organized by salespeople of brokerage companies rather than reading documents produced by sell-side analysts.

In Thierry's case, classical investment gave salespeople a key role in guiding the fund managers in their investment choices, based on relative valuation and with a temporal horizon of a few months, within which it was expected that stock price variations would help investments "beat the index." This valuation was thus somewhat close to speculative valuation, defined as the attempt to analyze how other participants to the exchange take into account public announcements about the listed company's accounts. The depersonalization of valuation with classical investment did not give the sell-side analysts, working for the brokers, any greater power in the ability to attract fund managers' fees. As we can see in the case of the team on which Thierry worked, these fees were still mainly connected to the work of salespeople, who had a stronger influence on the choices of fund managers, in part due to the very widespread explanation of a "lack of time" to do fundamental valuation. This limitation on the contribution of sell-side analysts was combined with the short-term pressure on buy-side analysts like Thierry. His recommendations were supposed to produce positive results within the three months that marked the rounds of assessment of the investment team's performance, just as it was for Yves's team, as described previously.

Carla, who expressed her passion about the "stories" of companies in whose stocks she invested, retired before seeing the implementation of what she called the "mix" between index replication and personal investment that defined the classical investment method. She deplored the evolutions after her departure and said, at the time of our interview in 2003, that there was no opportunity for her to invest personally in listed companies. After the "internet bubble," she said, constant price variations meant that stock exchanges were a "market of trading"—i.e., a market where speculation dominated and price was disconnected from fundamental value, the determination of which had constituted her expertise as a fund manager. Stressing the role of trading and speculation was a way to diminish the legitimacy of the new investment method. According to Carla and to many of the employees I observed, the growing role of the classical investment method increased the importance of trading and reduced the role not only of financial analysts but also of fund managers and salespeople in the search for true value.

The role of trading grew with the development of classical investment because of their potential contribution to produce gains when trying to "beat the index." As we have seen, fund managers applying the "classical," or "mixed," approach were situated in a tension between two opposing lines of reasoning. On the one hand, they were supposed to obtain short-term gains to beat the index that they replicated under the presupposition of market efficiency. And on the other hand, their procedures presupposed that prices reflected a true fundamental value in the long run, which challenged the legitimacy of speculating on daily price variations. Because traders were supposed to obtain gains by speculating on short-term, sometimes intraday, price variation, their work could become crucial to obtaining gains that were visible during the three-month time horizon within which fund management teams were evaluated. Jérôme, who managed a fund based on long-term investment, said he did ask traders to find the best price of the day but only as a "matter of principle" because that was their job. But he claimed that he did not see any influence of daily price variations on the performance of his investment. Yves explained that, on the contrary, the way in which traders executed buy and sell orders was very important in his strategy:

The beautiful years when we do 30 percent, you don't give a damn about a difference of 1 percent. But when you're at 1 percent or 2 percent since the beginning of the year,[40] the execution,[41] where sometimes you can go up to 1 percent, just in the execution, and sometimes more[42] depending on the moments of the day, etc., so then you watch it closely! So we are fighting with some basis points at the end of the year to beat the index! So, so . . . no, no, no, the execution is really important. It's true that if you're really right, in the long run, you don't care at all. But that's over two or three years. And today, we are not in a business over two to three years. The business is quarterly and yearly, it's very important. That's what matters, the quarters and the year.

As we have seen, at Brokers Inc. and other brokerage houses, salespeople and traders worked in tandem for the same client, so that it was not possible to determine exactly for whose service the fees were paying. The increasing importance of trading in classical investment changed the relation between the forms of expertise of each profession and the understanding of their influence on the company's income.

The new organization limited the importance of the personal relationship between fund managers and salespeople, and gave the teams of buy-side traders more leeway and ability to distribute fees to the teams of sell-side traders. This happened through a rating system based on a vote, where fund managers on the same team had to establish a ranked list of the brokers from whom they bought services, distinguishing between analysts and salespeople. Each fund manager indicated the amount he wanted to give to each salesperson, thereby directly affecting his bonus. Since these amounts were paid only through the buy and sell orders issued through traders, the implementation of this list was in the hands of the trading team. This was the case with Yves's team, as he told me in my interview with him, and I heard very similar descriptions in other interviews. Yves explained that in his case, the management team drew up a list of brokers and transmitted it to the trading team. He pointed out that at Acme, traders had some role in the decision on how to distribute fees. They were not required to assign fees exactly as they appeared on the list his team had sent them. This is what Pascal was saying about buy-side traders in the United States in the excerpt quoted earlier when he explained that they could "help [their] buddies" but within certain guidelines. However, according to Yves, fund managers had the last word in the negotiation with the trading team. This was because fees had to reflect the importance that the expertise of salespeople and analysts had for fund managers rather than the expertise of traders:

> Currently, the desk[43] so far has had a lot, a lot of freedom within certain guidelines that the management[44] gives them. That is, they could overallocate or severely cut our allocations. So, because there have been large volumes, and we, we vote in absolute, not in percentage, we arrive, generally, with good volumes, to pay everyone properly. But they overpay some people a lot. That is, the increase, which was not expected at the beginning of the year, in the volumes of transactions, well, it's going to overpay those who have liquidity . . . that's it! So, sometimes, there are problems because the good desks, in the sell-side, do not correspond to the good research, where we have put our points. When it fits, it's okay, and when it does not match, we do not like, for example, the research or the service, and we give them a lot of money because these people take risks, or give good prices, it causes problems because the message is not entirely consistent.

While Yves insisted on the importance of trading, he considered that fees were "consistent" because they paid for the quality of the work of analysts and salespeople, not that of traders. The vote of each manager and buy-side analyst remained nominal; i.e., it named a person in particular. However, valuation was collective for the core fund. It was carried out by fund managers and analysts, with the last word given to a team of three senior employees. This diluted the importance of the personal relation between each salesperson and each fund manager. Juliette, the senior salesperson at Brokers Inc., found that the new organization of management transformed her work, removing this direct relationship and therefore the "added value" that justified her bonus:

> When I started, it was the beginning of Americans who were starting to invest internationally. [. . .] Before, you had one or two big structured funds, like Fidelity, and the rest were more kind of boutiques, people, two or three people, who had set up their fund and then who . . . It became very much a process, and they have standardized asset management, and they have become big funds, with fifty, sixty analysts, structured . . . usually structured by sector, and things like that. [. . .] Well it changes, because instead of talking to someone who decides and who says to buy this or that stock, you have to talk to sixty people, by sector, by things like that. And you have some kind of . . . of vote, every six months they vote, and they pay you according to the votes that you had, instead of having someone on the phone and telling him: "You have to buy this idea" . . . "Buy this stock," who buys it, and who gives the order[45] right away.

As we saw in chapter 2, André used the uncertainty about the respective importance of traders and salespeople for the income of Brokers Inc. as a way to sustain pressure on all employees to increase, maintain, and strengthen relations with clients. In this tension, traders like Luke and Pascal would claim the legitimacy of their expertise by diminishing that of fundamental and relative valuations. Salespeople, analysts, and fund managers, in contrast, would assert their expertise by proposing a balance between personal valuation and market efficiency that varied depending on the person, the situation, and the valuation and investment procedure under consideration. These relations must be analyzed not as a fixed state of the financial industry but rather as a dynamic process where the rules in the industry change and employees make sense of transformations in relation to their own career trajectories.

Employees held different and often conflicting views about the expansion of classical investment that, as I could observe, was happening at the same time at Acme in Paris and at Brokers Inc. in New York. But the diversity of views was organized by a common problematization concerning the interdependence and opposition between personal valuation and market efficiency. The increased importance of classical investment was perceived as diminishing the role of those professions most associated with personal valuation in the search for the true value of listed companies, such as fund managers, financial analysts, and salespeople. At the same time, the standardization of classical investment and the quarterly and yearly evaluations of fund managers foregrounded the role of traders. Their work was supposed to potentially help achieve performance results, even if it was based on speculative valuation that could reject the market efficiency on which classical investment was based. Thus, the concrete ways in which the financial industry was designated as the social space where market efficiency is or can be realized were shaped as part of the shifting relations among employees, professions, and companies. Market efficiency was invoked to justify multiple practices, which corresponded to forms of expertise that were differentiated and distinguished hierarchically within the financial industry. This concept remains a rallying point, a final justification that employees had to put forward to defend their personal trajectory, with the different emotional or moral components that it could entail.

The word *market* has many meanings in the everyday practices of the financial industry. Yet, important uses of the word concern the designation of the financial industry itself, problematized in terms of market efficiency as it is formalized in financial methods and lines of reasoning. I have therefore proposed here not to use the word *market*, however defined, as an analytical concept to study the financial industry. Instead, I have tried to understand the importance of the uses of the concept of market efficiency and the designation of the financial industry as markets for the organization of the financial industry itself, as I observed it through the everyday practices of employees like those of Brokers Inc. in New York and Acme in Paris.

In these practices, the concept of market efficiency is a fundamental presupposition for the assertion that there is a financial value that can be analyzed and problematized in terms of its truth. In the procedures of valuation and investment, this concept is used to designate prices as meaningful data. It is also used to determine the concept of the "investment universe"—i.e., the totality of what is valuable for the financial industry—as well as hierarchies in the access to money managed by the financial industry. In these procedures, the concept of market efficiency is established in a tense and sometimes contradictory relation to the concept of the independent investor, the other main supposed source of valuation explored in this book. This tension organizes the possibilities of investment, as the most widespread investment method, the "classical method," occupies a contradictory position within the extremes of software-based index replication and the rejection of market efficiency in the name of personal expertise, for instance by certain hedge funds and traders. In this problematization of investment, the social space of market efficiency is identified as the financial industry, the place where legitimate valuation and investment methods are used for the totality of available assets worldwide. This designation, with more labile and vague meanings, is also important for the way in which employees understand their professional space. The financial industry is designated as "the market," with a reference to market efficiency, when employees consider certain data reliable in the search for the true value of companies or when they make sense of the professional relations in which they engage—for instance, to "feel the market." In these cases, the word "market" may designate certain sources of information, certain methods, or certain segments of the financial industry. But in all these instances, the use of the word refers to the search for the true value of assets, itself formalized in the concept of market efficiency. The designation of the financial industry as the space where market efficiency is realized is thus not straightforward or univocal. It happens through the implementation of procedures, the use of data, and the identification of particular practices in a shifting relation among employees, professions, and companies.

As we saw in the previous chapters, the notion of market efficiency is coconstituted with the notion of an independent investor trying to maximize returns. These two concepts stand in a tense relation that takes different shapes in the different definitions of value: fundamental, relative, and speculative. They organize the legitimacy of classical investment and of the definition of the totality of available financial assets as the "investment universe" where the financial industry would contribute to a socially optimal allocation of resources worldwide. In chapter 1, I described how the concepts of investor, efficient market, and value are political imaginaries that articulate a legitimization of the hierarchical distribution of money within listed companies, between listed companies, and between those that are included in the investment universe and those that are not. These hierarchies, and the role of the different definitions of value in them, concern not only listed companies but also all the social activities that are viewed as financial assets in the financial industry and put into competition, as we observed it in Acme's Allocation Department.

The designation of the practices of each employee as the acts of an independent investor and the designation of the financial industry as the social space where market efficiency is realized are thus part of the political imaginaries that contribute to organize and legitimize the global distributive role of the financial industry. This role is not an aftereffect of the application of otherwise politically neutral techniques. As I will argue in the next chapter, these political imaginaries play an important role in organizing these methods in spite of their fragmented and contradictory character.

4

FINANCIAL VALUE AS POLITICAL
ASSEMBLAGE

N this chapter, I highlight the importance of the political
meanings of the concepts of investor, market, and value in
everyday practices in the financial industry. Previous chapters
have highlighted the multiple and contradictory ways value is
considered to be the product of individual independent investors
and efficient markets. This is visible in the formalized expression
of valuation and investment procedures in professional manuals, in the concrete procedures that employees apply in everyday
practice, and in the way employees use these concepts to make
sense of their professional identities and the place of work in
their personal trajectories. Political imaginaries, I argue in this
chapter, play a crucial role in how this multiplicity holds together.

As we saw in chapter 1, financial value is defined in three different ways. These definitions of value are partly contradictory, as
they presuppose different definitions of the efficient market, the
investor, and the object of investment. But they are also interdependent, as each method uses numbers and lines of reasoning
produced by the other two. In all of them, the figure of the investor is said to have the power to extract money from the activities in which it invests, with the support of state sovereignty. In
this conceptual frame, the relation between the investor and

the efficient market is tense and dynamic: independent investors are necessary for markets to be efficient and reflect true
value in prices, but they become superfluous once this efficiency
is attained. And market efficiency needs both people who think
markets are not efficient and continue to search for new information and people who think markets are efficient and thus use
prices as signals, supposedly leading to a socially optimal allocation of resources. This dynamic tension becomes a contradiction
in financial formulas that presuppose at the same time that markets are and are not efficient.

Chapters 2 and 3 then showed how employees applied these
tensions and contradictions in everyday practice and used them
to make sense of their professional spaces and identities. In chapter 2, we saw how the figure of the investor is disseminated in
employees' procedures, where its multiple and contradictory definitions can be used together by the same person and in the same
act of valuation and investment. Through these contradictions,
employees constantly reassert the moral injunction to enact this
figure by expressing opinions that are expected to be personal,
sincere, and independent from the potential threats of friendship,
fees, and entertaining outings. In chapter 3, we saw that multiple
and contradictory definitions of market efficiency are also disseminated in procedures. Just like the figure of the investor, the
concept of market efficiency is considered a fundamental source
for the definition of the true value of financial assets. Employees use the concept to legitimize certain forms of data and their
sources and to define the financial industry itself using meanings
that can be more labile and vague.

The first section of this chapter brings together the analyses
of the previous chapters to show how valuation and investment
practices combine different epistemological and ontological presuppositions. They organize different, partly disconnected and

contradictory definitions of the truth of value that prices supposedly reflect. The following sections then consider how the idea of value and the presupposition that it can be true are stabilized not by creating a unified epistemological or ontological framework but by making reference to the moral and political meanings of the concepts of value, investor, and market that are used to organize all procedures.

The second section shows how, across this multiplicity, these presuppositions all refer to the same moral and political imaginaries connecting the concepts of investor, market, and value. These concepts are distributed in all the practices of valuation and investment, and employees use them to claim consistency in their own practice and to legitimize the distributive effects of the financial industry. In this section, I explore the notion of *financial crisis* to show how these political meanings can become explicit without erasing their multiplicity and contradictions.

The final section proposes a reflexive exploration of the analytical status of the political imaginaries of investor, market, and value in the financial industry developed in this book. It considers the limitations of critical analyses that focus solely on epistemological questions or that propose substantive definitions of the concepts of investor and market. It also examines the usefulness of the concept of multiplicity to address this issue, stressing that it needs to be combined with a problematization of the global hierarchies produced in part by the financial industry.

EPISTEMOLOGICAL AND ONTOLOGICAL MULTIPLICITY

As we saw in previous chapters, financial professionals recognize each other as enacting the figure of the investor and the financial industry as comprising the social space where market efficiency is or could be achieved. This recognition is in large part based on the idea that this social space is composed of professionals who apply the standardized methods of financial valuation and investment, which I have referred to as financial theory in this book. Financial regulatory frameworks tend to incorporate this understanding of financial professionals and the financial industry through the concept of the qualified investor, among others. According to the circularity of financial theory, investors act according to the best definition of themselves only if they apply this theory, and when they do, they contribute to the market efficiency that the theory itself presupposes. This endows prices with the quality of being the most accurate representation of the value of financial assets because they reflect all available information about these assets. In this section, I revisit the epistemological and ontological contradictions and disconnections in financial theory in order to ask how the idea that financial assets have a true value makes sense in this ontological and epistemological multiplicity. I do this by analyzing this epistemological and ontological multiplicity in the formalized presentation of procedures; I then explore how it is applied organizationally.

Among the many methods and lines of reasoning mobilized by employees, some deserve to be highlighted because they constitute regular references with which employees make sense of their practices in general terms and justify their social distributive effects. This is the case for the idea that the truth of value reflected in prices is determined by using information that is itself epistemologically accurate. In this claim, the methods used by employees actually mobilize various epistemologies.

On the one hand, the free will of the individual evaluator is a principle of valuation. Valuation formulas and lines of reasoning are always designed from the point of view of an independent investor. But for these formulas and lines of reasoning to allow value to be reflected as true, their application should also appear as the product of belief, conviction, sincerity, and authenticity, the strictly personal character of which is crucial. In this line of reasoning, salespeople, analysts, traders, and fund managers must be able to realize this intimate commitment, which is an explicit injunction of the procedures and the sanctions that may ensue from lack of compliance. This mobilizes a subjectivist epistemology where the valuating gaze is the sole source of valuation and each subject may establish a different value. It situates valuation in a temporality of the immediate present: valuation is valid only for the moment when it is uttered because as the valuating gaze integrates new information, the true value he utters changes.

On the other hand, the truth of value is supposed to be expressed by prices obtained in an efficient market. In this case, the epistemology is objectivist: some data that is produced beyond the subject's reach has to be accepted as true. However, this notion of a market that could be efficient itself includes different epistemological and ontological presuppositions.

The market is sometimes considered a set of personal opinions established according to different methods. The data can be a price resulting from opinions reflected in acts of purchase and sale. But data can also be a "market consensus," determined by the statistical processing of opinions collected from employees. In addition, the market can be considered something that can be reflected by a fraction of its participants, those who are perceived as representative or as the ones who shape the opinion of others. This is the case for employees who meet during joint outings, for financial media, or for other sources of specialized information or analysis that professionals consider important for themselves and/or for their colleagues. In this case, the market is shaped by the temporality of the encounters between individualities and is projected into the future as the social promise that these encounters will happen again.

The market is also seen as an entity that resembles a nature that is defined by regularities that correspond to relations established in statistics. The representative character of prices presupposed in the liberal logic of efficient markets gives these prices the character of discrete data, based on the idea that there is just one price for each transaction. These encounters are then treated as equally weighted events with a normal distribution. This is the basis for the calculation of averages, standard deviations, correlations, and other mathematical relations between prices or between data produced by the statistical processing of prices. Therefore, the market is considered a series of equally weighted discrete events, occurring in an infinite time, where the laws of probabilities hold for the past, the present, and the future.

Another source of supposedly true information to be reflected in the price are the specific professional groups whose methodological expertise is considered legitimate. This is the case for intergovernmental and academic organizations that publish data about business sectors or the economy in general that employees use more or less systematically, such as central banks of rich states, the OECD, the IMF, and the BIS. It is also the case of some prestigious companies in the financial industry, such as major auditing companies and investment banks.

Different and partly related definitions of the concept of state also play several fundamental roles in the production of this truth. States are supposed to guarantee the production of accounting data and to forbid fraud in the dissemination of both public and private information. Accounting standards themselves thereby play a crucial role. They delimit what a company is from the point of view of the investor and establish a temporality for assessing its activities. They also provide the categories used to determine what cash flows can be appropriated by the investor and how companies can be compared to each other from the point of view of this appropriation. State sovereignty backs and enforces a form of expertise that endows accounting categories and numbers with their own form of truth. A different definition of the state plays a fundamental role in the definition of the so-called risk-free interest rate. Rich states set the first standard, which the valuating gaze uses to determine whether or not a social activity deserves to be considered an object of valuation and investment. In both definitions of the state, the numbers produced with these lines of reasoning acquire an objective status in relation to the valuating gaze, who must just accept them as part of the information that should be reflected in the price. Modification of this data by employees happens, but it is intended to make these numbers more accurate according to the epistemology used in their official production. In the case of the state as guarantor of information, it is the state's capacity to enforce its rules that establishes the possibility of truth. In the case of the risk-free rate of return, the possibility of truth is based on presuppositions about the state's ability to collect taxes and give priority to investors over other social actors. The concept of risk-free presupposes a neutralization of probabilities, since the latter would imply a risk, even though minimal. The presupposed sovereignty of the state would therefore extend into infinity in a continuous way.

We can thus observe multiple epistemologies at play—that of a sovereign state that institutes truth, that of recognized forms of expertise, that of the laws of nature defined by statistics, and that of the will of a valuating subject—whether isolated or combined. Each of these epistemologies mobilizes specific presuppositions concerning time and the realities about which a truth could be said.

These ontologies and epistemologies articulate different power relations between the figure of the investor and the other actors concerned by the company under valuation, such as the company's employees, business partners, and environment. These are reduced to the status of objects defined by the free will of the investor. At the same time, the investor is viewed partly as having to abide by the objectivity imposed by the market's true prices and partly as having the capacity to beat the market, either because it will become efficient or, more marginally, because it will not be efficient at all. The authority of the market is defined, in turn, as a more or less contradictory combination of the laws of nature as defined by statistics and the combination of subjective opinions.

Financial theory presupposes that it acts itself as the cognitive mediator that renders all these relations among investor, market, and financial asset possible. This gives it an ambivalent status according to its own presuppositions. On the one hand, the freedom of valuating investors is fundamental to the notion of market efficiency. On the other hand, these investors are perceived as free only if they apply financial theory as their method of valuation. For employees, deviations from this order may result in dismissal or a more serious penalty. Expertise in a specific theoretical corpus, with its contradictions and its conceptual and epistemological fragmentations, remains the mandatory framework for financial valuation and investment. The radical freedom of the investor presupposed in financial theory is at the same time negated by his obligation to apply these methods and asserted as the result of this application. This ambivalent status is put to test in the occasional debates that occur when new methods of analysis are proposed and either rejected or integrated into the corpus.

The power attributed to the state in these methods is also ambivalent. On the one hand, according to liberal reasoning, the state is supposed to play the role of external guarantor of the rules of the game, ensuring that the necessary information for valuation is available equally and freely to all and is not manipulated to

favor particular interests. On the other hand, the state is understood as a full-fledged actor in the exchange, as it issues and sells
its own debt securities. However, despite the absolute nature
attributed to the sovereignty of the state in these forms of reasoning, the state is also limited by the creditor rights of the figure
of the investor. The investor is given a position of power over its
object of investment, whether it be in listed companies or in the
state that guarantees his rights. States are thus defined in terms
of an ambivalent sovereignty. This sovereignty imposes itself
on investors in order to guarantee the rules of the game. It also
imposes itself on the rest of society—but only in order to extract
taxes to ensure that debts are repaid to investors, whose creditor
rights are defined as the ultimate limitation of sovereignty. The
continuous and infinite risk-free time of state sovereignty is thus
a basis for the discrete infinity of the market where the freedom
of the investor is realized.

These various epistemological and ontological presuppositions are usually combined in valuation and investment practice.
Two examples, the discounted cash flows (DCF) and the classical investment method, are worth reviewing here because of their
extensive use in the financial industry. In the calculation of the
discount rate for the DCF, stock and bond prices are considered
representative of the listed company's value because in efficient
markets, prices reflect all the information gathered by market
participants. As representative of true value, these prices are also
considered to follow the rules of statistics, so it makes sense to
calculate averages, standard deviations, and correlations between
them. In the DCF method, this presupposition about the representative character of current prices is used to find a value of
the company different from the current price. This corresponds
to the idea that the market is inefficient in the present and will
be corrected in the future. Correction results from using the same

procedure to assemble the disciplining truth of market efficiency based on statistical rules and on the combination of personal opinions, together with the superiority of individual conviction and sincerity for the determination of value—but only as long as financial theory controls that process. In a contradictory way, the DCF method implies that the market is and is not efficient when it uses current prices to calculate the weight of equity in relation to debt. And in all these calculations, the presuppositions about state sovereignty present in the concept of risk-free rate remain central. The company under consideration would be immediately discarded if it seemed to promise returns lower than the rate paid by bonds issued by rich states.

In the case of the classical investment method, applying the modern portfolio theory (MPT) implies using statistics to analyze prices considered as data because they would be the product of an efficient market that must be replicated. This is combined with a strategy aiming to "beat the market" by a margin that even if small, is based on the presupposition that the market is not efficient. The efficiency of markets is further denied by the requirement to realize gains over a three-month time horizon, implying that classical investment pay attention to short-term price movements. This temporality differs from the supposedly random temporality of new information that would affect market prices. But also the focus on short-term price movements strengthens the role of traders in the investment method—due, in particular, to their supposed ability to make winning transactions without taking into account the fundamental valuation that supposedly should be reflected by prices in efficient markets.

These combinations do not just appear in the formalized definition of procedures. They are also used to organize the tasks of employees and the commercial relations between companies. The organization of the financial industry itself is thus partly shaped by the way in which these multiple epistemologies and ontologies are combined in procedures of valuation and investment. Within and between companies, this diversity is organized in relations that are at the same time cooperative, competitive, and hierarchical, in which employees, teams, professions, and companies tend to defend their expertise. It is worth recalling some examples from Brokers Inc. and Acme that show how widespread and constitutive this combination is for the financial industry.

The fund managers who were clients of Brokers Inc. jointly paid for the analysis produced by its analysts, whose reports they could download from the company's website; for the work of its salespeople, who personally filtered and transformed that analysis; and for the activity of its traders, through which fees were transferred. The reasons for paying Brokers Inc. could vary from one investment management company to another and from one fund manager to another. This organized conflicts among the different professions inside the brokerage company. But it was together, with their conflicts included, that these professions and activities were complementary, providing a service that was sold by Brokers Inc.

The diversity of combinations was greater at Acme, where many valuation and investment methods were used for a large number of asset types and for a wide variety of clients. In the same company, there were employees who used classic investment methods, employees who programmed software to replicate indexes, and employees who rejected the idea of market efficiency. This diversity of definitions of value, used for a multiplicity of financial assets, was combined in the overall investment strategy proposed by the company to its biggest customers. This broader investment method was in large part based on modern portfolio theory as adapted in the calculations of the Allocation Department. In this case, diversification was used according to the classical investment method, and the whole world was defined as a single efficient market. But this overall portfolio offered for bigger clients also included other investment approaches developed by the company, some of which rejected market efficiency but were included as way to further diversify investment. Thus, the company proposed to integrate the epistemological diversity and contradictions described here into one contract of fund management, defined as a strategy developed from the point of view of an independent investor facing a potentially efficient market.

While DCF and classical investment are very widely used, a greater variety of combinations is possible in the financial industry as long as the same methods are mobilized. An organizational space where this diversity can be found is that of the methods called "alternative investment," defined as such because they depart from the classic investment method. At Hedge Consulting, a consulting investment firm where I did fieldwork in 2003,[1] the team developed software that issued buy and sell orders for stocks of companies listed on exchanges based in western Europe, the United States, and Japan. The software used statistics to process data published by Bloomberg, Reuters, Yahoo!, and other publicly available sources. The team was not allowed to issue a buy or sell order that was not prescribed by the software developed by the engineer on the team. Valuation and investment work consisted mainly of designing the software. The software included most standard valuation methods and used available information to produce theoretical prices orienting the weights and positions to be given to listed companies. These different valuation methods had different weights, which the software revised at regular intervals in order to bet on price changes. The team revised the software periodically, making changes if it was not leading to gains. This combined the epistemological and ontological presuppositions present in the methods of valuation and investment integrated into the software, a presupposition about the statistical regularity of stock price movements that the software was supposed to detect, and a presupposition about the supremacy of the individual valuating gaze of the members of the team, who could reset the whole process according to their own and their clients' opinions.

These combinations also vary over time, as we saw in the case of the extension of the classic investment method. In this process, the companies that determined the indexes became more important for the definition of value, and the position of traders was strengthened, since they could influence the short-term performance of investment. At the same time, professions whose legitimacy was more connected to the expression of a personal opinion about fundamental and relative values were weakened by arguments asserting that markets are efficient. However, because of their mutual interdependence, none of these definitions of value became redundant. This process was rather a reorganization of the power relations between professions and forms of expertise that reproduced the epistemological and ontological multiplicity described here.

The epistemological and ontological presuppositions of valuation and investment practices are partly disconnected and contradictory. But almost all these presuppositions assert that prices, as the product of the valuation of investors in more or less efficient markets, could reveal a true value of the social activities funded by the financial industry. The truth of the value supposedly asserted in prices does not stand on one consistent or homogeneous epistemological and ontological basis. Rather, it is asserted in almost all of the many different and partly contradictory epistemological and ontological presuppositions of financial theory. This multiplicity is reproduced and reshaped in every act of valuation and investment. These constant repetitions and transformations are partly organized by the relations between employees and between companies that exist within regulatory frames that often change slowly. The next section explores the central the role in this process played by the moral and political meanings of the assertion about the existence of a true value that is reflected in prices produced by efficient markets.

MORAL AND POLITICAL IMAGINARIES

This section addresses the relation between the technical aspects of valuation and investment methods and the moral and political imaginaries that connect the concepts of investor, market, and value. It shows that although employees may separate the technical meanings of their practices from these moral and political imaginaries, these imaginaries are present and become relevant in different ways in everyday practice. They are disseminated in all procedures, contributing to hold together the multiple and partly contradictory epistemological and ontological presuppositions used in the search for true value. And they are mobilized as explicit moral and political meanings of everyday practices when employees seek to justify their work—for instance, in order to account for what they perceive as a crisis. In this process, employees tend to assert their right to manage money for the rest of society based on what they perceive as a technical expertise that contributes to a socially optimal allocation of resources.

Previous chapters have shown how employees tend to problematize as a technical matter their capacity to find the truth of value and to guess how price will reflect that value in the future. Their work consists of applying standardized procedures correctly to reliable data that demands interpretation based on expert technical knowledge. Except on particular occasions, they may not feel the need to reflect about the distributive effects of their practices worldwide. They may not understand all the conceptual connections between the methods they and their colleagues apply.[2] And they may not care about the multiple connections between their own practices and what happens in segments of the financial industry that seem too distant to them. Rather, employees justify their valuation and investment methods mainly as a way to increase their salaries, bonuses, and prestige.[3] Part of the meaning of these practices for employees comes from the recognition by peers that they apply official professional rules correctly.[4] And they can do this with various emotional connections to their professional life, including different forms of adherence, rejection, and indifference.[5]

At the same time, the supposed accuracy of valuation and investment methods results from a combination of epistemological and ontological presuppositions that are disconnected and partly contradictory. They imply different definitions of value, investor, and markets that employees mobilize in their conflicts and assert in their specializations within the financial industry. Through this multiplicity, nevertheless, all these procedures reassert the political imaginaries in which there is a true value that is reflected in prices obtained by the interaction of independent investors in efficient markets. This connects everyday practices to moral and political imaginaries that are also formalized in financial theory and in financial regulation, as I discussed in chapter 1. The political meaning of this connection is found in the idea that this kind of market efficiency leads to a socially optimal allocation of resources. The moral meaning is found in the requirement that each person play his part in applying the procedures so that this political horizon can be realized. In everyday practice, these moral and political meanings are present and gain importance in different ways. As we have seen, these meanings are implicit in the choices of variables, in the lines of reasoning that organize procedures, and in the organization of tasks within and between companies. Employees may refer to these meanings as part of the technical features of their practice or as a way to justify their practice as the correct application of professional rules. But employees may also bring forward these moral and political meanings more explicitly—for instance, when conflicts between employees arise or when there is a broad consensus within the financial industry that there is a "crisis" that concerns these moral injunctions and their political horizons. In this section, I show the fundamental role of these moral and political meanings by exploring these various occurrences.

Arjaliès et al. describe an instance where a coalition of investment companies, whose clients included trade unions, attempted to pressure a listed company that was preventing trade unions from organizing within its walls.[6] The authors show that even though there was a general consensus among the top managers of these investment companies that it was necessary for them to take this step, legal contracts prevented them from doing so. Just like we saw for Acme, in this case each financial company has several contracts with different clients, so that changing valuation and investment for one client would have broken the contracts with the others. These methods are thus mandatory for all companies and employees, without there being one unified authority to enforce them. They are reproduced within each company according to contractual obligations and regulatory requirements. As we saw for each employee and team within companies like Brokers Inc. and Acme, this does not result in the embodiment of the figure of the investor in some employee who would then determine prices in markets that would constitute the core of the financial industry. On the contrary, the roles and definitions of investor, market, and value are present in all the procedures.[7]

The political imaginary according to which prices reflect a true value in the case of market efficiency is thus a shared reference disseminated in procedures and contracts. This shared imaginary contributes to hold together the epistemological and ontological fragmentations and contradictions that employees work with in everyday practice.

We can analyze each act of investment and valuation in this way. For instance, as part of his job, Paul, the fund manager on the team directed by Yves at Acme, had to buy and sell stocks for the core fund of the team. He did this by sending an order to the desk of the team's traders, who then passed it on to sell-side traders working for brokerage companies with whom the team had contractual relations. In the case of an order to buy, Paul's opinion about the soundness of the transaction was officially based on the idea that the price was low compared to the true value that the efficient market would later reflect. Paul's decision to purchase, officially based on his personal opinion, was also the result of acts of valuation and investment by other employees within and outside Acme. It was partly the result of negotiations between fund managers and traders on the European big caps team at Acme. It also resulted from the analysis sold by salespeople and analysts working for the brokers used by the team, who themselves used other sources of information and lines of reasoning, such as those produced by the specialized press or other institutions. The relation between Paul and the salespeople of brokerage firms, whether resulting from telephone conversations or evenings at the opera, and the relation between Acme's traders and the sell-side traders were only some of the components of this purchase. Paul's decision was also the result of allocation decisions made at Acme at several other hierarchical levels, affecting, for instance, the amount allotted to European big caps, using modern portfolio theory to assess the whole world as a single market. And this strategy was itself negotiated by Acme's management with major clients.

In all these cases, employees applied multiple epistemological and ontological presuppositions that asserted the problematization of prices as the reflection of true value through the encounter of investors in efficient markets. They were thereby respecting their labor and commercial contracts and financial regulation. The legal owners of the money that was thus distributed were not represented by a person who was identified as the investor. This process resulted rather from the assemblage of a multitude of definitions of the investor's gaze and of the efficient market disseminated in the procedures that employees, organized in teams and companies, carried out in everyday interactions.

In all the relations implied in Paul's order to buy a stock, employees could consider that they were applying procedures whose technical character may not have needed to be moral or political. But as we saw in chapters 2 and 3, employees were also supposed to assert in different ways some of the moral features of the definition of the individual investor, as well as of the truth of the financial value they looked for, which prices were supposed to reflect through market efficiency. As I showed in chapter 2, employees had to assert that their valuation and decision to invest were the result of a personal opinion based on sincerity and conviction. These qualities refer to the independence of the figure of the investor, serving as moral markers that assert this figure is the source of the definition of true value as long as he cares about maximizing his own returns. Procedures regulating the relation between fund managers and salespeople—for instance, for short conversations or for outings—stress the importance of this cognitive and emotional independence if prices are to reflect all available information and hence approximate true value. The negation of market efficiency and the assertion that transactions are conducted with friends or as payment for outings appear as marginal cases, problematized in the moral terms of the requirement for conviction and sincerity.

In chapter 3, we saw that the confrontation among employees, professions, and companies caused by the expansion of classical investment mobilized concerns about the respect for market efficiency. At stake was the capacity of the financial industry to represent the true value of social activities in prices. The expansion of classical investment was itself justified as the most adequate approach to valuation and investment in markets already considered efficient. Its critics asserted it posed a danger to market efficiency, either because the new organization did not give enough importance to personalized valuation or because it gave too much importance to the work of traders. Again, rejection of market efficiency, as in the methods bundled into the segment of alternative investment, was considered acceptable only as a marginal approach. In companies like Acme, however, these alternative techniques were included in the general portfolio as part of the diversification strategy organized by the idea of market efficiency.

For employees, their everyday professional practices may have a character of self-evidence that does not call for reflection about the legitimacy of valuation and investment. This contributes to reinforcing the idea that the effects these practices promise, such as market efficiency, are already a reality. It is only in special cases that employees need to justify what they do. As we saw in previous examples, these can include situations involving conflicts among employees, teams, companies, and forms of expertise. They can also extend to interviews with an anthropologist when employees are asked to discuss the place of work in their personal lives. But employees can also mobilize more explicit moral and political justifications for their involvement in the global distributive effects of the financial industry. This was the case at the time of my observations, which occurred shortly after the so-called "dot.com crisis" or "internet bubble." The definition of "crisis" itself was organized by the moral and political imaginaries connecting investors, markets, and value that I have described so far, making it a way to reassert these imaginaries, with calls for their defense or restoration.[8]

In 1996, the stock prices of companies related to the internet, then considered a new technology, started to rise. That year the U.S. Federal Reserve started increasing interest rates in an attempt to stem this rise, which its chair, Alan Greenspan, claimed was excessive. The rise in prices continued until March 2000; prices then fell almost continuously for the next two years. Between 2000 and 2002, the capitalization of these companies decreased by $5 trillion, and the Nasdaq Composite Index fell around 75 percent.[9] At the beginning of my observations, in 2002, the prices of some stocks were increasing, but many companies had gone bankrupt, and several scandals involving financial fraud had erupted, like those at Enron and WorldCom. Between 2002 and 2005, the employees I observed often took a stance in relation to the "internet bubble."

The organization of work, dividing tasks within a hierarchy that was partly determined by wages and bonuses, meant that each person's work was partly legitimized by the income it provided to his employer and to himself. If these incomes remained stable or increased, employees could consider that they were performing their tasks properly and contributing thereby to a socially optimal allocation of resources. In everyday practice, employees usually referred to these monetary gains using the term "value creation," which connects with the political imaginary of market efficiency. According to this line of reasoning, prices produced by efficient markets work as signals orienting investment in a socially optimal way so that listed companies and society at large can develop to their maximum economic potential. The increase in employee bonuses, the financial industry's profits, and the prices of financial assets is thus considered part of the same process of "value creation," as well as proof that value is indeed being created.[10] The collapse of stock prices in 2000 led to reduced gains in the financial industry, smaller employee bonuses, and employee firings, as André remarked in order to distance himself from Brokers SA. According to Jérôme, the fund manager quoted in chapter 2, the collapse of prices meant a "destruction of value," an expression used by other employees I encountered during fieldwork. Very evident in my interactions with employees at the time of my observations, the "internet bubble" seemed to challenge this self-evident character of their everyday practices, if only in part, and to call for more elaborate justifications.

In this context, employees defined the notion of crisis with reference to market efficiency. The word implied an erroneous valuation of listed companies, which gave them prices much higher than their true values. The fall in prices was thus said to be a correction, and the price variation, first up and then down, was considered part of the trial-and-error process of market efficiency through which the truth of value would be revealed. The employees I observed used the term "crisis" to refer to this upward movement judged erroneous a posteriori. According to the same line of reasoning, when the fall of prices is considered a crisis, it is usually also considered to be caused by erroneous valuation, but now it is referred to as a "crash" instead of a "bubble." Thus, in both cases it is a price deviation from true value that causes the crisis and that can end only with a market correction and the restoration of efficiency. Thus, the terms *crisis*, *bubble*, and *crash* are all used to refer to what is understood as the normalcy of market efficiency. Such movements gave employees the opportunity to put forward justifications about their own activity or about the

professional environment in which they reaffirmed the importance of respecting professional rules, now described using the
moral and political imaginaries linking the concepts of investor,
value, and market that I described earlier.

Yves, the director of the Acme team investing in European big
caps whom I interviewed in 2004, had been a fund manager at the
end of the 1990s. Classical investing constituted his main expertise and was supposed to justify his professional position and
income. He had applied this know-how for many years before
becoming the director of a team at Acme. However, he attributed
his inability to express a personal opinion during the "bubble" to
this method:

> The problem is that those who did not agree, well, in general, they
> lost their job . . . if they were out of the internet companies, in
> 99, 2000, they broke their track record,[11] in three months it was
> finished for three years. That's it, it came down to that level of
> things. Well then, a year later, it started to correct itself, two years
> later, they were heroes, three years later they had . . . [. . .] I was,
> I wasn't . . . I wasn't a hero, I mean, I just followed the bubble.

As we saw in the parts of this interview I quoted previously,
Yves defended the importance of fundamental valuation based
on a personal opinion according to the reasoning of the classical investment method. But when talking about the "internet
bubble," he pointed to one of the requirements contradicting this
method—his having to follow an index—in order to justify his
participation in what he would later describe as an error. The idea
that the market would "correct itself" referred to the adequate
reflection of value in prices due to market efficiency. According to
Yves, this adequate reflection depended on those market participants whose moral qualities allowed them to remain independent

of the hype and labor pressures to follow the index. This difficulty granted them the moral qualification of "heroes" of valuation and investment.

Yves mobilized the moral imaginary of an independent investor, whose freedom of opinion is the condition that enables market efficiency to lead to a socially optimal allocation of resources. However, he did not feel obliged to continue this reasoning much further in his argument. His goal, in the interview, was to justify his past without having to question it fundamentally. He used the figure of the "hero" to clear himself, at least in part, of the responsibility for the wrong to which he claimed he had contributed. He did this by stating that his breach of the morality of the independent investor was due not to his personal moral rejection of this figure but rather to the need to preserve his source of income in a procedural professional space. Nicolas, the analyst at Brokers Inc., used very similar reasoning in the interview that I quoted in chapter 1. In that interview, he claimed that the marginal position of the DCF method, which he so explicitly lamented, was all the more unfortunate because the DCF "protects you from bubbles, it protects you from crashes . . . so sometimes the problem is that the DCF puts you completely out of phase." In his argument, he attacked relative valuation using the examples of Amazon and Yahoo!, which at the time were explicit references to the "internet bubble." At the same time, he explained that he had to use all methods of valuation, even if it went against his preference for the DCF, which was "there only because everybody knows that it is the only way to evaluate a company." Indeed, being "completely out of phase" could mean not being considered "seriously" enough to be given a promotion or, as Yves explained, losing your job.

Nicolas and Yves thus used the moral imaginary of the figure of the investor to make sense of the "bubble" as a price deviation from true value. Their narrative called for a restoration of this morality in a way that would further legitimize what they considered the core of their professional expertise. In other situations, employees referred to the political imaginary of market efficiency to describe the "bubble." This was the case with Fernand, the director of the Allocation Department at Acme. He oversaw the analysts that established hierarchies of assets from all over the world as if they were part of one global efficient market. This analysis determined the guidelines for the investment portfolio that Acme offered to its biggest clients—i.e., those that entrusted the company with amounts large enough to be diversified in a wide number of assets. The work in the Allocation Department was also the result of negotiations between departments and teams within Acme, all of which tried to assume a bigger role in distributing the €300 billion managed by the company. According to Fernand, this distribution of money was to be made according to the true value expressed in prices that resulted from the market efficiency produced by the financial industry.

Fernand had started his career thirty years earlier, in the 1970s, as a specialist in the fundamental valuation of listed companies. When he agreed to an interview with me, he was about to be replaced as part of a conflict within the company. His approaching departure, which I knew nothing about during the interview, perhaps explained why he spent so much time with me and offered long explanations about the financial industry, where he had spent all his career. In this context, he addressed the "bubble" as part of the history of the financial industry he had experienced personally. In doing so, he repeated the political justification used by government authorities to explain the regulatory changes that had occurred since the 1980s. Like Yves, Fernand considered that the procedural organization of classical investment conflicted with the importance of personal opinion:

You explain that you are a long-term manager, but in fact people watch the perf[12] every week. Every Friday night, they tell themselves: "It's annoying, he did twelve bp,[13] you did ten, two bp is not bad, right?!" So there is something that adds on to itself, it is the industry itself that makes, by the pressure that it puts, by the competition that it organizes, by the way in which it needs, I would say, all this, it is [the financial industry] that puts pressure in an investment that we don't really need. You, if you are my customer, as a life insurance customer, you have absolutely no need for your life insurance product to go up every week. You give me 100 francs,[14] with the hope that there will be 200 in ten years, when you will actually arrive at the end of your contract. And if by any chance you had to die, you wish that, indeed, the capital [will] be protected, that you can leave 130, 150, or 180 to your heirs. The idea that it performs less well during the month of May is absolutely irrelevant. And yet it is the essential part of the life of [fund] managers today. So, why? Because the competition is stronger, because there are more companies, because there is someone who will tell you: "Did you see your contract? It hasn't moved during the month of May. If you had been at the Banque des Champs, they did three bp during the month of May, and you did only one! Maybe, you should give it a look." That is to say, it must provoke the turnover of assets, provoke the turnover of portfolios, the turnover of clients, the turnover of mandates. All this formidable brokerage industry, which has grown considerably for some twenty years, it needs the turnstile to keep turning. There must be a flow, if you wish, these people have to live off a flow. And me too, a little bit . . . but less than them. I could very well live without a benchmark, with indeed a horizon of several years, for insurance companies, for our clients, etc. And two-thirds of my time goes to trying to explain to customers that, indeed, last month, we have two bp less than the competition, but it doesn't matter, because we did this, we did that, we'll catch up, and so on.

Despite this critique, Fernand said the financial organization where he worked was legitimate because it imposed discipline on companies on a global scale, pushing them to increase their returns in order to access the money managed by the financial industry:

It seems to me that we have tremendously expanded our management universe. That is to say, in this company, there are people who are interested in buying bonds issued by a Thai brewery or by an Argentinean bank. Again, maybe I'm going to talk to you about my life for too long, but me, when I came in, I had the choice between the bonds of EDF or Gaz de France,[15] and I had to choose between the stocks of Michelin or Peugeot. Thailand, I didn't know where it was, so I didn't ask myself the question. [. . .] You see, it was a totally different world. Today, any diversified mutual fund manager has the whole world at his disposal with a screen that provides him with ongoing price quotations of 25,000 stocks if he wants. [. . .] So this horizon has widened, and at same time, I find that the pressure on performance has terribly narrowed. [. . .] The financial market [. . .] has imposed the discipline of the hierarchy of returns. We who manage money for third parties, for example, for pension funds, and well, we don't have the right not to invest in companies that provide 25 percent on the capital invested, for example, in IT, Microsoft, etc., even if we like Michelin because Michelin it's 6 percent or 7 percent on equity and well, it's better 25 than 6! And people are going to say to us: "Yes, but 25, you take it with a certain risk!" And we will say: "Yes, but as long as it's there, we take it." And since we are not judged on what will happen in ten years, we will indeed take it.

According to Fernand, the fact that employees may not be considered personally responsible for their errors in the long term meant that they would probably not respect the moral injunction present in the definition of the figure of the investor. He considered that it was during this search for high returns that the financial industry, seeking the truth of the value of available future cash flows, made some valuation errors that led to the "bubble":

> So you had, if you want, there was a change in the flows of money, which were poured on activities promising 15, 20, 25 percent returns. Ten years ago,[16] if you wanted to do a capital increase in the steel industry, a capital increase for Moulinex, no one came. But in 1999, you could do a capital increase for any company called X or Y.com, you said that with two genius friends in a garage you had invented a new internet-this thing that would allow you to indeed have the circulation of goods, products, I don't know what, that you could buy your groceries and that the caddy would arrive directly by your elevator through the internet portal, I mean, the bullshit, excuse my word, that we could say at that time, in which we participated like the others! Because we said: "Well, yes, after all we don't realize, maybe it's true" [. . .] and so, the market was capable of convincing [others] and of convincing itself, it is both at the same time, that, indeed, there were there profits that were capable of attracting a capital, which asked for nothing but being allowed to plunge in.

Fernand asserts that the "bubble" is part of the movement of that which "maybe [is] true" according to the process of trial and error supposed to lead to market efficiency, once participants in the exchange have correctly integrated all available information. In this line of reasoning, the fall in prices is a return to market efficiency after the new information has been integrated. Thus,

Fernand said that after the correction, stock prices could indeed reflect the true value of the new technologies and economic transformations of the 1990s:

> So we can see all this strength of the system, that is, its capacity to define a hierarchy among returns and therefore to impose a true discipline, a true rigor. [. . .] We have been able to create hierarchies, but at the same time we have been able to make collective mistakes in a proportion, I would say, in hindsight, that seems incredible for the blindness, the stupidity, the bandwagoning, what you wish. . . . Because, indeed, any fund which did not have in its portfolio 30 percent of ".com" stocks or whatever, in the years 1999 and 2000 actually seemed totally tacky, outdated, with quarterly performances that could cost you losing your clients. [. . .] The financial industry, because of its globalization and because it set itself in competition with itself, has exaggerated. And I think that it is a fundamental feature of this activity. I think that in its trends it does not make mistakes, but on the other hand, it always exaggerates. The market wasn't wrong, it did see that globalization was a tremendous revaluation of capital. [. . .] So it is true that financial markets have had the role of . . . I would say, in a certain way, they have increased the rigor of profitability in the markets, they have increased the level of requirements, they have imposed better movements of transparency, they have provoked a better efficiency of capital, as we say, but indeed there have been situations of excess.

In this discussion, the notion of crisis was defined in relation to the concepts of market efficiency and the figure of a maximizing investor, and the financial industry was designated as the place where they are realized. Fernand combined several of the lines of reasoning of financial theory to express this. The "bubble" and its "explosion" were presented as stronger-than-usual price variations in the trial-and-error process of the search for truth characteristic of market efficiency. Using the statistical reasoning formalized in modern portfolio theory, Fernand asserted that true value is reflected in prices' "trends," while short-term variations were indeed inevitably erroneous, since they were part of the movement of revelation. He considered that procedural rigidity and hyped competition in the financial industry may impose short-term bias on valuation but that this does not hamper the capacity of the financial industry to reflect true value in prices and fulfill its political role on a global scale. States are totally absent in the analysis; in this global space, only the financial industry should determine the value of social activities and establish hierarchies among them in order to support or discard them.

It is important to analyze this kind of discourse in relation to the situation in which it is produced and within the professional rules of the financial industry. I did not observe Fernand relating these assertions to his everyday practices. The overwhelming majority of people I observed in the financial industry did not relate to their work in political terms. They may have held views about the economy and society associated with conservatism or neoliberalism, although that was not always the case.[17] Expanding business and income most likely were more important than considerations about the financial industry's political role. This may have been the case with Fernand as well. His reflections about his own life experience in his interview were also partly related to his imminent departure, which probably signaled the beginning of retirement. But they are significant for the analysis presented here because they reproduce, in a slightly more systematic way, the shared moral and political imaginaries that are used to organize valuation and investment procedures and that employees mobilize when they look for justifications. These imaginaries are used in such way that they provide justifications that are considered consistent enough, without addressing or challenging the multiple epistemological and ontological presuppositions that they bring together.

As we saw at Acme, employees mobilized divergent and conflicting definitions of financial value and market efficiency. Fernand claimed that market efficiency was as a long-term trend based on individual fundamental valuation, an assertion contradicted, at the very moment he was speaking to me, by the practices of most of the employees to whom his department entrusted the money of Acme's customers. He more or less explicitly distanced himself from the classical investment method, but his insistence on the need for individual valuation challenged Sébastien's development of software to replicate indexes based on modern portfolio theory, and he clearly disagreed with the rejection of market efficiency by some of Acme's hedge fund managers. However, Fernand's argument did not try to account for each Acme employee's procedures or even for the way he himself, as director of the Allocation Department, dealt with the different groups of employees fighting over fees and bonuses in the company. He sought to assert the legitimacy of what he presented as a system, of which he was a part and the merit of which was its ability to tell a truth of value, at a moment when the "bubble" or the "crisis" seemed to call this into question. In a similar way, when Juliette and Carla sought to justify their personal trajectories and criticized the changes that challenged their expertise, they did not try to find an epistemological or ontological consistency amidst the different uses of the concepts of investor and market efficiency. The political and moral imaginaries available in these concepts played that role instead.

These moral and political justifications may serve mainly as tools to take stances in concrete situations. During my observations at Brokers Inc., Hedge Consulting, and Acme between 2002 and 2005, employees increasingly asserted the "crisis" was over. Proof of this was the increasing asset prices and the increasing profits of the financial industry, which translated into revenue for teams and employees in the form of fees, salaries, and bonuses. The global hierarchies resulting from the collection, production, and distribution of money by the financial industry could be considered the technically accurate and politically legitimate result of market efficiency without further need for justifications. The sharp fall in credit derivative prices in 2007–2008 and the return to profits in the financial industry a few years after that constituted a new round of this kind of argument.

As we saw in chapter 3, employees tended to consider that the financial industry is the social place where market efficiency is realized. The way Fernand used the word "we" to assert that the financial industry contributes to an optimal allocation of money worldwide was not the result of chance. It was an instance that makes explicit the connection between the technical legitimacy and the political legitimacy of expertise in financial methods. Financial regulation and professional rules restrict the social space of valuation and investment to the financial industry, where knowledge of financial theory is a fundamental barrier to entry. Each new employee must establish that he legitimately belongs in the professional setting by learning and proving proficiency in these methods. This filter plays an important role, enabling professionals to view their own practices and those of their colleagues as legitimate in a process of mutual recognition in a hierarchical organization.

Ho has highlighted how front-office employees in the financial industry emphasize their elite education as proof of their intellectual superiority. This, they tend to argue, justifies the fact that they occupy a social role in which they can influence where the money goes for the rest of society.[18] Along the same lines, Godechot shows how, in negotiating for higher salaries and bonuses, traders seek professional legitimacy by claiming mastery, and even ownership, of trading algorithms and methods that could be developed only with their know-how.[19] In many of these cases, employees consider as their personal achievement what broader sociological analysis would attribute to the social conditions of their upbringing—in particular, the wealth necessary to obtain a successful education at a prestigious institution.[20] Most employees I observed and interviewed at Brokers Inc., Acme, and Hedge Consulting and in the rest of the financial industry had indeed graduated from such schools and universities.

Employees may thus consider that their official position among the social elite also justifies the central role they play in the distribution of money worldwide. According to financial regulation and financial theory, they are the experts on the only form of knowledge that leads to a socially optimal allocation of resources in the global space of operations of the financial industry. This is explicit in Fernand's discourse quoted earlier. But it is also more or less explicit or implicit when employees justify their income and their legitimacy within the financial industry by claiming that they contribute to market efficiency and the representation of the true value of assets worldwide. As we saw, this was the case for all the employees who did not reject market efficiency explicitly. Those who did reject the possibility of market efficiency altogether had to justify why they did so and were confined to a marginal, albeit legitimate, position. The extension of the use of indexes in valuation and investment was accompanied by a reaffirmation of the technical and political legitimacies of this expert knowledge and hence of the social group that masters and applies it.

This elitism may be combined with other political imaginaries. We saw that this was the case for the way in which employees at

Brokers Inc. understood their identities in terms of age, gender, and class. But other forms of elite identity may be at stake. The case of national identity is significant because it connects with hierarchies among nation-states that relate to the history of colonialism, the Cold War, and the growth of manufacturing in China that I discussed in the introduction to this book. For instance, Ailon shows how trading instructors in Israel mobilize the elitism of the Jewish Israeli identity in their practice. They teach students to situate the elitist sense this identity gives them in their everyday lives within a global financial hierarchy where the United States occupies the top position.[21] Pitluck explains how financial professionals in Malaysia operate differently depending on the perceived national identity of their counterparts. They situate their elite position in terms of Malaysian national identity within global hierarchies that give financial meanings to the distinction between Malaysian and foreigner.[22] Chong demonstrates how employees of a major global consultancy firm draw particular distinctions between Chinese and Western identities when they apply management methods to promote the maximization of shareholder value in state-owned companies in northern China.[23] They define these identities in relation to the different meanings given to financial methods within the consultancy firm and in state-owned companies, where they are supposed to increase operational efficiency not for private owners but for the state. These identities thus partly result from the way in which financial methods to maximize shareholder value are defined in the power relations between Chinese and foreign nationals employed by the consultancy and between employees of the consultancy and Chinese state and Communist Party officials. The imaginaries of national identity are different in each of these cases, and elitism can be more or less explicit or implicit. But in all cases, employees combine the elitism and hierarchies that relate to national identity with the elitism that relates to a form of financial knowledge that asserts their legitimacy to decide where money must go in society at large.[24]

The moral and political imaginaries of valuation and investment assert that investors meeting in efficient markets produce a correct representation of the true value of assets that leads to a socially optimal allocation of resources. These imaginaries are present across the multiple and partly contradictory epistemological and ontological presuppositions about the truth of value formalized in financial methods. They are disseminated in the procedures applied by all employees, who also mobilize these meanings to assert their positions in interactions at work and to make sense of the global distributive effects of the financial industry. In the political discourses that accompanied the formulation of financial regulation, the notions of investor and efficient markets were used explicitly to justify a political project. At once technical, moral, and political, these concepts remain the general set of references that employees use to understand their practices and the global space of the financial industry.

TRUTH AS THE REALITY OF VALUE: A POLITICAL ASSEMBLAGE

This section explores theoretical possibilities that could account for the status of the concepts of investor, efficient market, and value in the financial industry. As we have seen, these concepts have many definitions in financial procedures. Nevertheless, through that multiplicity, they are repeatedly connected through imaginaries concerning the legitimacy of their role in the social distribution of resources. This legitimacy is premised on the capacity of prices to serve as signals in the allocation of resources because they would represent the true value of social activities. This representation results from the application of supposedly politically neutral techniques—i.e., the standardized valuation and investment procedures I have described. The price is considered true both as a product of the adequate application of valuation and investment procedures and as the legitimate expression and organization of the social hierarchies resulting from this application. Foucault showed that for ordoliberals, the state was supposed to produce such a system in order to require that every citizen act as a maximizing investor. This would then guarantee that prices were the best possible representation of the social value of the objects of the exchange. The political aim was to establish an organization in which social justice depended on the application of techniques of economic calculation that were defined as deprived of any political or moral content. In the following pages, I look at the limitations of the analytical strategies that critique the financial industry by focusing only on the epistemological and ontological questions concerning the definition of value. I then address the problems posed by critical approaches that use the concepts of investor and markets as analytical categories. Finally, I propose to address this political role of the assertion of a true value by focusing on the multiplicity of meanings in everyday practice and on the role that political imaginaries play in the production of social hierarchies through the collection, production, and distribution of money.

As we have seen, fundamental, relative, and speculative valuations define the value of financial assets as an amount of money the investor could obtain from the money he already owns. In textbooks, in the marketing materials in the financial industry, and in daily exchanges between employees, obtaining this money is usually referred to with the expression "creating value." For instance, one of the supplementary manuals I was given to prepare for the exams to obtain the certified international investment analyst (CIIA) credential simply stated: "The purpose of finance is to create value."[25] Within the relations among investor, market, and value established in financial theory, this gain indicates not only individual but also social "value," the distribution of which would be politically legitimate. Employees of the financial industry could thus consider "value creation" as including their own gains, the profits of the financial industry, the rise in asset prices, and the distributive effects of the financial industry. The monetary gain is considered the effect, and therefore the proof, of this social "value creation."[26]

For Adam Smith, in a free market the price of a good or service represented the cost of reproducing the work that was accumulated in it.[27] Despite this anchoring of value in a substance that would be observable in principle, Smith considered that it was very difficult to find a better representation of it than that proposed by the market price itself.[28] But financial theory does not provide a substantive definition of what this wealth or value could be apart from its representation by a sum of money.[29] The manual of financial analysis that Nicolas, the senior analyst at Brokers Inc., gave me when I arrived at the company thus stated:

> George Bernard Shaw once observed that "Economists know the price of everything and the value of nothing." And in a very real sense he is correct, since to an economist the value of an asset is nothing more or less than the price at which informed buyers and sellers are willing to trade it. The question of whether an asset has value beyond its selling price is one economists are content to leave to philosophers.[30]

In this line of reasoning, the monetary gain of the investor is "value" because it is defined as such by the efficient market. As

Levy shows, the notion of profit in management theories has changed over time, and in the last forty to fifty years, it has come to be defined as the gains for the shareholder.[31] Similar trends are present in the definition of the value of companies' assets in international accounting standards.[32] From a regulatory point of view, since the financial industry is designated as the space of implementation of the figure of the investor, and therefore of efficient markets, the prices it produces are considered the best signals for orienting money. The value that these prices would reflect as true is understood to be both the gain that can be obtained by the investor and the legitimate place of the social activity thus funded within the global hierarchy of access to money. In this perspective, true value exists because there are prices that represent it.

The problematization of value as something that is central in the distribution of money in society and that results from a technical operation of representation has been the focus of many critical studies on the epistemological and ontological presuppositions of this relation of representation. These studies have analyzed the multiplicities, contradictions, and uncertainties of financial professional practice. For instance, Riles shows how the concept of collateral is marked by an intrinsic absence,[33] Bruegger and Knorr Cetina highlight the technological infrastructure of the representation of time and the world in trading methods,[34] and Lépinay examines how different departments of the same bank define financial derivatives in different and hardly compatible ways.[35] In this book, I have also analyzed epistemological and ontological inconsistencies in the definitions of financial value in the financial industry. However, the sole focus on the representative character of prices does not address the concrete distribution of money by the financial industry. It even risks reproducing part of the neoclassical problematization of markets, which considers that distributive effects must be mainly addressed as issues concerning access to information.[36] This could come close to saying that the problem with valuation and investment is that they are misguided for technical reasons, implicitly presupposing that if the epistemological problems were settled, a socially optimal allocation of resources could ensue. This is the meaning of regulatory reforms that, during so-called financial crises, focus, for example, on enhancing the transparency of information and risk control, both matters that concern the accuracy of calculation techniques.[37]

Addressing the definition of value as an epistemological concern risks encapsulating the analysis within problematizations concerning the best way to represent value, such as those proposed by financial theory and financial regulation. There is a similar risk for the approaches that study the financial industry using the concepts of investor and market as analytic categories. In the work of Adam Smith, for instance, these categories were used to refer to individual people meeting in physical places where they would negotiate prices to maximize their gains. These people and markets were certainly idealized but referred to moral subjects with property rights whose social relations were supposed to compose the polity.[38] This frame is repeated conceptually in several critiques of finance that address the financial industry as a social space where investors meet. But since the end of the nineteenth century, critical observers remarked that in the relation between financial institutions and society, the figure of the investor had become increasingly disembodied. Retaining the figure of the investor in these analyses meant then problematizing its actions as well as its absence.

This is the case with Marx's critique. In his 1844 writings, capitalist relations place in opposition embodied subjects with different social roles, capitalists and proletarians, who will all be liberated by the socialization of ownership of the means of production.[39] The revolution called for in *The Communist Manifesto* was still one to be conducted against a particular class of people.[40] But some twenty years later Marx considered that stock companies had established a new relation of production—with exploitation but without private property. The bourgeois, as embodied owners of the means of production, had disappeared behind financial intermediaries, for whom Marx does not hide his contempt but who had only a secondary role in the capitalist process:

> This is the abolition of the capitalist mode of production within the capitalist mode of production itself, and hence a self-abolishing contradiction, which presents itself prima facie as a mere point of transition to a new form of production. It presents itself as such a contradiction even in appearance. It gives rise to monopoly in certain spheres and hence provokes state intervention. It reproduces a new financial aristocracy, a new kind of parasite in the guise of company promoters, speculators and merely nominal directors; an entire system of swindling and cheating with respect to the promotion of companies, issue of shares and share dealings. It is private production unchecked by private ownership.[41]

Commenting on this passage, Engels considered that the disappearance of the private owners of the means of production announced their total socialization and the disappearance of capitalism itself.

At the beginning of the twentieth century, major founders of the social sciences used the category of an embodied subject owning money to address financial inequalities. Mauss and Keynes developed an idealized image of the financial investor as owner of capital in order to problematize monetary inequalities. For Mauss, these "financial guardians [*trésoriers*] for their fellow citizens" are obliged to give back what society has given them, according to the logic of the gift.[42] For Keynes, they have to be eliminated from the financial system because they impose rates of return that are too high and depress investment and employment.[43] Simmel considered that this figure is not found in the organization of the distribution of money and of the ownership of companies but proposes nevertheless to retain it as an ideal in an explicit neo-Kantian teleology. The alienation and inequality of the relations of production would be resolved in a development that is at once political, moral, and economic, in which every individual will realize himself as an autonomous subject through monetary exchanges.[44]

Skeptical about any teleology of the realization of the free subject, Weber takes up the Marxian analysis of exploitation without owners and integrates it in a problematization of bureaucracy. Yet, he still problematizes the financial sector in relation to the embodied investor, only to find its absence and hence the impossibility of ethical action in finance:

> In this case [hierocratic domination], interests that are personal and flexible are at play within broad limits, and purely personal action and the will can change in a decisive way the relation and the situation of the participants. On the other hand, the director of a company with shareholders will find it very hard to establish that kind of relation with the workers in the factory, because it is his duty to defend the interest of the shareholders as his true "masters"; and this will be almost impossible for the director of the bank that finances the company, in his relation to the factory workers, or for the owner of a mortgage credit in his relation to the owner of the good that serves as collateral for the credit given by the bank. Behavior is here determined in a decisive manner by "competition," by the market (labor market, money market, and

goods markets), by "objective" considerations that being neither ethical nor anti-ethical, but simply non-ethical, seem absurd to any ethics, i.e. by factors that all introduce impersonal instances between the people concerned. From an ethical point of view, this "slavery without master" in which capitalism enmeshes the worker or the debtor of a mortgage, can only be discussed as an institution. But, by principle, this discussion cannot concern the personal behavior of the participant, whether he be dominant or dominated. Under the threat of disappearing because he would be, from any point of view, economically useless, this behavior is prescribed to him essentially in objective relations and—this is the decisive point—it is characterized as a "service" with an impersonal *objective aim.*[45]

In what constitutes an extreme case in his analytic framework, Weber determines that the financial bureaucracy is a social universe in which all ethics—i.e., all value rationality—is "absurd." He frames the financial industry, and companies and activities that some would today call financialized, in an analytic problematization that both presupposes the need of individual subjects to conduct action and highlights their absence: employees are obliged to follow procedures in order to survive, and critical analysis can concern itself only with institutions that are described as a series of functional tasks without ethical subjects. Retaining the idea that investment must be analyzed as though it was done by independent investors finding themselves in markets, the empirical social sciences can only conclude that the figure of the investor is absent, which is even more paradoxical because that figure is constantly invoked by the professionals of finance themselves, by financial regulation, and by a large number of political and media discourses.

In neoclassical economics and financial theory, the figure of the investor is also idealized. Since the first half of the twentieth century, management scholars also have noted that the owners of corporations have disappeared from their daily management. This analysis became the basis, after World War II, for theories asserting that although shareholders did not manage the corporation anymore, its aim had to be the maximization of shareholders' monetary income, also called the maximization of shareholder value. The investor here was partly an embodied social group, the owners of stocks, and partly an ideal image defined by increasingly formalized financial methods.[46] Foucault remarked that this ideal character of the investor was part of an explicitly political project for ordoliberalism. In this frame, the investor and the markets are not descriptive categories but regulatory ideas supposed to orient observation in order to detect processes that would allow for the social realization of these concepts through institutional construction. Foucault showed that for ordoliberals, the state was supposed to produce such a system in order to require that every citizen act as a maximizing investor. This would then guarantee that prices were the best possible representation of the social value of the objects of the exchange. The political aim was to establish an organization in which social justice depended on the application of techniques of economic calculation that were defined as deprived of any political or moral content.[47]

This conceptual character of investors and markets in the financial industry may be missed in analyses that focus all the attention on the practices where prices are negotiated.[48] There are indeed price negotiations in the financial industry. But as we saw in the previous chapters, the activity of traders is only a part of a much wider set of labor and commercial relations. The definition of what prices must represent is set by different professions according to a shared set of valuation and investment methods, and political imaginaries play a fundamental role in their organization. Studying this process as a confrontation of maximizing individuals in market settings erases the institutional rules that hold the process together, make the transactions possible, and inscribe them in the global hierarchies of access to money on which these transactions themselves depend.

Weber's description of the financial industry is echoed in the way in which Foucault analyzes the relation between knowledge and power in psychiatric clinics and prisons. According to Foucault, when psychiatric clinics were established, madness was defined in opposition to the politically and morally defined ideal behavior of a theoretical rational subject. The institutions of psychiatry appeared to treat the deviances from this ideal in a way that viewed madness as a human condition that would be identifiable thanks to the procedural methods for its treatment. These methods were themselves designed in relation to an epistemological discourse, so their moral and political aspects were forgotten but remained fundamentally a part of what then appeared as a matter of scientific truth: "*The manner in which the mad were alienated* was forgotten, only to reappear as the *nature of their alienation*."[49] From the same perspective, Foucault proposed to understand how the institution of prison was established in relation to the moral and religious concept of the soul. In this process, the soul

> is produced permanently around, on, within the body by the functioning of a power that is exercised on those punished—and, in a more general way, on those one supervises, trains and corrects [. . .] over those who are stuck at a machine and supervised for the rest of their lives [. . .]. This real, noncorporal soul is not a substance; it is the element in which are articulated the effects of a certain type of power and the reference of a certain type of knowledge [. . .]. The soul is the effect and instrument of a political anatomy [. . .].[50]

The way in which the concepts of investor, market efficiency, and true value are presupposed in procedures has a similar effect on the way in which they are taken as adequate categories to describe what happens in the financial industry, even by some of its harshest critics.

Foucault proposes instead to study how these categories are operational in power relations. Carried out procedurally, the figure of the investor is not a subject with a will but seems closer to what Foucault called an "intentionality":

> Power relations are both intentional and nonsubjective. If in fact they are intelligible, this is not because they are the effect of another instance that "explains" them, but rather because they are imbued, through and through, with calculation: there is no power that is exercised without a series of aims and objectives. But this does not mean that it results from the choice or decision of an individual subject; [. . .] the rationality of power is characterized by tactics that are often quite explicit at the restricted level where they are inscribed (the local cynicism of power), tactics which, becoming connected to one another, attracting and propagating one another, but finding their base of support and their condition elsewhere, end by forming comprehensive settings [*dispositifs d'ensemble*]: the logic is perfectly clear, the aims decipherable, and yet it is often the case that no one is there to have invented them, and few who can be said to have formulated them.[51]

These insights are useful for highlighting the importance of concepts like those of investor, market, and value without using them as analytic categories to assess how they are used in everyday practice. These passages also allow for addressing the fragmented and contradictory character of the definitions of value, which could be obscured with Foucault's later interest in the notion of governmentality.

However, this figure of the investor is not only, as in Foucault's view, a reason immanent in a series of procedures. As we saw in the previous chapters, employees are expected to display moral adherence, conviction, sincerity, passion, and pain in relation to the concepts of investor, market efficiency, and financial value. At the same time, they may have varying relations to their professional life—i.e., attachment, rejection, or indifference—and they may be more or less ethically committed to or cynical about the application of procedures in everyday practice. And in all cases, they situate their professional practice in relation to their other social identities, as many analyses have shown in relation to imaginaries of age, gender, class, race, nationality, and religion, among others.

In this respect, Roitman's study of the ethics of road bandits is useful in addressing an important aspect of how employees in the financial industry relate to their work. The people she observed applied what they called the code of road banditry in nightly attacks that could end with the killing of recalcitrant victims. But they also referred to other imaginaries of duty and ethical obligation. They claimed that they were observant religious practitioners during the day, as well as public servants, heads of households, and citizens. She shows how they mobilized these conflicting ethical codes in different situations without needing to unify them in one consistent morality and without having to determine with certainty how sincere or authentic their feelings were about each of them.[52] Instead of trying to subsume all these practices in one rationale, it is more fruitful to address them as a multiplicity. The imaginaries of investor, markets, and value combine a multiplicity of epistemologies and ontologies, along with assertions about fairness and the desired order of global society. But in everyday practice, employees mobilize them in combination with varying emotional, moral, and political attachments.

And their application is coconstituted with the organizational rules that relate employees, companies, financial regulation, and academic formalizations of financial theory.

The notion of multiplicity does not imply a flattening of all elements into a level playing field. Some elements may be more prevalent and can contribute to organize the rest. This is important in addressing the notions of value, investor, and market in the financial industry. The political imaginaries connecting these concepts play an organizing role in the definition of procedures, the choice of data, the division of tasks, the relations within and between companies, and financial regulation. Employees of the financial industry use the concepts of investor and efficient market to give meaning to their own practices and the social space where they work. They can thus claim to be qualified to determine where the money managed by the financial industry should go because this determination is based on their personal expertise and on the socially optimal resource allocation that the financial industry is supposed to realize. These meanings are important for how employees make sense of their practice and repeat acts of valuation and investment one day after another, leading to the global distributive effects I mentioned in the introduction to this book.

As we have seen, there are no actors who can be singled out as the embodied investor because investment and valuation decisions are disseminated in all the tasks. Transactions—for instance, those that constitute the expertise of traders—are only part of a much broader set of social relations that determine where the money should go and according to which lines of reasoning. Focusing on these instances in order to consider the financial industry as a marketplace misses the much broader social process whereby money is hierarchically distributed worldwide. Prices are, of course, an important part of the process, but they are not the primary determinant of the way value is defined, which gives preeminence to the figure of the investor, and of the way investment is oriented, in which diversification is a fundamental line of reasoning. In this process, value is defined in multiple and contradictory ways, so it does not constitute a single line of reasoning that orients the money managed by the financial industry. Yet, as we have seen, the political imaginaries of investor, market, and value do establish a hierarchy where the figure of the investor is given priority and where the distribution of money by the financial industry is endowed with political legitimacy as the result of market efficiency and the sidelining of the state.

Worldwide, the practices of the financial industry connect with a variety of power relations. The over $200 trillion managed by the financial industry is concentrated in former colonial centers, the United States, Japan, and, increasingly, China. This geography reflects geopolitical confrontations in a historical process where imaginaries of racism, sexism, nationalism, imperialism, and corporate profit were mutually established. Reducing this complex intersection of power relations in the financial industry to a single logic, be it that of neoliberalism, capitalism, or even financialization, misses the many power relations that both sustain and endanger it. Instead of looking at the financial industry as a series of investors meeting in markets according to the logic of value maximization, it is important to see how these categories are fundamental in the organization of this bureaucratic space, both internally and in the way in which it can connect to power relations outside of it. It is in this sense that I propose to consider the financial industry as a political institution and the procedures and meanings of the concepts of investor, market, and value as political imaginaries.

Due to the fortuities and limitations of my fieldwork, the observations presented in this book have focused on the valuation of listed companies, but it is important to point out that the same lines of reasoning and most formulas, with minor modifications, are used for the valuation of other financial assets. The presupposition that there is a truth of value that is revealed in prices, defined at the same time as a technical matter and as the legitimization of hierarchies in the distribution of resources, far exceeds the social space of the financial industry. At the same time, it constitutes just one of the ways to account for contemporary monetary relations. But the fact that this truth is supposed to be the product of established forms of expertise applied in the financial industry and that it is supposed to be identified as the effect of the activity of investors in efficient markets contributes to the legitimization of these hierarchies. The truth of the financial value of social activities, supposed to be realized in prices that are then also considered the proof of its existence, must be understood as a political assemblage, in which the practices of the financial industry play a crucial role—but one that depends on the place that it is granted in global power relations concerning the production and distribution of money.

CONCLUSION

THE practices addressed in this book primarily concern listed companies. But the financial methods I have described are applied to all assets in very similar terms. At the time of my observations, between 2002 and 2005, employees and part of the press still talked about the "internet bubble" as the "biggest financial crisis since 1929." A few years later a large part of the press and many governments attributed this title to the "subprime crisis." As I write this, the Covid-19 pandemic keeps spreading, and there is no such talk of financial crisis, at least as of yet. From the point of view of financial regulation and the financial practices described in this book, this means that the financial industry is fulfilling its role by contributing to a socially optimal allocation of resources. The inequalities I described at the beginning of the book, which are worsening with the Covid-19 pandemic, nevertheless attest to the contrary. In concluding this book, it may therefore be useful to come back to what the case of listed companies says about the financial industry at large.

THE TRUTH OF VALUE AS PRACTICE IN THE FINANCIAL INDUSTRY

For some forty years, in a very diverse set of jurisdictions around the world, financial regulation has given the financial industry a central role in the distribution of money, taking as a reference the financial theory standardized after World War II. According to this conceptual framework, when independent investors use the cognitive tools developed in standard financial theory, they contribute to achieving market efficiency. Prices reflect the true value of traded assets and serve as signals for a socially optimal allocation of resources. Financial regulation distinguishes the category of qualified investors, essentially employees of the financial industry who have been so designated based on their knowledge of financial theory and the means they have to apply it. Regulation establishes thus that the optimal allocation of money should be the result of these investors meeting in efficient markets within the financial industry.

As we have seen, this theory is the product of an intellectual history that assembles several ontologies and epistemologies that are more or less disconnected or contradictory. It mobilizes both a subjectivist epistemology, based on the freedom of the valuating gaze, and an objectivist epistemology, where the truth of the price is imposed on these subjects either as a social construct in a market or as a phenomenon of nature that is defined in relation to the rules of statistics. This theory gives the state a central role in determining of the standard of all value while also establishing that it should play no role in decisions about the distribution of money beyond guaranteeing a minimum revenue to the figure of the investor. The theory also implies using other sources of data, with their own ontologies and epistemologies, that are considered to provide legitimate information because they are the product of legitimate technical expertise, which is the only methodological corpus with which valuation is possible.

This theory is used to define the tasks of employees, specialized in different ways to define the value of assets and invest in them. The activities of valuation and investment are the product of salaried jobs in a commercial network of companies. The theory is part of career trajectories that occur through relations of hierarchy, cooperation, and competition within and between companies. In this process, the formulas and lines of reasoning of financial theory are considered the best tools for representing the interests of the legal owners of the money managed by financial employees. The increase in income, wages, and bonuses is supposed to reward the skillful application of the procedures of valuation and investment.

In these practices, employees must see themselves as bearing the investor's gaze and as facing efficient markets. This places them in a tension in which the individual valuation of the investor is necessary to achieve market efficiency but becomes superfluous once that efficiency is reached. This tension becomes a contradiction when efficiency is both negated and asserted in the same formulas or in the same valuation or investment procedures.

Depending on their specialization, employees assemble in different ways the three definitions of financial value—fundamental, relative, and speculative—which are at the same time interdependent and opposed to each other; in addition, each of them contains its own different tensions and contradictions. On the one hand, employees express opinions on value that are supposed to be personal and to imply their conviction, their sincerity, their beliefs, or even their passion—something they do with different emotional relations to their work, whether attachment, rejection, ambivalence, or indifference. On the other hand, the procedures they follow presuppose the efficiency of markets. Procedures like the classical investment method thus ask employees to use their personal opinions to beat the indexes that are used based on the presupposition of market efficiency.

In this setting, financial value is defined by the future monetary gains of the owners of money. The idea that this value has a truth is based on the presupposition that this truth is revealed in prices resulting from investors' exchanges in efficient markets. Recognizing themselves as the experts who apply this figure of the investor, employees can consider, as financial regulation does, that their professional space is where the efficient markets they presuppose in their procedures are realized. When procedures are applied correctly, the prices they lead to are seen as proof that this value and its truth are revealed and that the social effects of this valuation are legitimate. The financial industry is thus reasserted in everyday practice as the place where financial value is represented in a way that is true, so that this representation of value must be imposed on the rest of society as the signal leading to a socially optimal allocation of resources. The truth of value expressed in prices is thus considered to be both the result of a politically neutral technique and a standard of social justice in a political project instituted in financial regulation.

In order to give meaning to their practices, employees mobilize the political and moral references present in their methods. This is reinforced in situations considered crises, which are understood to call for justifications regarding the daily activity and the professional space of employees. This space is not the open arena where they meet to exchange as free and equal subjects, presupposed in liberal utopias, but rather an assemblage of companies, the entry to which requires mastering a method that is applied only in a salaried relation. Yet, it is by making reference to the political meanings of investor, efficient market, and value that these practices are justified for employees and, more importantly, for financial regulation and for those who accept its distributive effects.

There are many ways in which these lines of reasoning are challenged today within the financial industry. Here I mention three that have become increasingly important since I did the research on which this book is based. One concerns Islamic finance. As Rudnyckyj shows, Islamic finance is carried out as a global project by financial experts who combine the methods and lines of reasoning described in this book with religious precepts.[1] They do so in order to expand their presence both within and outside the financial industry. They thus pose a challenge to the main financial imaginaries described in this book but can also appear as a new segment of the financial industry with which they are intimately connected.

Another development concerns the use of algorithms in investment and valuation. While algorithms are widely used in trading,[2] they are also increasingly used as methods of valuation and investment. In this process, they may replace some of the professions that used to conduct these activities. This was, as we saw, Sébastien's understanding of the impact of his software on investment management. But algorithms may also be used to change the lines of reasoning of valuation and investment methods, connecting financial data to other forms of data in statistical relations that are possible only for machines with high computing capabilities. Some companies are specializing in this approach, which tends to attribute to valuation and investment a new form of legitimacy, that of digitization and machine learning.[3]

Finally, another challenge is posed by the development of the Chinese financial industry. Its financial regulation enforces the methods and lines of reasoning described in this book, but financial companies are mainly state owned, and their explicit aim is to contribute to a nationally oriented state policy under the control of the Chinese Communist Party.[4]

In these three cases, the practices described in this book are present, but they are combined with others, and so are their political imaginaries. So far, the money managed through these approaches, although amounting to several trillion dollars, remains a fraction of all the money managed by the financial industry. Besides, algorithmic valuation and investment can be integrated in all of them. In any case, they partly escape the descriptions proposed in this book. Yet, they can still be subject to analysis in terms of their role in the global distribution of resources, which has been the analytic approach proposed in this book.

THE ACTIVITY OF THE FINANCIAL INDUSTRY AS A POLITICAL ISSUE

The assertion that there is a truth of value matters because institutions in charge of financial regulation and practitioners in the financial industry itself use it to legitimize the social hierarchies that the financial industry contributes to establish by the way it distributes money. Focus on the epistemological and ontological limitations of valuation and investment methods, which are infused with contradictions and heterogeneity, certainly contributes to the critique of the financial industry's social roles. But it also risks disregarding the fact that the social existence of this assertion about the truth of value lies not only in the theoretical debates that formalize it but also, and especially, in the social relations of power that reproduce it in everyday practice. Valuation and investment done by employees like those described in this book are a political issue because they play a fundamental role in the production of global social hierarchies.

In the financial industry, the truth of financial value is invoked as both a technical and a political justification of relations of power concerning any specific asset and concerning the relation among all assets and activities that are excluded from the money managed by the financial industry. In the analysis of listed companies, the point of view of shareholders and bondholders is given priority over that of other participants in the activity of the listed company. The analysis presupposes not only that the cash flow produced by the company has to go to the figure of the investor but also that the activity of the company itself must be oriented toward maximizing this income. This reasoning is not unique to the valuation of listed companies. It is actually central in all asset valuation and investment methods formalized in financial theory. In the analysis of the debts of states, for instance, the figure of the investor is given priority over the other members of society—such as taxpayers, recipients of state aid, public-sector employees, and generally anyone directly or indirectly benefiting from public expenditure. In the valuation of credit derivatives, commodities, and all other financial assets, it is again the income of the figure of the investor that must be secured first. In all these cases, investment is defined as individual income sought by the owner of money, and his gaze is imposed over that of any other participant in the activity that is financed.

Valuation and investment also establish power relations among social activities that compete to access the money managed by the financial industry. When employees describe a company as a potential investment, they systematically compare it with other listed companies and with other financial assets. This happens in many ways. In the valuation of a single asset, the asset is compared to the risk-free rate of return and to a sector or index of reference. In the classical investment method and in relative valuation in general, all activities are potentially compared to each other. The

biggest investment management companies thus develop investment and valuation strategies that attempt to include all financial
assets in the world. Although there may not be any investment
management company that indeed invests in all these assets at
the same time, this possibility is a technical presupposition of
valuation and investment methods. In the process, some social
activities are totally excluded from the money managed by the
financial industry. They risk disappearing if they cannot transform themselves according to investment and valuation lines of
reasoning—for example, by generating more money for the figure
of the investor. The transformations that an activity may have to
undergo in order to be included in the investment universe can
end up being as damaging as or even worse than the consequences
of exclusion from the money managed by the financial industry.

From the point of view of financial regulation, these transformations of social activities and their inclusion in or exclusion
from the hierarchy of access to money managed by the financial
industry are the desirable result of a regime of truth that allows
for a socially optimal allocation of resources. The financial industry, considered to represent individual interests defined according to the methods formalized in financial theory, would thus
contribute to a global common good. This setting gives states
an ambiguous role. The state should only guarantee the rules of
exchange without taking any part in it. However, states are also
expected to use their sovereignty in order to guarantee a minimum income for the owners of money and thereby establish a
standard of value that is imposed on all other social activities that
may be funded by the financial industry.

It is therefore analytically fruitful to consider the financial
industry as a political institution instead of as a series of markets
where investors meet. The vast amounts of money produced, collected, and distributed by the financial industry connect with a
variety of other institutions and power relations worldwide. The

financial industry thus plays an important role in sustaining these power relations and is shaped by them in return. The assertion of the preeminence of the figure of the investor and of the truth produced by market efficiency connects with many other power relations that cannot be subsumed under a single logic. The role of states is central in this process. For centuries, the development of rich states has been inseparable from that of the financial industry. Colonial empires and large financial institutions have spread around the planet together. If after World War II the financial industry seemed under the control of rich states, it was given a central role in global exchanges after regulatory changes in the 1970s and 1980s. Today, as we see at Brokers Inc. in the relation between Frédéric and his clients or in the investment strategies developed at Acme, the employees of the financial industry operate with the whole world as their horizon of valuation and investment. In the particular geography of this global space, financial regulation, despite its relative homogeneity from the point of view of content, is fragmented by the limitations of geographical jurisdictions and of the mandates specific to each supervisory body. In contrast, the financial industry shares valuation and investment methods and rules of labor and commercial organization across the world. These shared rules contribute to its capacity to manage a hierarchical distribution of money on a global scale through commercial relations among the companies that compose it. In so doing, it contributes to constituting this global space as a political space. It thus operates as a global political institution.

THE TRUTH OF VALUE FROM CRISIS TO CRISIS

The term "financial crisis" is often used to refer to a heterogeneous set of events, such as falling stock prices in the United States or

Europe; the default on state debts by the government of Mexico, Russia, or Argentina; or the default of mortgage borrowers based in the United States. Systematically, financial regulation and the financial industry have mobilized the conceptual framework of market efficiency to define what these crises were and the solutions they required. Repeatedly, it was concluded that the crisis resulted from erroneous asset valuation.

In this setting, the crisis is conceived as a moment of deviation and correction in the process whereby prices reflect true value. Since the end of the 1980s, proposed solutions have generally tended to strengthen the control of the quality of information—for example, by asking participants to provide more data about their activities. They have also tended to strengthen the relation of representation between clients of the financial industry and the employees responsible for representing their interests. This is how valuation and investment procedures have become increasingly standardized and mandatory for employees and how the bonus system has been formalized as part of the principal-agent relation.

At the time of my observations, the "crisis" of the "internet bubble," which officially took place from 1996 to 2003, was accompanied by the bankruptcy of companies related to the telecommunications sector, which had grown with the money invested in their listed shares. Some of these companies had not complied with regulations concerning disclosure of their activities and accounting data. The cases of Enron and WorldCom were then presented as symbolizing the greed of business leaders who had committed fraud at the expense of the entire financial industry and the shareholders who gave them their money. This resulted in regulatory changes, imposing more detailed tax and financial statements, especially concerning financial derivatives, which had been particularly designed in order not to appear clearly on balance sheets.

The "subprime crisis" began a few years later, in 2007. In the United States, banks had securitized their loans, mostly mortgages, which allowed them to issue more loans by circumventing regulations specifically aimed at preventing them from doing so. Real estate prices, which had risen with this process, started dropping as many low-income borrowers started defaulting. Banks increasingly accumulated houses with falling prices and loans in default. After letting the investment bank Lehman Brothers go bankrupt, the U.S. government decided to help other banks to prevent them from going bankrupt in turn, as all banks are both borrowers from and lenders to each other. In this case, too, the crisis was determined to be the result of erroneous valuations of credit derivatives, either because these assets were deemed too complex to be understood or because acts of fraud hid information from the employees of rating agencies and the financial industry at large.

As before, there were calls for more transparency, as well as for a review of the compensation system, in order to ensure that the interests of the employees of the financial industry aligned with those of their customers and to prevent fraud. Although the United States and some European countries had to nationalize banks, they did not influence their procedures of valuation and investment. The conceptual framework according to which these institutions could continue to operate as a gathering of investors in efficient markets remained intact.

In the United States and Europe, the return of profits for financial institutions and their payment of penalties for past fraud, as well as GDP growth and decreased unemployment rates, were interpreted as evidence that the subprime crisis was over. This reinforced the discourse according to which, after trial and error in valuation, the distribution of resources by the financial industry was again close to social optimality based on market efficiency. The global inequalities that existed before the crisis and continued after it was over were thereby legitimized and perpetuated.

Money is today a fundamental element in the production of global hierarchies. Used with imaginaries that vary from one situation to another, money constitutes social relations as much as these relations determine what money itself is. The financial industry, as one of the major institutions organizing the production and distribution of money worldwide, plays an important role in this process. As it creates hierarchies worldwide, it contributes to establishing a global political space. And it does so by mobilizing imaginaries about the identity of the actors who determine this distribution and about the justice of the social inequalities that ensue from it. In this setting, financial regulation, standard academic production in economics, the financial press, part of the general press, and a large fraction of political discourse consider the financial industry's utterance of value part of a legitimate regime of truth. The anthropology and the sociology of money have highlighted that money can be used in an open-ended variety of social relations—not only to create hierarchies but also to destroy them. The analysis proposed in this book thus hopes to contributes to this endeavor, offering a critique of the imaginaries that organize and legitimize the role of the financial industry in the production of global social hierarchies.

NOTES

INTRODUCTION

1. All dollar amounts given in this book are denominated in U.S. dollars unless otherwise indicated.

2. It can be useful to use female pronouns to refer to gender-neutral actors, if only to remind one of the gendered traps of language, but the financial industry, which is far from unique in this respect, is generally organized with a gendered division of labor in which high-ranked positions tend to be held by people identified as male. I will therefore use masculine pronouns when speaking in general about these kinds of employees because using female pronouns could give the misleading impression that this gendered hierarchy is not in place. For studies that focus on this issue, see Melissa Fisher, *Wall Street Women* (Durham, NC: Duke University Press, 2012); Karen Ho, *Liquidated: An Ethnography of Wall Street* (Durham, NC: Duke University Press, 2009); Louise Roth, *Selling Women Short: Gender and Inequality on Wall Street* (Princeton, NJ: Princeton University Press, 2006); Leslie Salzinger, "Re-making Men: Masculinity as a Terrain of the Neoliberal Economy," *Critical Historical Studies* 3, no. 1 (2016): 1–25; and Daniel Souleles, *Songs of Profit, Songs of Loss. Private Equity, Wealth and Inequality* (Lincoln: University of Nebraska Press, 2019).

3. I will discuss the notion of financial asset in chapter 1.

4. Sabine Montagne and Horacio Ortiz, "Sociologie de l'agence financière: enjeux et perspectives," *Sociétés Contemporaines* 92, no. 4 (2013):

7–33; Horacio Ortiz, "A Political Anthropology of Finance: Studying the Distribution of Money in the Financial Industry as a Political Process," *Anthropological Theory* 21, no. 1 (2021): 3–27.

5. Liam Kennedy, "Top 400 Asset Managers," *Investment and Pensions Europe*, June 2018, 21–23, https://www.ipe.com/reports/special-reports /top-400-asset-managers/top-400-asset-managers-2018-10-years-of -asset-growth/10025004.article.

6. Capitalization is determined by multiplying the number of assets by their listed price. It does not represent the price at which all the assets would be purchased, since prices would probably change with those acts of buying and selling.

7. For numbers on stock exchanges, see "Statistics," World Federation of Exchanges, accessed December 20, 2018, https://www.world-exchanges .org/our-work/statistics.

8. For numbers on debt securities and derivatives, see "Statistics," Bank of International Settlements, accessed December 20, 2018, https://www .bis.org/statistics/index.htm.

9. A derivative contract is usually a commitment to exchange a notional amount in the future that is much higher than the price of the contract itself. In general, this nominal amount is not exchanged because different contracts are used to cancel each other out before the commitment must be fulfilled.

10. For numbers on gross domestic product see "Database," World Bank Group, accessed December 20, 2018, https://data.worldbank.org/indicator /NY.GDP.MKTP.CD.

11. For numbers on state budgets and monetary mass, see Central Intelligence Agency, *The World Factbook*," accessed December 20, 2018, https:// www.cia.gov/library/publications/resources/the-world-factbook/geos /xx.html. Narrow monetary mass refers to bills, coins and short-term bank deposits. Broad monetary mass includes the narrow monetary mass plus longer-term deposits. Of course, the comparison must take into account the fact that state budgets describe yearly flows, while the assets held by the financial industry constitute a more static amount.

12. FAO, IFAD, UNICEF, WFP, and WHO, *The State of Food Security and Nutrition in the World 2018: Building Climate Resilience for Food Security and Nutrition* (Rome: FAO, 2018), http://www.fao.org/policy-support /tools-and-publications/resources-details/en/c/1152267/.

13. World Bank Group, *Reaching the Global Target to Reduce Stunting: How Much Will It Cost and How Can We Pay for It?*, accessed December 20, 2018, http://pubdocs.worldbank.org/en/460861439997767818/Stunting-Costing-and-Financing-Overview-Brief.pdf; International Institute for Sustainable Development, *Ending Hunger: What Would It Cost?*, October 2016, https://www.iisd.org/sites/default/files/publications/ending-hunger-what-would-it-cost.pdf.

14. Amartya Sen, *Development as Freedom* (Oxford: Oxford University Press, 1999); Göran Therborn, *The Killing Fields of Inequality* (Cambridge: Polity Press, 2013).

15. Laura Bear, "Capital and Time: Uncertainty and Qualitative Measures of Inequality," *British Journal of Sociology* 65, no. 4 (2014): 639–49; Jane Guyer, "The Eruption of Tradition: On Ordinality and Calculation," *Anthropological Theory* 10, no. 1–2 (2010): 121–31; Keith Hart, "Models of Statistical Distribution: A Window on Social History," *Anthropological Theory* 10, no. 1–2 (2010): 67–74; Federico Neiburg and Jane Guyer, "The Real in the Real Economy," *HAU: Journal of Ethnographic Theory* 7, no. 3 (2017): 261–79.

16. Eric Helleiner, "The Southern Side of Embedded Liberalism: The Politics of Postwar Monetary Policy in the Third World," in *Monetary Orders: Ambiguous Economics, Ubiquitous Politics*, ed. Jonathan Kirshner (Ithaca, NY: Cornell University Press, 2003), 57–77; Barry Eichengreen, *Globalizing Capital: A History of the International Monetary System* (Princeton NJ: Princeton University Press, 1996).

17. Giulia Dal Maso, *Risky Expertise in Chinese Financialisation: Returned Labor and the State-Finance Nexus* (Singapore: Palgrave Macmillan, 2020); Ellen Hertz, *The Trading Crowd: An Ethnography of the Shanghai Stock Market* (Cambridge: Cambridge University Press, 1998); Johannes Petry, "Financialization with Chinese Characteristics? Exchanges, Control and Capital Markets in Authoritarian Capitalism," *Economy and Society* 49, no. 2 (2020): 213–38; Yingyao Wang, "The Rise of the 'Shareholding State': Financialization of Economic Management in China," *Socio-economic Review* 13, no. 3 (2015): 603–25.

18. Greta Krippner, *Capitalizing on Crisis: The Political Origins of the Rise of Finance* (Cambridge, MA: Harvard University Press, 2011); Thomas Piketty, *Capital in the XXIst Century*, trans. Arthur Goldhammer (Cambridge, MA: Harvard University Press, 2014).

19. Brigitte Young, Isabella Bakker, and Diane Elson, *Questioning Financial Governance from a Feminist Perspective* (London: Routledge, 2011); Adrienne Roberts, "Gender, Financial Deepening and the Production of Embodied Finance: Towards a Critical Feminist Analysis," *Global Society* 29, no. 1 (2015): 107–27.

20. Neil Fligstein, *The Transformation of Corporate Control* (Cambridge, MA: Harvard University Press, 1990), and *The Architecture of Markets: An Economic Sociology of Twenty-First-Century Capitalist Societies* (Princeton, NJ: Princeton University Press, 2001); Mahmoud Ezzamel, Hugh Wilmott, and Frank Worthington, "Manufacturing Shareholder Value: The Role of Accounting in Organizational Transformation," *Accounting, Organizations and Society* 33, no. 2–3 (2008): 107–40; Karen Ho, *Liquidated*; John Roberts et al., "In the Mirror of the Market: The Disciplinary Effects of Company/Fund Manager Meetings," *Accounting, Organizations and Society* 31, no. 3 (2006): 277–94.

21. Olivier Godechot, "Financialization Is Marketization! A Study of the Respective Impact of Various Dimensions of Financialization on the Increase in Global Inequality," *Sociological Science* 3, no. 30 (2016): 495–519; Ken-Hou Lin and Donald Tomaskovic-Devey, "Financialization and U.S. Income Inequality, 1970–2008," *American Journal of Sociology* 118, no. 5 (2013): 1284–329.

22. Daniela Gabor, "The Wall Street Consensus," *Development and Change*, first published online (2021): doi: 10.1111/dech.12645; Helleiner, "The Southern Side of Embedded Liberalism"; Bernhard Reinsberg et al., "The World System and the Hollowing Out of State Capacity: How Structural Adjustment Programs Affect Bureaucratic Quality in Developing Countries," *American Journal of Sociology* 124, no. 4 (2019): 1222–57; Joseph Stiglitz, *Making Globalization Work* (London: Penguin, 2006).

23. Noelle Stout, *Dispossessed: How Predatory Bureaucracy Foreclosed on the American Middle Class* (Oakland: University of California Press, 2019).

24. Philip McMichael, "A Food Regime Analysis of the 'World Food Crisis,'" *Agriculture and Human Values* 26, no. 4 (2009): 281–95.

25. Eileen Appelbaum and Rosemary Batt, *Private Equity at Work: When Wall Street Manages Main Street* (New York: Russell Sage Foundation, 2014).

26. Geoffrey Lawrence, Sarah Sippel, and David Burch, "The Financialisation of Food and Farming," in *Handbook on the Globalisation of*

Agriculture, ed. Guy Robinson and Doris Carson (Cheltenham, UK: Edward Elgar, 2015), 309–27; Ben White et al., "The New Enclosures: Critical Perspectives on Corporate Land Deals," *Journal of Peasant Studies* 39, no. 3–4 (2012): 619–47.

27. Andrew Leyshon and Nigel Thrift, "The Capitalization of Almost Everything: The Future of Finance and Capitalism," *Theory, Culture and Society* 24, no. 7–8 (2007): 97–115; Eve Chiapello, "Financialisation of Valuation," *Human Studies* 38, no. 1 (2015): 13–35; Wai Fong Chua, "Experts, Networks and Inscriptions in the Fabrication of Accounting Images: A Story of the Representation of Three Public Hospitals," *Accounting, Organizations and Society* 23, no. 2–3 (1995): 111–45.

28. Krippner, *Capitalizing on Crisis*.

29. Rawi Abdelal, *Capital Rules: The Construction of Global Finance* (Cambridge, MA: Harvard University Press, 2007).

30. Jennifer Amyx, *Japan's Financial Crisis: Institutional Rigidity and Reluctant Change* (Princeton, NJ: Princeton University Press, 2004).

31. Yaga Reddy, *India and the Global Financial Crisis: Managing Money and Finance* (London: Anthem Press, 2009).

32. Hertz, *The Trading Crowd*.

33. Maria Chaves Jardim, *Syndicats et fonds de pension durant le gouvernement Lula* (Paris: L'Harmattan, 2013); Lúcia Müller, *Mercado Exemplar: um estudo antropológico sobre a Bolsa de Valores* (Porto Alegre, Brazil: Zouk, 2006).

34. Michel Aglietta and Antoine Rebérioux, *Dérives du capitalisme financier* (Paris: Albin Michel, 2004); Mark Blyth, "The Political Power of Financial Ideas: Transparency, Risk, and Distribution in Global Finance," in Kirshner, *Monetary Orders*, 239–59; Helleiner, "The Southern Side of Embedded Liberalism"; Stiglitz, *Making Globalization Work*.

35. Simone Polillo and Mauro F. Guillén, "Globalization Pressures and the State: The Worldwide Spread of Central Bank Independence," *American Journal of Sociology* 110, no. 6 (2005): 1764–802; Paul Langley, *Liquidity Lost: The Governance of the Financial Crisis* (Oxford: Oxford University Press, 2015).

36. Howard Davies and David Green, *Global Financial Regulation: The Essential Guide* (Cambridge: Polity Press, 2011).

37. Horacio Ortiz, "Marchés efficients, investisseurs libres et Etats garants: trames du politique dans les pratiques financières professionnelles,"

Politix 95, no. 3 (2011): 155–80, and "The Limits of Financial Imagination: Free Investors, Efficient Markets and Crisis," *American Anthropologist* 116, no. 1 (2014): 38–50.

38. The definition of "qualified" or "sophisticated investor" usually also includes wealthy individuals, who play a marginal role in financial exchanges worldwide. The European Securities and Markets Authority uses the expression "professional investor."

39. Gordon L. Clark, *Pension Fund Capitalism* (Oxford: Oxford University Press, 2000); Ismail Erturk et al., "Against Agency: A Positional Critique," *Economy and Society* 36, no. 1 (2007): 51–77; Sabine Montagne, *Les Fonds de Pension: Entre protection sociale et spéculation financière* (Paris: Odile Jacob, 2006); Dominique Plihon and Jean-Pierre Ponssard, eds., *La montée en puissance des fonds d'investissement* (Paris: La Documentation Française, 2002).

40. Horacio Ortiz, "Investir: une décision disséminée; Enquête de terrain sur les dérivés de credit," *Sociétés Contemporaines*, no. 92 (2013): 35–57.

41. Georges Balandier, *Anthropologie Politique* (Paris: Presses Universitaires de France, 1967); Ortiz, "A Political Anthropology of Finance."

42. Natascha Van der Zwan, "Making Sense of Financialization," *Socio-economic Review* 12, no. 1 (2014): 99–129; Rajesh Venugopal, "Neoliberalism as Concept," *Economy and Society* 44, no. 2 (2015): 165–87.

43. Gilles Deleuze and Félix Guattari, *Capitalisme ou Schizophrénie 2: Mille Plateaux* (Paris: Les Editions de Minuit, 1980); see also Stephen Collier and Aihwa Ong, "Global Assemblages, Political Problems," in *Global Assemblages: Technology, Politics, and Ethics as Anthropological Problems*, ed. Stephen Collier and Aihwa Ong (Oxford: Blackwell, 2005), 3–21.

44. Saskia Sassen, "Global Finance and Its Institutional Spaces," in *The Oxford Handbook of the Sociology of Finance*, ed. Karin Knorr Cetina and Alex Preda (Oxford: Oxford University Press, 2012), 13–32.

45. Deleuze and Guattari, *Capitalisme ou Schizophrénie 2*.

46. See also José Luis Escalona Victoria, "Anthropology of Power: Beyond State-Centric Politics," *Anthropological Theory* 16, no. 2–3 (2016): 249–62; Michel Foucault, *Histoire de la sexualité 1 La volonté de savoir* (Paris: Gallimard, 1976).

47. See also Diane-Laure Arjaliès et al., *Chains of Finance: How Investment Management Is Shaped* (Oxford: Oxford University Press, 2017); Gordon L. Clark and Nigel Thrift, "The Return of Bureaucracy: Managing

Dispersed Knowledge in Global Finance," in Cetina and Preda, *The Sociology of Financial Markets*, 229–49; Richard Whitley, "The Transformation of Business Finance Into Financial Economics: The Roles of Academic Expansion and Changes in U.S. Capital Markets," *Accounting, Organizations and Society* 11, no. 2 (1986): 171–92.

48. Marc Abélès, "Pour une anthropologie des institutions," *L'Homme*, no. 135 (1995): 65–85.

49. Andrea Mennicken and Peter Miller, "Accounting, Territorialization and Power," *Foucault Studies*, no. 13 (2012): 4–24.

50. Marieke De Goede, *Virtue, Fortune and Faith: A Genealogy of Finance* (Minneapolis: University of Minnesota Press, 2005).

51. Langley, *Liquidity Lost*.

52. Michel Foucault, *History of Madness*, trans. Jonathan Murphy and Jean Khalfa (New York: Routledge, 2006 [1972]).

53. Nina Bandelj, Fred Wherry, and Viviana Zelizer, "Advancing Money Talks," in *Money Talks: Explaining How Money Really Works*, ed. Nina Bandelj, Fred Wherry, and Viviana Zelizer (Princeton, NJ: Princeton University Press, 2017), 1–22; Jane Guyer, *Legacies, Logics, Logistics: Essays in the Anthropology of the Platform Economy* (Chicago: University of Chicago Press, 2016); Keith Hart and Horacio Ortiz, "The Anthropology of Money and Finance: Between Ethnography and World History," *Annual Review of Anthropology* 43 (2014): 465–82; Bill Maurer, "The Anthropology of Money," *Annual Review of Anthropology* 35 (2006): 15–36; Simone Polillo, "Money, Moral Authority and the Politics of Creditworthiness," *American Sociological Review* 76, no. 3 (2011): 437–64; Vivana Zelizer, *Economic Lives: How Culture Shapes the Economy* (Princeton, NJ: Princeton University Press, 2009).

54. Viviana Zelizer, *The Purchase of Intimacy* (Princeton, NJ: Princeton University Press, 2005).

55. Keith Hart, "Heads or Tails? The Two Sides of the Coin," *Man*, n.s., 21, no. 4 (1986): 637–56; Hertz, *The Trading Crowd*; Federico Neiburg, "Inflation: Economists and Economic Cultures in Brazil and Argentina," *Comparative Studies of Society and History* 48, no. 3 (2006): 604–33.

56. Marion Fourcade, "Cents and Sensibility: Economic Valuation and the Nature of 'Nature,'" *American Journal of Sociology* 116, no. 6 (2011): 1721–77.

57. Julie Chu, *Cosmologies of Credit: Transnational Mobility and the Politics of Destination in China* (Durham, NC: Duke University Press, 2010).

58. David Stark, "What's Valuable," in *The Worth of Goods: Valuation and Pricing in the Economy*, ed. Patrick Aspers and Jens Beckert (Oxford: Oxford University Press, 2011), 319–38.

59. Caitlin Zaloom, "The Evangelical Financial Ethic: Double Forms and the Search for God in the Economic World," *American Ethnologist* 43, no. 2 (2016): 325–38.

60. Jane Guyer, *Marginal Gains: Monetary Transactions in Atlantic Africa* (Chicago: University of Chicago Press, 2004), and *Legacies, Logics, Logistics*.

61. See also Bill Maurer, *How Would You Like to Pay? How Technology Is Changing the Future of Money* (Durham, NC: Duke University Press, 2015).

62. Guyer, *Legacies, Logics, Logistics*; see also Marcel Mauss, *The Gift*, trans. W. D. Halls (London: Routledge, 2002 [1923–1924]); Marshall Sahlins, "On the Culture of Material Value and the Cosmography of Riches," *HAU: Journal of Ethnographic Theory* 3, no. 2 (2013): 161–95.

63. Gustav Peebles, "The Anthropology of Credit and Debt," *Annual Review of Anthropology* 39 (2010): 225–40.

64. Guyer, *Marginal Gains*; Jonathan Parry and Maurice Bloch, "Introduction: Money and the Morality of Exchange," in *Money and the Morality of Exchange*, ed. Jonathan Parry and Maurice Bloch (Cambridge: Cambridge University Press, 1989), 1–32;, Michel-Rolph Trouillot, *Global Transformations: Anthropology and the Modern World* (New York: Palgrave Macmillan, 2003).

65. Karl Marx, *Capital: A Critique of Political Economy*, vol. 1, trans. Ben Fowkes (London: Penguin and New Left Review, 1992); see also Michel Foucault, *Les mots et les choses* (Paris: Gallimard, 1966).

66. Pierre Klossowski, *La monnaie vivante* (Paris: Payot & Rivages, 1997 [1970]); Herbert Marcuse, *Eros and Civilization: A Philosophical Enquiry Into Freud* (Boston: Beacon Press, 1955).

67. Georg Simmel, *The Philosophy of Money* (New York: Routledge, 1978 [1900]).

68. Mauss, *The Gift*, 70.

69. Nigel Dodd, *The Social Life of Money* (Princeton, NJ: Princeton University Press, 2014); Keith Hart, *The Memory Bank: Money in an Unequal*

World (London: Profile, 2000); Keith Hart, "Introduction," in *Economy for and Against Democracy*, ed. Keith Hart (New York: Berghahn Press, 2015), 1–15.

70. Benedict Anderson, *Imagined Communities: Reflections on the Origin and Spread of Nationalism* (London: Verso, 2006 [1983]); Eric Helleiner, *The Making of National Money: Territorial Currencies in Historical Perspective* (Ithaca, NY: Cornell University Press, 2003).

71. Laura Bear et al., "Gens: A Feminist Manifesto for the Study of Capitalism," *Theorizing the Contemporary, Fieldsights*, March 30, 2015, https://culanth.org/fieldsights/gens-a-feminist-manifesto-for-the -study-of-capitalism.

72. Guyer, *Marginal Gains*, and *Legacies, Logics, Logistics*. This also echoes Stark's analysis of how multiple definitions of "worth" can connect or disconnect; see David Stark, "For What It's Worth," in *Research in the Sociology of Organizations*, vol. 52, ed. Charlotte Cloutier, Jean-Pascal Gond, and Bernard Leca (Bingley, UK: Emerald, 2017), 383–97.

73. Kimberly Chong, *Best Practice: Management Consulting and the Ethics of Financialization in China* (Durham, NC: Duke University Press, 2018); John Dewey, *Theory of Valuation* (Chicago: University of Chicago Press, 1939); Martin Kornberger et al., "Introduction: Making Things Valuable," in *Making Things Valuable*, ed. Martin Kornberger et al. (Oxford: Oxford University Press, 2015), 1–22; Fabian Muniesa, "A Flank Movement in the Understanding of Valuation," *Sociological Review* 59, no. 2 (2011): 24–38; Horacio Ortiz, "Financial Value: Economic, Moral, Political, Global," *HAU: Journal of Ethnographic Theory* 3, no. 1 (2013): 64–79. I would consider that the same could be said of the word "valuation."

74. For a critical review of this opposition, see Neiburg and Guyer, "The Real in the Real Economy."

75. Max Weber, "Politics as a Vocation," in *From Max Weber, Essays in Sociology*, ed. and trans. Hans Gerth and C. Wright Mills (Oxford: Oxford University Press, 1958 [1917]), 77–128.

76. Louis Dumont, *Homo Hierarchicus: The Caste System and Its implications*, trans. Mark Sainsbury, Louis Dumont, and Basia Gulati (Oxford: Oxford University Press, 1990 [1970]); Joel Robbins, "Monism, Pluralism, and the Structure of Value Relations: A Dumontian Contribution to the Contemporary Study of Value," *HAU: Journal of Ethnographic Theory* 3, no. 1 (2013): 99–115.

77. Michael Lambek, "The Value of (Performative) Acts," *HAU: Journal of Ethnographic Theory* 3, no. 1 (2013): 141–60.

78. See, for instance, James Scott, *The Moral Economy of the Peasants: Rebellion and Subsistence in South-East Asia* (New Haven, CT: Yale University Press, 1976).

79. Anna Tsing, "Sorting Out Commodities: How Capitalist Value Is Made Through Gifts," *HAU: Journal of Ethnographic Theory* 3, no. 1 (2013): 21–43.

80. David Graeber, "It Is Value That Brings Universes Into Being," *HAU: Journal of Ethnographic Theory* 3, no. 2 (2013): 219–43; Daniel Miller, "The uses of value," *Geoforum* 39 (2008):1122–32; David Pedersen, "Introduction: Towards a Value Theory of Anthropology," *Anthropological Theory* 8, no. 1 (2008): 5–8.

81. Weber, "Politics as a Vocation."

82. Michel De Certeau, *L'invention du quotidien 1: Arts de faire* (Paris: Gallimard, 1990 [1980]); William James, "Pragmatism and Common Sense," in *The Writings of William James*, ed. John McDermott (Chicago: University of Chicago Press, 1977 [1907]), 418–28, and "Pragmatism's Conception of Truth," in McDermott, *The Writings of William James*, 429–43; Horacio Ortiz, "Wittgenstein's Critique of Representation and the Ethical Reflexivity of Anthropological Discourse," in *Reflecting on Reflexivity: The Human Condition as an Ontological Surprise*, ed. Terry Evens, Don Handelman, and Christopher Roberts (New York: Berghahn Press, 2016), 124–41.

83. Horacio Ortiz, "Hedge Funds and the Limit of Market Efficiency as a Regulatory Concept," in *Financial Cultures and Crisis Dynamics*, ed. Bob Jessop, Brigitte Young, and Christoph Scherrer (New York: Routledge, 2015), 191–207.

84. Ortiz, "Financial Value," and "The Limits of Financial Imagination: Free Investors, Efficient Markets and Crisis," *American Anthropologist* 116, no. 1 (2014): 38–50.

85. Horacio Ortiz and Fabian Muniesa, "Business Schools, the Anxiety of Finance and the Order of the 'Middle Tier,'" *Journal of Cultural Economy* 11, no. 1 (2018): 1–19.

86. Horacio Ortiz, "A Political Anthropology of Finance: Profits, States and Cultures in Cross-Border Investment in Shanghai," *HAU: Journal of Ethnographic Theory* 7, no. 3 (2017): 325–45.

87. There is a bias here, that is in great part due to the sites of my observations. States would probably need to be more prominent in the analysis if I were describing valuation and investment in bonds.

88. Judith Butler, *Gender Trouble: Feminism and the Subversion of Identity* (New York: Routledge, 1990).

1. THE ORGANIZATIONAL SPACE
OF FINANCIAL VALUE

1. Diane-Laure Arjaliès et al., *Chains of Finance: How Investment Management Is Shaped* (Oxford: Oxford University Press, 2017).

2. Colin Hoag, "Assembling Partial Perspectives: Thoughts on the Anthropology of Bureaucracy," *PoLAR: Political and Legal Anthropological Review* 34, no. 1 (2011): 81–94; Max Weber, *Economy and Society: An Outline of Interpretive Sociology*, ed. Guenther Roth and Claus Wittich, trans. Ephraim Fischoff et al. (Berkeley: University of California Press, 1978).

3. Viviana Zelizer, *The Purchase of Intimacy* (Princeton, NJ: Princeton University Press, 2005).

4. Karen Ho, *Liquidated: An Ethnography of Wall Street* (Durham, NC: Duke University Press, 2009); Stefan Leins, *Stories of Capitalism: Inside the Role of Financial Analysts* (Chicago: University of Chicago Press, 2018); Caitlin Zaloom, *Out of the Pits: Traders and Technology from Chicago to London* (Chicago: University of Chicago Press, 2006).

5. Kimberly Chong, *Best Practice: Management Consulting and the Ethics of Financialization in China* (Durham, NC: Duke University Press, 2018); Leins, *Stories of Capitalism*; Hirokazu Miyazaki, "Economy of Dreams: Hope in Global Capitalism and Its Critiques," *Cultural Anthropology* 21, no. 2 (2006): 147–72; Zaloom, *Out of the Pits*.

6. Zaloom, *Out of the Pits*.

7. Olivier Godechot, *Les Traders: Essai de sociologie des marchés financiers* (Paris: La Découverte, 2001).

8. Ho, *Liquidated*.

9. Galit Ailon, "Bracketing the Nation: Lay Financial Trading in Israel," *Current Anthropology* 60, no. 2 (2019): 245–61; Aaron Pitluck, "Watching Foreigners: How Counterparties Enable Herds, Crowds, and Generate Liquidity in Financial Markets," *Socio-economic Review* 12, no. 1 (2014): 5–31.

10. Melissa Fisher, *Wall Street Women* (Durham, NC: Duke University Press, 2012); Ho, *Liquidated*; Louise Roth, *Selling Women Short: Gender and Inequality on Wall Street* (Princeton, NJ: Princeton University Press, 2006); Leslie Salzinger, "Re-making Men: Masculinity as a Terrain of the Neoliberal Economy," *Critical Historical Studies* 3, no. 1 (2016): 1–25; Daniel Souleles, *Songs of Profit, Songs of Loss. Private Equity, Wealth and Inequality* (Lincoln: University of Nebraska Press, 2019); and Zaloom, *Out of the Pits*.

11. Mitchel Abolafia, *Making Markets: Opportunism and Restraint on Wall Street* (Cambridge, MA: Harvard University Press, 1996); Arjaliès et al., *Chains of Finance*; Godechot, *Les Traders*; Olivier Godechot, *Wages, Bonuses and Appropriation of Profit in the Financial Industry: The Working Rich* (New York: Routledge, 2016); Horacio Ortiz, "The Limits of Financial Imagination: Free Investors, Efficient Markets and Crisis," *American Anthropologist* 116, no. 1 (2014): 38–50; Zaloom, *Out of the Pits*.

12. Peter Miller and Nikolas Rose, "Political Power Beyond the State: Problematics of Government," *British Journal of Sociology* 43, no. 2 (1992): 173–205.

13. Marieke De Goede, *Virtue, Fortune and Faith: A Genealogy of Finance* (Minneapolis: University of Minnesota Press, 2005); Donald MacKenzie, *An Engine, Not a Camera: How Financial Models Shape Markets* (Cambridge, MA: MIT Press, 2006).

14. Miller and Rose, "Political Power Beyond the State."

15. Peter Miller and Ted O'Leary, "Mediating Instruments and Making Markets: Capital Budgeting, Science and the Economy," *Accounting, Organizations and Society* 32, no. 7–8 (2007): 701–34.

16. Andrea Mennicken and Peter Miller, "Accounting, Territorialization and Power," *Foucault Studies*, no. 13 (2012): 4–24.

17. Sabine Montagne and Horacio Ortiz, "Sociologie de l'agence financière: enjeux et perspectives," *Sociétés Contemporaines* 92, no. 4 (2013): 7–33.

18. Jézabel Couppey-Soubeyran, Dominique Plihon, and Dhafer Saïdane, *Les banques, acteurs de la globalisation financière* (Paris: La Documentation Française, 2006); Olivier Godechot and Paul Lagneau-Ymonet, "D'un rapport salarial favorable à un autre: Les professionnels de la bourse 1970–2000," in *Le salariat bancaire: Enjeux sociaux et pratiques de*

gestion, ed. Patrice Baubeau, Chantal Cossalter, and Catherine Omnès (Nanterre: Presses de l'université Paris Ouest, 2009), 193–220.

19. Neil Fligstein, *The Transformation of Corporate Control* (Cambridge, MA: Harvard University Press, 1990); William Lazonik and Mary O'Sullivan, "Maximizing Shareholder Value: A New Ideology for Corporate Governance," *Economy and Society* 29, no. 1 (2000): 13–35; Frédéric Lordon, "La 'création de valeur' comme rhétorique et comme pratique: Généalogie et sociologie de la 'valeur actionnariale,'" *L'Année de la régulation* 4 (2000): 117–65; Dominique Plihon and Jean-Pierre Ponssard, eds., *La montée en puissance des fonds d'investissement* (Paris: La Documentation Française, 2002).

20. Arjaliès et al., *Chains of Finance*.

21. Ismail Erturk et al., "Against Agency: A Positional Critique," *Economy and Society* 36, no. 1 (2007): 51–77; Sabine Montagne, "Investing Prudently: How Financialization Puts a Legal Standard to Use," *Sociologie du travail* 55, no. 1 (2013): 48–66.

22. Gordon L. Clark, *Pension Fund Capitalism* (Oxford: Oxford University Press, 2000); Sabine Montagne, *Les Fonds de Pension: Entre protection sociale et spéculation financière* (Paris: Odile Jacob, 2006).

23. As I said in the introduction, capitalization is defined as the quoted price of a share of stock multiplied by the number of existing shares. It is one of the measures of the size of a company. However, the price would probably vary widely if all the stocks were exchanged at the same time.

24. This tension is often problematized as a "conflict of interest"; cf., for example, Richard Swedberg, "Conflicts of Interests in the US Brokerage Industry," in *The Sociology of Financial Markets*, ed. Karin Knorr Cetina and Alex Preda (Oxford: Oxford University Press, 2005), 187–203. As we see in the following pages, this idea of conflict implies a definition of the actors and their interests that is too univocal and clear-cut; see Arjaliès et al., *Chains of Finance*; Erturk et al., "Against Agency."

25. As I describe later in the book, a smaller team that accounted for less than 10 percent of the company's revenues sold information about companies listed in the United States to customers based in Europe.

26. As we will see, the work of traders could be very different elsewhere.

27. See also Arjaliès et al., *Chains of Finance*.

28. A basis point, or bp, corresponds to 0.01 percent.

29. Like all social identities, these identities were relational and changed depending on the situation; see Judith Butler, *Gender Trouble: Feminism and the Subversion of Identity* (New York: Routledge, 1990); Sarah Mazouz, "Faire des differences. Ce que l'ethnographie nous apprend sur l'articulation des modes pluriels d'assignation," *Raisons Politiques* 58, n. 2 (2015): 75–89; and Marilyn Strathern, "Naturalism and the Invention of Identity," *Social Analysis* 61, no. 2 (2017): 15–30. In this book, I study these forms of discrimination not systematically but only in relation to the practices of valuation and investment. For more systematic approaches, see Fisher, *Wall Street Women*; Ho, *Liquidated*; Roth, *Selling Women Short*; Salzinger, "Re-making Men"; Souleles, *Songs of Profit, Songs of Loss*; and Zaloom, *Out of the Pits*;

30. Income could be much higher for hedge fund managers, with higher bonuses calculated partly in relation to the profits obtained by the investment. But hedge funds constitute a small segment of the financial industry that is generally identified as a privileged exception; see Horacio Ortiz, "Hedge Funds and the Limit of Market Efficiency as a Regulatory Concept," in *Financial Cultures and Crisis Dynamics*, ed. Bob Jessop, Brigitte Young, and Christoph Scherrer (New York: Routledge, 2015), 191–207.

31. Kean Birch and Fabian Muniesa, "Introduction: Assetization and Technoscientific Capitalism," in *Assetization: Turnings Things Into Assets in Technoscientific Capitalism*, ed. Kean Birch and Fabian Muniesa (Cambridge, MA: MIT Press, 2020), 1–41.

32. Hendrik Vollmer, "How to Do More with Numbers: Elementary Stakes, Framing, Keying, and the Three-Dimensional Character of Numerical Signs," *Accounting, Organizations and Society* 32, no. 6 (2007): 577–600.

33. Jens Beckert and Richard Bronk, "An Introduction to *Uncertain Futures*," in *Uncertain Futures: Imaginaries, Narratives and Calculation in the Economy*, ed. Jens Beckert and Richard Bronk (Oxford: Oxford University Press, 2018), 1–36.

34. Jane Guyer et al., "Introduction: Number as Inventive Frontier," *Anthropological Theory* 10, no. 1–2 (2010): 36–61.

35. Jane Guyer, *Legacies, Logics, Logistics: Essays in the Anthropology of the Platform Economy* (Chicago: University of Chicago Press, 2016).

36. Bill Maurer, "Repressed Futures: Financial Derivatives' Theological Unconscious," *Economy and Society* 31, no. 1 (2002): 15–36.

37. Jane Guyer, "The Eruption of Tradition: On Ordinality and Calculation," *Anthropological Theory* 10, no. 1–2 (2010): 121–31.

38. Keith Hart, "Models of Statistical Distribution: A Window on Social
   History," *Anthropological Theory* 10, no. 1–2 (2010): 67–74.

39. See also Marion Fourcade, "Ordinalization," *Sociological Theory* 34, no. 3
   (2016): 175–95.

40. Liliana Doganova, "Discounting the Future: A Political Technology,"
   Economic Sociology_The European Electronic Newsletter 19, no. 2 (2018):
   4–9.

41. https://www.cfainstitute.org. I will use the following manuals, which
   are divided for the three levels of certification awarded by the association: *Schweser Notes: CFA Level 1* (La Crosse, WI: Kaplan Schweser,
   2007); *Schweser Notes: CFA Level 2* (La Crosse, WI: Kaplan Schweser,
   2007); and *Schweser Notes: CFA Level 3* (La Crosse, WI: Kaplan Schweser, 2009), hereafter cited as *CFA Level 1*, *CFA Level 2*, and *CFA Level 3*,
   respectively.

42. https://www.aciia.org. I will use the following manual: *Course Manual*
   (Geneva: International Learning Platform for Investment Professionals, 2009), hereafter cited as *CIIA*.

43. See, for instance, *CFA Level 1*, bk. 4, pp. 179 and 187. Cf. *CIIA*, "Portfolio
   Management," ch. 1, p. 42.

44. See, for instance, *CFA Level 3*, "Levels 1 and 2 Refresher: Contents," pp.
   36 and following; and *CIIA*, "Equity," ch. 4, pp. 17 and following.

45. I explore these issues with more detail in Horacio Ortiz, "Political
   Imaginaries of the Weighted Average Cost of Capital. A Conceptual
   Analysis," *Valuation Studies* in press (2021); see also Anthony Hopwood,
   "On Trying to Study Accounting in the Contexts in Which It Oper-
   ates," *Accounting, Organizations and Society* 8, no. 2–3 (1983): 287–305;
   Paolo Quattrone, "Books to Be Practiced: Memory, the Power of the
   Visual, and the Success of Accounting," *Accounting, Organizations and
   Society* 34, no. 4 (2009): 85–118, and "Governing Social Orders, Unfolding
   Rationality, and Jesuit Accounting Practices: A Procedural Approach to
   Institutional Logics," *Administrative Science Quarterly* 60, no. 3 (2015):
   411–45; John Roberts et al., "In the Mirror of the Market: The Dis-
   ciplinary Effects of Company/Fund Manager Meetings," *Accounting,
   Organizations and Society* 31, no. 3 (2006): 277–94; Sadao Takatera and
   Norio Sawabe, "Time and Space in Income Accounting," *Accounting,*

Organizations and Society 25, no. 8 (2000): 787–98; James Williams, "Regulatory Technologies, Risky Subjects, and Financial Boundaries: Governing 'Fraud' in the Financial Markets," *Accounting, Organizations and Society* 38, no. 6–7 (2013): 544–58.

46. *CFA Level 2*, bk. 4, pp. 169 and following; *CIIA*, "Equity," ch. 4, pp. 7–13.

47. *CFA Level 2*, bk. 4, p. 169.

48. Thus, $100 invested today at 10 percent a year is calculated to be worth $110 in a year. And $110 received one year from now and discounted at a rate of 10 percent is considered to be worth $100 today. Thus, for a discount rate of 10 percent, $100 is referred to as the "present value" of $110 received in one year.

49. *CFA Level 1*, bk. 4, p. 35; *CIIA*, "Equity," ch. 4, p. 15.

50. *CIIA*, "Equity," ch. 4, p. 10; *CFA Level 2*, bk. 4, p. 172.

51. *CFA Level 1*, bk. 4, p. 178; *CIIA*, "Equity Questions II," p. 4.

52. *CFA Level 1*, bk. 4, p. 279; *CIIA*, "Equity Solutions II," p. 8.

53. *CIIA*, "Equity," ch. 4, p. 35.

54. De Goede, *Virtue, Fortune and Faith*.; Marion Fourcade and Rakesh Khurana, "From Social Control to Financial Economics: The Linked Ecologies of Economics and Business in Twentieth Century America," *Theory and Society* 42, no. 2 (2013): 121–59, and "The Social Trajectory of a Finance Professor and the Common Sense of Capital," *History of Political Economy* 49, no. 2 (2017): 347–81; Johan Heilbron, Jochem Verheul, and Sander Quak, "The Origins and Early Diffusion of 'Shareholder Value' in the United States," *Theory and Society* 43, no. 1 (2014): 1–22; Maurer, "Repressed Futures"; MacKenzie, *An Engine, Not a Camera*; Simone Polillo, "Market Efficiency as a Revolution in Data Analysis," *Economic Anthropology* 5, no. 2 (2018): 198–209; Alex Preda, *Framing Finance: The Boundaries of Markets and Modern Capitalism* (Chicago: University of Chicago Press, 2009); Richard Whitley, "The Transformation of Business Finance Into Financial Economics: The Roles of Academic Expansion and Changes in U.S. Capital Markets," *Accounting, Organizations and Society* 11, no. 2 (1986): 171–92.

55. Fabian Muniesa, "Market Technologies and the Pragmatics of Prices," *Economy and Society* 36, no. 3 (2007): 377–95.

56. *CIIA*, "Portfolio Management," ch. 1, p. 46; *CFA Level 1*, bk. 4, pp. 130 and following.

57. See, for instance, *CIIA*, "Portfolio Management," ch. 1, p. 42.

58. *CFA Level 1*, bk. 4, p. 133.

59. *CIIA*, "Portfolio Management," ch. 1, p. 67.

60. Miller and O'Leary, "Mediating Instruments and Making Markets"; Caroline Lambert and Eric Pezet, "The Making of the Management Accountant—Becoming the Producer of Truthful Knowledge," *Accounting, Organizations and Society* 35, no. 1 (2010): 10–30; Michael Power, "Accounting and Finance," in *The Oxford Handbook of the Sociology of Finance*, ed. Karin Knorr Cetina and Alex Preda (Oxford: Oxford University Press, 2012), 291–314; Keith Robson, "Accounting as 'Inscription': Action at a Distance and the Development of Accounting," *Accounting, Organizations and Society* 17, no. 7 (1992): 685–708; Roberts et al., "In the Mirror of the Market."

61. Earnings before interest, tax, depreciation, and amortization.

62. Earnings before interest and tax.

63. See, for instance, *CFA Level 2*, bk. 3, pp. 208–210; *CIIA*, "Accounting," ch. 10, pp. 1–12.

64. See, for instance, *CFA Level 2*, bk. 4; and *CIIA*, "Equity," ch. 4, pp. 32–38.

65. *CFA Level 2*, bk. 4, p. 125; *CIIA*, "Equity," ch. 4, p. 37.

66. Ortiz, "Hedge Funds and the Limit of Market Efficiency."

67. De Goede, *Virtue, Fortune and Faith*; Paul Langley, *Liquidity Lost: The Governance of the Financial Crisis* (Oxford: Oxford University Press, 2015); Pierre-Charles Pradier, *La notion de risque en économie* (Paris: La Découverte, 2006).

68. See, for instance, Beckert and Bronk, "An Introduction to *Uncertain Futures*."

69. *CIIA*, "Fixed Income," ch. 2, p. 18; *CFA*, bk. 5, p. 85.

70. The London interbank offered rate. This is the official interest rate at which the biggest banks lend to each other. It closely follows the interest rates offered by central banks and paid by rich states on their sovereign bonds.

71. *CIIA*, "Fixed Income," ch. 2, p. 35, states: "The yield spread between a given security and the corresponding Government security has the nature of risk premium because it reflects the risks (lower liquidity, higher credit risk . . .) that an investor has to face when he invests in non-Government securities." See also *CFA*, bk. 5, p. 85.

72. Nina Boy, "Sovereign Safety," *Security Dialogue* 46, no. 6 (2015): 530–47; Horacio Ortiz, "Marchés efficients, investisseurs libres et Etats garants:

trames du politique dans les pratiques financières professionnelles."
Politix 95, no.3 (2011): 155–80.

73. For the following explanations of the use of the capital asset pricing model for relative valuation, cf. *CFA Level 1*, bk. 4, p. 135, and *CIIA*, "Portfolio Management," ch. 1, p. 74.

74. Henri Markovitz and William Sharpe received the Sveriges Riksbank Prize in Economic Sciences in Memory of Alfred Nobel in 1990 for developing, respectively, modern portfolio theory and the capital asset pricing model. Eugene Fama, credited with establishing the notion of a "random walk" of asset prices, received the Nobel Prize in 2013.

75. John Keynes, *The General Theory of Employment, Interest and Money* (London: Macmillan, 1936; New York: Prometheus, 1997), 156.

76. *CFA Level 3*, "Level 1 and 2 Refresher: Contents," p. 12; see also *CIIA*, "Portfolio Management," ch. 1, pp. 31–35.

77. *CFA Level 3*, "Level 1 and 2 Refresher: Contents," p. 12; see also *CIIA*, "Portfolio Management," ch. 1, pp. 31–35 and 42.

78. See, for instance, *CFA Level 3*, "Level 1 and 2 Refresher: Contents," pp. 25–26.

79. *CFA Level 2*, bk. 4, p. 182; *CIIA*, "Corporate," ch. 1, p. 47.

80. *CIIA*, "Equity," ch. 4, p. 15. See Horacio Ortiz, "Political Imaginaries of the Weighted Average Cost of Capital."

81. *CIIA*, "Corporate," ch. 1, p. 1.

82. Mahmoud Ezzamel, Hugh Wilmott, and Frank Worthington, "Manufacturing Shareholder Value: The Role of Accounting in Organizational Transformation," *Accounting, Organizations and Society* 33, no. 2–3 (2008): 107–40; Fligstein, *The Transformation of Corporate Control*; Ho, *Liquidated*; Lazonik and O'Sullivan, "Maximizing Shareholder Value"; Lordon, "La 'création de valeur' comme rhétorique et comme pratique"; Plihon and Ponssard, *La montée en puissance des fonds d'investissement*; Roberts et al., "In the Mirror of the Market."

83. Chong, *Best Practice*; Ellen Hertz, *The Trading Crowd: An Ethnography of the Shanghai Stock Market* (Cambridge: Cambridge University Press, 1998); Johannes Petry, "Financialization with Chinese Characteristics? Exchanges, Control and Capital Markets in Authoritarian Capitalism," *Economy and Society* 49, no. 2 (2020): 213–38; Yingyao Wang, "The Rise of the 'Shareholding State': Financialization of Economic Management in China," *Socio-economic Review* 13, no. 3 (2015): 603–25.

84. This is due to the idea of reinvestment, or *capitalization*, of returns: after investing $100 now at 10 percent and obtaining $10 of interest in one year, the investor is supposed to reinvest the whole amount, $110, for one more year at the same rate of 10 percent. Thus, in two years, the investor has $110 + $11 = $121. The cash flow to be received in one year is discounted at a rate of $(1 + 0.10)$, that to be received in two years at $(1 + 0.10)^2$, and that to be received in year t at $(1 + 0.10)^t$. The further the valuation looks into the future, the higher the denominator and the lower the present value of the same amount of money.

85. Liliana Doganova, "Discounting and the Making of the Future: On Uncertainty in Forest Management and Drug Development," in *Uncertain Futures: Imaginaries, Narratives and Calculation in the Economy*, ed. Jens Beckert and Richard Bronk (Oxford: Oxford University Press, 2018), 278–97, and "Discounting the Future." See also Fabian Muniesa, Liliana Doganova, Horacio Ortiz, et al., *Capitalization. A Cultural Guide* (Paris: Presses des Mines, 2017).

86. Marion Fourcade, "State Metrology: The Rating of Sovereigns and the Judgment of Nations," in *The Many Hands of the State: Theorizing Political Authority and Social Control*, ed. Kimberly Morgan and Ann Orloff (Cambridge: Cambridge University Press, 2017), 103–27; Benjamin Lemoine, *L'ordre de la dette: Enquête sur les infortunes de l'état et la prospérité du marché* (Paris: La Découverte, 2016); Donald MacKenzie, "The Credit Crisis as a Problem in the Sociology of Knowledge," *American Journal of Sociology* 116, no. 6 (2011): 1778–841; Timothy Sinclair, *The New Masters of Capital: American Bond Rating Agencies and the Politics of Creditworthiness* (Ithaca, NY: Cornell University Press, 2005).

87. Joseph Stiglitz, *Making Globalization Work* (London: Penguin, 2006); Daniela Gabor, "The Wall Street Consensus," *Development and Change*, first published online (2021): doi: 10.1111/dech.12645.

88. *CIIA*, "Corporate," chap. 1, p. 2.

89. *CIIA*, "Corporate," chap. 1, p. 3.

2. VALUATION AS A PERSONAL OPINION

1. Marieke De Goede, *Virtue, Fortune and Faith: A Genealogy of Finance* (Minneapolis: University of Minnesota Press, 2005); Alex Preda, "The Investor as a Cultural Figure of Global Capitalism," in *The Sociology of*

Financial Markets, ed. Karin Knorr Cetina and Alex Preda (Oxford: Oxford University Press, 2005), 141–62, and *Framing Finance: The Boundaries of Markets and Modern Capitalism* (Chicago: University of Chicago Press, 2009); Viviana Zelizer, *Morals and Markets: The Development of Life Insurance in the United States* (New York: Columbia University Press, 1979).

2. Sabine Montagne, "Pouvoir financier vs. pouvoir salarial: Les fonds de pension américains; contribution du droit à la légitimité financière," *Annales: Histoire, sciences sociales* 60, no. 6 (2005): 1299–325; Noelle Stout. *Dispossessed: How Predatory Bureaucracy Foreclosed on the American Middle Class* (Oakland: University of California Press, 2019).

3. Gordon L. Clark, *Pension Fund Capitalism* (Oxford: Oxford University Press, 2000); Sabine Montagne, *Les Fonds de Pension: Entre protection sociale et spéculation financière* (Paris: Odile Jacob, 2006), and "Investing Prudently: How Financialization Puts a Legal Standard to Use," *Sociologie du travail* 55, no. 1 (2013): 48–66.

4. Clark, *Pension Fund Capitalism*; Ismail Erturk et al., "Against Agency: A Positional Critique," *Economy and Society* 36, no. 1 (2007): 51–77; Montagne, *Les Fonds de Pension*.

5. Donald MacKenzie, *An Engine, Not a Camera: How Financial Models Shape Markets* (Cambridge, MA: MIT Press, 2006); Richard Whitley, "The Transformation of Business Finance Into Financial Economics: The Roles of Academic Expansion and Changes in U.S. Capital Markets," *Accounting, Organizations and Society* 11, no. 2 (1986): 171–92.

6. Peter Miller and Nikolas Rose, "Political Power Beyond the State: Problematics of Government," *British Journal of Sociology* 43, no. 2 (1992): 173–205.

7. Horacio Ortiz, "Investir: une décision disséminée; Enquête de terrain sur les dérivés de credit," *Sociétés Contemporaines*, no. 92 (2013): 35–57.

8. Caitlin Zaloom, *Out of the Pits: Traders and Technology from Chicago to London* (Chicago: University of Chicago Press, 2006).

9. Catherine Aaron et al., "Les styles de gestion de portefeuille existent-ils?," *Revue d'Economie Financière* 81, no. 4 (2005): 171–88; Kimberly Chong and David Tuckett, "Constructing Conviction Through Action and Narrative: How Money Managers Manage Uncertainty and the Consequence for Financial Market Functioning," *Socio-economic Review* 13, no. 2 (2015): 309–30; Stefan Leins, *Stories of Capitalism: Inside the Role of Financial Analysts* (Chicago: University of Chicago Press, 2018).

10. The term *grandes écoles* is used to designate elite academic institutions in France.
11. This expression is used to say that at the current price the company is undervalued.
12. That is, the listed price is $5.
13. This is an average of several yearly price-to-earnings ratios. For a description of this ratio, see chapter 1.
14. The term *margins* refers to the listed company's earnings, earnings before interest and tax, and other such accounting data that need to be forecasted in order to do the DCF.
15. See Leslie Salzinger, "Re-making Men: Masculinity as a Terrain of the Neoliberal Economy," *Critical Historical Studies* 3, no. 1 (2016): 1–25; Zaloom, *Out of the Pits*.
16. *Central* refers to one of the top engineering schools in France.
17. A business school that does not belong to the top tier.
18. Robert C. Merton and Myron Scholes earned the Sveriges Riksbank Prize in Economic Sciences in Memory of Alfred Nobel in 1997 for this theory.
19. That is, the analysis provided by financial analysts.
20. Olivier Godechot, *Wages, Bonuses and Appropriation of Profit in the Financial Industry: The Working Rich* (New York: Routledge, 2016).
21. Hirokazu Miyazaki, "Economy of Dreams: Hope in Global Capitalism and Its Critiques," *Cultural Anthropology* 21, no. 2 (2006): 147–72; Hirokazu Miyazaki and Annelise Riles, "Failure as Endpoint," in *Global Assemblages: Technology, Politics, and Ethics as Anthropological Problems*, ed. Stephen Collier and Aihwa Ong (Oxford: Blackwell, 2005), 320–31.
22. Olivier Godechot, "What Do Heads of Dealing Rooms Do? The Social Capital of Internal Entrepreneurs," *Sociological Review* 56, no. 1 (2008): 145–61; Godechot, *Wages, Bonuses and Appropriation of Profit in the Financial Industry*.
23. That is, a potential client with whom the relation is not stable yet.
24. Karen Ho, *Liquidated: An Ethnography of Wall Street* (Durham, NC: Duke University Press, 2009).
25. Olivier Godechot, *Les Traders: Essai de sociologie des marchés financiers* (Paris: Editions La Découverte, 2001), and *Wages, Bonuses and Appropriation of Profit in the Financial Industry*.
26. Zaloom, *Out of the Pits*; see also Leins, *Stories of Capitalism*.

3. THE TRUTH OF VALUE AS THE RESULT OF EFFICIENT MARKETS

1. Adam Smith, *An Inquiry Into the Nature and Causes of the Wealth of Nations* (New York: Prometheus, 1991 [1776]), 38.

2. Michel Foucault, *Naissance de la Biopolitique: Cours au Collège de France, 1978–1979* (Paris: Gallimard, Seuil, 2004); Donald MacKenzie, *An Engine, Not a Camera: How Financial Models Shape Markets* (Cambridge, MA: MIT Press, 2006); Christian Walter, "Une histoire du concept d'efficience sur les marchés financiers," *Annales: Histoire, sciences sociales* 51, no. 4 (1996): 873–905.

3. For what follows in this paragraph, see Marieke De Goede, *Virtue, Fortune and Faith: A Genealogy of Finance* (Minneapolis: University of Minnesota Press, 2005); Alex Preda, *Framing Finance: The Boundaries of Markets and Modern Capitalism* (Chicago: University of Chicago Press, 2009).

4. Johannes Petry, Jan Fichtner, and Eelke Heemskerk, "Steering Capital: The Growing Private Authority of Index Providers in the Age of Passive Asset Management," *Review of International Political Economy* 28, no. 1 (2019): 152–76, https://doi.org/10.1080/09692290.2019.1699147.

5. Michel Callon, "Introduction: The Embeddedness of Economic Markets in Economics," in *The Laws of the Markets*, ed. Michel Callon (Oxford: Blackwell, 1998), 1–57.

6. Michel Callon, "Performativity, Misfires and Politics," *Journal of Cultural Economy* 3, no. 2 (2010): 166.

7. Melinda Cooper and Martijn Konings, "Pragmatics of Money and Finance: Beyond Performativity and Fundamental Value," *Journal of Cultural Economy* 9, no. 1 (2016): 2.

8. Judith Butler, "Performative Agency," *Journal of Cultural Economy* 3, no. 2 (2010): 147–61; Peter Miller, "Calculating Economic Life," *Journal of Cultural Economy* 1, no. 1:51–64 (2008); Peter Miller and Nikolas Rose, "Political Power Beyond the State: Problematics of Government," *British Journal of Sociology* 43, no. 2 (1992): 173–205; Fabian Muniesa, *The Provoked Economy: Economic Reality and the Performative Turn* (New York: Routledge, 2014).

9. Marion Fourcade, "Theories of Markets and Theories of Society," *American Behavioral Scientist* 50, no. 8 (2007):1015–34.

10. Viviana Zelizer, *The Social Meaning of Money: Pin Money, Paychecks, Poor Relief, and Other Currencies* (Princeton, NJ: Princeton University Press, 1997), and *The Purchase of Intimacy* (Princeton, NJ: Princeton University Press, 2005).

11. Jane Guyer, *Marginal Gains: Monetary Transactions in Atlantic Africa* (Chicago: University of Chicago Press, 2004), and *Legacies, Logics, Logistics: Essays in the Anthropology of the Platform Economy* (Chicago: University of Chicago Press, 2016).

12. Andrea Mennicken and Peter Miller, "Accounting, Territorialization and Power," *Foucault Studies*, no. 13 (2012): 4–24.

13. See also Peter Miller and Nikolas Rose, "Governing Economic Life," *Economy and Society* 19, no. 1 (1990): 1–31.

14. Petry, Fichtner, and Heemskerk, "Steering Capital," 11.

15. Benjamin Lemoine, *L'ordre de la dette: Enquête sur les infortunes de l'état et la prospérité du marché* (Paris: La Découverte, 2016).

16. Laura Bear, *Navigating Austerity: Currents of Debt Along a South Asian River* (Stanford, CA: Stanford University Press, 2015).

17. Janet Roitman, *Fiscal Disobedience: An Anthropology of Economic Regulation in Central Africa* (Princeton, NJ: Princeton University Press, 2004).

18. Ariel Wilkis, *The Moral Power of Money: Morality and Economy in the Life of the Poor* (Stanford CA: Stanford University Press, 2018).

19. Deborah James, *Money from Nothing: Indebtedness and Aspiration in South Africa* (Stanford, CA: Stanford University Press, 2014).

20. Index *futures* are contracts according to which Paul, for example, agrees to sell in three months at a price of €93 million all the shares present in the index, with their current weights in the index. If the price of this bundle of stocks goes from €93 million to €90 million during this period, on the date the contract expires, the person who engaged in the futures contract with Paul will have to buy these shares from him at a price that will therefore be higher than the current listed price at that time. Paul will then be able to buy these shares at the listed price (i.e., €90 million) and to sell them immediately at that higher price, which the counterparty of the futures contract is obliged to accept. In this fictitious example, Paul would make a profit of €3 million. Because prices can vary widely in a short time, the potential gains and losses are very big, and financial regulation worldwide aims at limiting instabilities that are considered too dangerous. In particular, financial regulation

imposes a mechanism whereby this gain or loss is calculated daily, and Paul has to keep a minimum amount of money, referred to as *margin*, in an account at the institution, usually a stock exchange, where he buys these contracts. In order to purchase a futures contract three months before its expiration, Paul must not pay €93 million but a much lower amount. Thus, Paul can at the same time invest most of the €90 million he manages in stocks that are part of the benchmark and use a small proportion of that money to bet on the evolution of the benchmark with futures contracts. Obliged to hold shares in the portfolio, with this method he can, for instance, hope to have a portfolio performance that is better than that of the index, and he can even obtain net profits in the case of a general decrease of stock prices.

21. Petry, Fichtner, and Heemskerk, "Steering Capital."
22. *Schweser Notes: CFA Level 2* (La Crosse, WI: Kaplan Schweser, 2007), bk. 2, p. 261; *Course Manual* (Geneva: International Learning Platform for Investment Professionals, 2009), "Portfolio Management," ch. 1, p. 41.
23. Petry, Fichtner, and Heemskerk, "Steering Capital," 2.
24. Jan Fichtner, Eelke Heemskerk, and Javier Garcia Bernardo, "Hidden Power of the Big Three? Passive Index Funds, Re-concentration of Corporate Ownership, and New Financial Risk," *Business and Politics* 19, no. 2 (2017): 298–326.
25. *Course Manual*, "Portfolio Management," ch. 1, p. 41.
26. Horacio Ortiz, "Hedge Funds and the Limit of Market Efficiency as a Regulatory Concept," in *Financial Cultures and Crisis Dynamics*, ed. Bob Jessop, Brigitte Young, and Christoph Scherrer (New York: Routledge, 2015), 191–207.
27. Short selling a financial asset is a way to bet on its price fall: it involves borrowing the asset, selling it immediately, and buying it back later, at a lower price, in order to return it to the lender. In the process, if the bet is successful, the strategy yields a profit, as the asset was sold at a high price and bought at a low price. An investment strategy called *long/short* is widely used by hedge funds investing in stock. It consists of attempting to detect, sometimes statistically, pairs of companies that, because of their business activities, are negatively correlated, so that, on average, the price of one rises when the price of the other falls.

28. Hirokazu Miyazaki, "Between Arbitrage and Speculation: An Economy of Belief and Doubt," *Economy and Society* 36, no. 3 (2007): 396–415; Ortiz, "Hedge Funds and the Limit of Market Efficiency."

29. David Cooper and Keith Robson, "Accounting, professions and regulation: Locating the sites of professionalization," *Accounting, Organizations and Society* 31 (2006): 415–44.

30. Olivier Godechot, *Les Traders: Essai de sociologie des marchés financiers* (Paris: Editions La Découverte, 2001); Horacio Ortiz and Fabian Muniesa, "Business Schools, the Anxiety of Finance and the Order of the 'Middle Tier,'" *Journal of Cultural Economy* 11, no. 1 (2018): 1–19.

31. Karen Ho, *Liquidated: An Ethnography of Wall Street* (Durham, NC: Duke University Press, 2009).

32. Marion Fourcade and Rakesh Khurana, "From Social Control to Financial Economics: The Linked Ecologies of Economics and Business in Twentieth Century America," *Theory and Society* 42, no. 2 (2013): 121–59; Javier Lezaun and Fabian Muniesa, "Twilight in the Leadership Playground: Subrealism and the Training of the Business Self," *Journal of Cultural Economy* 10, no. 3 (2017): 265–79; Ortiz and Muniesa, "Business Schools."

33. CFA Institute, *2011 Annual Report*, 2011, 24, http://annualreport.cfainstitute .org.s3-website-us-east-1.amazonaws.com/2011/downloads.html.

34. This means that for the same final fee, the trader has to perform many transactions and spend more time than he would if he had to perform just one big transaction.

35. The trader from Pascal's desk quoted earlier.

36. That is, the hunting trip.

37. Petry, Fichtner, and Heemskerk, "Steering Capital."

38. The interview took place in 2003.

39. Petry, Fichtner, and Heemskerk, "Steering Capital"; Timothy Sinclair, *The New Masters of Capital: American Bond Rating Agencies and the Politics of Creditworthiness* (Ithaca, NY: Cornell University Press, 2005).

40. That is, the price of the stocks making up the index increased by 1 to 2 percent since the beginning of the year.

41. That is, the concrete purchase and sale of stocks, which is the activity of traders.

42. That is, the trader can execute a buy order at a price that is lower than the price at the end of the day, which is used to calculate the value of the

index. If that price difference is above 1 percent, the investment for that particular stock has already attained the aims of the investment fund. If traders were successful at doing the same with all the stocks contained in the index, the investment would achieve its objective to beat the index by a margin of +1 percent, without relying at all on the valuation made by fund managers and analysts.

43. That is, the trading team, also called the "trading desk."

44. That is, the fund management team.

45. That is, the fund manager gives the purchase order to his traders, who give it to the traders of the salesperson, so that the fee is received immediately after the investment advice is given.

4. FINANCIAL VALUE AS POLITICAL ASSEMBLAGE

1. Horacio Ortiz, "Hedge Funds and the Limit of Market Efficiency as a Regulatory Concept," in *Financial Cultures and Crisis Dynamics*, ed. Bob Jessop, Brigitte Young, and Christoph Scherrer (New York: Routledge, 2015), 191–207.

2. Richard Barker and Sebastian Schulte, "Representing the Market Perspective: Fair Value Measurement for Non-financial Assets," *Accounting, Organizations and Society* 56 (2017): 55–67; Claire Dambrin and Keith Robson, "Tracing the Performance in the Pharmaceutical Industry: Ambivalence, Opacity and the Performativity of Flawed Measures," *Accounting, Organizations and Society* 36, no. 7 (2011): 428–55; Colin Hoag, "Assembling Partial Perspectives: Thoughts on the Anthropology of Bureaucracy," *PoLAR: Political and Legal Anthropological Review* 34, no. 1 (2011): 81–94.

3. Mitchel Abolafia, *Making Markets: Opportunism and Restraint on Wall Street* (Cambridge, MA: Harvard University Press, 1996); Diane-Laure Arjaliès et al., *Chains of Finance: How Investment Management Is Shaped* (Oxford: Oxford University Press, 2017); Olivier Godechot, *Les Traders: Essai de sociologie des marchés financiers* (Paris: La Découverte, 2001); Olivier Godechot, *Wages, Bonuses, and Appropriation of Profit in the Financial Industry: The Working Rich* (New York: Routledge, 2016); Horacio Ortiz, "The Limits of Financial Imagination: Free Investors, Efficient Markets and Crisis," *American Anthropologist* 116, no. 1 (2014): 38–50; Caitlin Zaloom, *Out of the Pits: Traders and Technology from Chicago to London* (Chicago: University of Chicago Press, 2006).

4. Karen Ho, *Liquidated: An Ethnography of Wall Street* (Durham, NC: Duke University Press, 2009); Stefan Leins, *Stories of Capitalism: Inside the Role of Financial Analysts* (Chicago: University of Chicago Press, 2018); Zaloom, *Out of the Pits.*

5. Kimberly Chong, *Best Practice: Management Consulting and the Ethics of Financialization in China* (Durham, NC: Duke University Press, 2018); Leins, *Stories of Capitalism*; Hirokazu Miyazaki, "Economy of Dreams: Hope in Global Capitalism and Its Critiques," *Cultural Anthropology* 21, no. 2 (2006): 147–72; Zaloom, *Out of the Pits.*

6. Arjaliès et al., *Chains of Finance.*

7. Horacio Ortiz, "Investir: une décision disséminée; Enquête de terrain sur les dérivés de credit," *Sociétés Contemporaines*, no. 92 (2013): 35–57.

8. Bill Maurer, "Credit Crisis Religion," *Religion and Society: Advances in Research* 1 (2010): 146–55; Horacio Ortiz, "Anthropology—of the Financial Crisis," in *Handbook of Economic Anthropology*, ed. James Carrier (Cheltenham, UK: Edward Elgar, 2012), 585–96, "The Limits of Financial Imagination," and "What Financial Crisis? The Global Politics of the Financial Industry: Distributional Consequences and Legitimizing Narratives," in *Economy for and Against Democracy*, ed. Keith Hart and John Sharp (New York: Berghahn Press, 2015), 39–57; Janet Roitman, *Anti-Crisis* (Durham, NC: Duke University Press, 2014).

9. Most companies in the "new technologies" sector were listed on the National Association of Securities Dealers Automated Quotations (Nasdaq).

10. Frédéric Lordon, "La 'création de valeur' comme rhétorique et comme pratique: Généalogie et sociologie de la 'valeur actionnariale,'" *L'Année de la régulation* 4 (2000): 117–65; Fabian Muniesa, "On the Political Vernaculars of Value Creation," *Science as Culture* 26, no. 4 (2017): 445–54; Horacio Ortiz, "Marchés efficients, investisseurs libres et Etats garants: trames du politique dans les pratiques financières professionnelles," *Politix* 95, no. 3 (2011): 155–80.

11. That is, they veered too far away from the performance of the index they were supposed to track and slightly outperform.

12. That is, the performance of the investment fund.

13. 12 basis points, or 0.12 percent, of gains in relation to the beginning of the week.

14. Fernand uses the former French currency, which had already been replaced by Euro at the time of the interview.

15. Electricité de France (EDF) and Gaz de France were state-owned monopolies providing electricity and gas in France at the time when Fernand started working in the financial industry.

16. The interview was conducted in 2004.

17. Cf. Leins, *Stories of Capitalism*.

18. Ho, *Liquidated*.

19. Godechot, *Les Traders; Wages, Bonuses and Appropriation of Profit in the Financial Industry: The Working Rich* (New York: Routledge, 2016).

20. Shamus Khan, "The Sociology of Elites," *Annual Review of Sociology* 38 (2012): 361–77.

21. Galit Ailon, "Bracketing the Nation: Lay Financial Trading in Israel," *Current Anthropology* 60, no. 2 (2019): 245–61.

22. Aaron Pitluck, "Watching Foreigners: How Counterparties Enable Herds, Crowds, and Generate Liquidity in Financial Markets," *Socio-economic Review* 12, no. 1 (2014): 5–31.

23. Kimberly Chong, *Best Practice: Management Consulting and the Ethics of Financialization in China* (Durham, NC: Duke University Press, 2018).

24. Rudnyckyj explores comparable combinations between religious elitism and financial expertise; see Daromir Rudnyckyj, *Beyond Debt: Islamic Experiments in Global Finance* (Chicago: University of Chicago Press, 2019).

25. Pierre Vernimmen et al., *Corporate Finance: Theory and Practice* (London: Wiley, 2011), 513.

26. Lordon, "La 'création de valeur' comme rhétorique et comme pratique"; Muniesa, "On the Political Vernaculars of Value Creation"; Ortiz, "Marchés efficients, investisseurs libres et Etats garants."

27. For Smith, because work always has the same value for the subject, it is the only standard that measures all goods and gives them a "real" or "natural" price; see Adam Smith, *An Inquiry Into the Nature and Causes of the Wealth of Nations* (New York: Prometheus, 1991 [1776]), 39.

28. Smith, *An Inquiry Into the Nature*, 37.

29. Christian Walter, "Une histoire du concept d'efficience sur les marchés financiers," *Annales: Histoire, sciences sociales* 51, no. 4 (1996): 873–905.

30. Robert Higgins, *Analysis for Financial Management* (Boston: Irwin McGraw-Hill, 2001 [1984]), 324.

31. Jonathan Levy, "Accounting for Profit and the History of Capital," *Critical Historical Studies* 1, no. 2 (2014): 171–214.

32. Joni Young, "Making Up Users," *Accounting, Organizations and Society* 31, no. 6 (2006): 579–600; Barker and Schulte, "Representing the Market Perspective."

33. Annelise Riles, *Collateral Knowledge: Legal Reasoning in the Global Financial Markets* (Chicago: University of Chicago Press, 2011).

34. Urs Bruegger and Karin Knorr Cetina, "Inhabiting Technology: The Global Lifeform of Financial Markets," *Current Sociology* 50, no. 3 (2001): 389–405.

35. Vincent Lépinay, *Codes of Finance: Engineering Derivatives in a Global Bank* (Princeton, NJ: Princeton University Press, 2011).

36. Part of the text in the following paragraphs initially appeared in Sabine Montagne and Horacio Ortiz, "Sociologie de l'agence financière: enjeux et perspectives," *Sociétés Contemporaines* 92, no. 4 (2013): 7–33.

37. Keith Hart and Horacio Ortiz, "The Anthropology of Money and Finance: Between Ethnography and World History," *Annual Review of Anthropology* 43 (2014): 465–82; Ortiz, "Anthropology—of the Financial Crisis."

38. Smith, *An Inquiry Into the Nature.*

39. Karl Marx, *Economics and Philosophical Manuscripts of 1844* (Moscow: Progress, 1977 [1844]).

40. Karl Marx and Friedrich Engels, *The Communist Manifesto*, trans. Eric Hobsbawm (London: Verso, 1998 [1848]).

41. Karl Marx, *Capital: A Critique of Political Economy*, vol. 3, trans. David Fernbach (London: Penguin and New Left Review, 1992 [1894]), 569.

42. Marcel Mauss, *The Gift*, trans. W. D. Halls (London: Routledge, 2002 [1923–1924]), 88.

43. John Keynes, *The General Theory of Employment, Interest and Money* (New York: Prometheus, 1997 [1936].

44. Georg Simmel, *The Philosophy of Money* (New York: Routledge, 1978 [1900]).

45. Max Weber, *Wirtschaft und Gesellschaft: Grundriss der Verstehenden Soziologie*, ed. Johannes Winckelmann (Tübingen: J. C. B. Mohr [Siebeck P], 1990 [1922]), 709. My translation, original italics and quotation marks.

46. William Lazonik and Mary O'Sullivan, "Maximizing Shareholder Value: A New Ideology for Corporate Governance," *Economy and Society* 29, no. 1 (2000): 13–35; Sabine Montagne, "Go-go managers contre futurs prix Nobel d'économie: genèse de l'investisseur professionnel moderne," *Sociétés Contemporaines* 93, no. 1 (2014): 9–37.

47. Michel Foucault, *Naissance de la Biopolitique: Cours au Collège de France,
1978–1979* (Paris: Gallimard, Seuil, 2004).

48. Cf., for instance, Abolafia, *Making Markets*; Charles Smith, *Success and
Survival on Wall Street: Understanding the Mind of the Market* (New
York: Roman & Littlefield, 1999).

49. Michel Foucault, *History of Madness*, trans. Jonathan Murphy and Jean
Khalfa (New York: Routledge, 2006 [1972]), 438.

50. Michel Foucault, *Discipline and Punish: The Birth of Prison*, trans. Alan
Sheridan (New York: Vintage, 1995 [1975]), 29–30.

51. Michel Foucault, *The History of Sexuality*, vol. 1, *An Introduction*, trans.
Robert Hurley (New York: Pantheon, 1978 [1976]), 94–95. Translation
modified; cf. Michel Foucault, *Histoire de la sexualité 1 La volonté de
savoir* Paris: Gallimard, 1976), 125–26.

52. Janet Roitman, *Fiscal Disobedience: An Anthropology of Economic Regulation in Central Africa* (Princeton, NJ: Princeton University Press, 2004).

CONCLUSION

1. Daromir Rudnyckyj, *Beyond Debt: Islamic Experiments in Global Finance*
(Chicago: University of Chicago Press, 2019).

2. Ann-Christina Lange, Marc Lenglet, and Robert Seyfert, "Cultures
of High-Frequency Trading: Mapping the Landscape of Algorithmic
Developments in Contemporary Financial Markets," *Economy and Society* 45, no. 2 (2016): 149–65; Fabian Muniesa, "Market Technologies and
the Pragmatics of Prices," *Economy and Society* 36, no. 3 (2007): 377–95.

3. Sudeep Doshi, Ju-Hon Kwek, and Joseph Lai, "Advanced Analytics in Asset
Management: Beyond the Buzz," McKinsey & Company, March 20, 2019,
https://www.mckinsey.com/industries/financial-services/our-insights
/advanced-analytics-in-asset-management-beyond-the-buzz.

4. Kimberly Chong, *Best Practice: Management Consulting and the Ethics of Financialization in China* (Durham, NC: Duke University Press,
2018); Johannes Petry, "Financialization with Chinese Characteristics?
Exchanges, Control and Capital Markets in Authoritarian Capitalism,"
Economy and Society 49, no. 2 (2020): 213–38; Yingyao Wang, "The Rise
of the 'Shareholding State': Financialization of Economic Management in China," *Socio-economic Review* 13, no. 3 (2015): 603–25.

BIBLIOGRAPHY

Aaron, Catherine, Isabelle Bilon, Sébastien Galanti, and Yamina Tadjeddine. "Les styles de gestion de portefeuille existent-ils?" *Revue d'Economie Financière* 81, no. 4 (2005): 171–88.

Abdelal, Rawi. *Capital Rules: The Construction of Global Finance.* Cambridge, MA: Harvard University Press, 2007.

Abélès, Marc. "Pour une anthropologie des institutions." *L'Homme*, no. 135 (1995): 65–85.

Abolafia, Mitchel. *Making Markets: Opportunism and Restraint on Wall Street.* Cambridge, MA: Harvard University Press, 1996.

Aglietta, Michel, and Antoine Rebérioux. *Dérives du capitalisme financier.* Paris: Albin Michel, 2004.

Ailon, Galit. "Bracketing the Nation: Lay Financial Trading in Israel." *Current Anthropology* 60, no. 2 (2019): 245–61.

Amyx, Jennifer. *Japan's Financial Crisis: Institutional Rigidity and Reluctant Change.* Princeton, NJ: Princeton University Press, 2004.

Anderson, Benedict. *Imagined Communities: Reflections on the Origin and Spread of Nationalism.* London: Verso, 2006 [1983].

Appelbaum, Eileen, and Rosemary Batt. *Private Equity at Work: When Wall Street Manages Main Street.* New York: Russell Sage Foundation, 2014.

Arjaliès, Diane-Laure, Philip Grant, Iain Hardie, Donald MacKenzie, and Ekaterina Svetlova. *Chains of Finance: How Investment Management Is Shaped.* Oxford: Oxford University Press, 2017.

Balandier, Georges. *Anthropologie Politique.* Paris: Presses Universitaires de France, 1967.

Bandelj, Nina, Fred Wherry, and Viviana Zelizer. "Advancing Money Talks." In *Money Talks: Explaining How Money Really Works*, ed. Nina Bandelj, Fred Wherry, and Viviana Zelizer, 1–22. Princeton, NJ: Princeton University Press, 2017.

Bank of International Settlements. "Statistics." Accessed December 20, 2018. https://www.bis.org/statistics/index.htm.

Barker, Richard, and Sebastian Schulte. "Representing the Market Perspective: Fair Value Measurement for Non-financial Assets." *Accounting, Organizations and Society* 56 (2017): 55–67.

Bear, Laura. "Capital and Time: Uncertainty and Qualitative Measures of Inequality." *British Journal of Sociology* 65, no. 4 (2014): 639–49.

——. *Navigating Austerity: Currents of Debt Along a South Asian River*. Stanford, CA: Stanford University Press, 2015.

Bear, Laura, Karen Ho, Anna Lowenhaupt Tsing, and Sylvia Yanagisako. "Gens: A Feminist Manifesto for the Study of capitalism." *Theorizing the Contemporary, Fieldsights*, March 30, 2015. https://culanth.org/fieldsights /gens-a-feminist-manifesto-for-the-study-of-capitalism.

Beckert, Jens, and Richard Bronk. "An Introduction to *Uncertain Futures*." In *Uncertain Futures: Imaginaries, Narratives and Calculation in the Economy*, ed. Jens Beckert and Richard Bronk, 1–36. Oxford: Oxford University Press, 2018.

Birch, Kean, and Fabian Muniesa. "Introduction: Assetization and Technoscientific Capitalism." In *Assetization: Turnings Things Into Assets in Technoscientific Capitalism*, ed. Kean Birch and Fabian Muniesa, 1–41. Cambridge, MA: MIT Press, 2020.

Blyth, Mark. "The Political Power of Financial Ideas: Transparency, Risk, and Distribution in Global Finance." In *Monetary Orders: Ambiguous Economics, Ubiquitous Politics*, ed. Jonathan Kirshner, 239–59. Ithaca, NY: Cornell University Press, 2003.

Boy, Nina. "Sovereign Safety." *Security Dialogue* 46, no. 6 (2015): 530–47.

Bruegger, Urs, and Karin Knorr Cetina. "Inhabiting Technology: The Global Lifeform of Financial Markets." *Current Sociology* 50, no. 3 (2001): 389–405.

Butler, Judith. *Gender Trouble: Feminism and the Subversion of Identity*. New York: Routledge, 1990.

——. "Performative Agency." *Journal of Cultural Economy* 3, no. 2 (2010): 147–61.

Callon, Michel. "Introduction: The Embeddedness of Economic Markets in Economics." In *The Laws of the Markets*, ed. Michel Callon, 1–57. Oxford: Blackwell, 1998.

——. "Performativity, Misfires and Politics." *Journal of Cultural Economy* 3, no. 2 (2010): 163–69.

Central Intelligence Agency. *The World Factbook*. Accessed December 20, 2018. https://www.cia.gov/library/publications/resources/the-world-factbook /geos/xx.html.

CFA Institute. *2011 Annual Report*. 2011. http://annualreport.cfainstitute.org .s3-website-us-east-1.amazonaws.com/2011/downloads.html.

Chaves Jardim, Maria. *Syndicats et fonds de pension durant le gouvernement Lula*. Paris: L'Harmattan, 2013.

Chiapello, Eve. "Financialisation of Valuation." *Human Studies* 38, no. 1 (2015): 13–35.

Chong, Kimberly. *Best Practice: Management Consulting and the Ethics of Financialization in China*. Durham, NC: Duke University Press, 2018.

Chong, Kimberly, and David Tuckett. "Constructing Conviction Through Action and Narrative: How Money Managers Manage Uncertainty and the Consequence for Financial Market Functioning." *Socio-economic Review* 13, no. 2 (2015): 309–30.

Chu, Julie. *Cosmologies of Credit: Transnational Mobility and the Politics of Destination in China*. Durham, NC: Duke University Press, 2010.

Chua, Wai Fong. "Experts, Networks and Inscriptions in the Fabrication of Accounting Images: A Story of the Representation of Three Public Hospitals." *Accounting, Organizations and Society* 23, no. 2–3 (1995): 111–45.

Clark, Gordon L. *Pension Fund Capitalism*. Oxford: Oxford University Press, 2000.

Clark, Gordon L., and Nigel Thrift. "The Return of Bureaucracy: Managing Dispersed Knowledge in Global Finance." In *The Sociology of Financial Markets*, ed. Karin Knorr Cetina and Alex Preda, 229–49. Oxford: Oxford University Press, 2005.

Collier, Stephen, and Aihwa Ong. "Global Assemblages, Political Problems." In *Global Assemblages: Technology, Politics, and Ethics as Anthropological Problems*, ed. Stephen Collier and Aihwa Ong, 3–21. Oxford: Blackwell, 2005.

Cooper, David and Keith Robson. "Accounting, professions and regulation: Locating the sites of professionalization." *Accounting, Organizations and Society*, 31(2006): 415–44.

Cooper, Melinda, and Martijn Konings. "Pragmatics of Money and Finance: Beyond Performativity and Fundamental Value." *Journal of Cultural Economy* 9, no. 1 (2016): 1–4.

Couppey-Soubeyran, Jézabel, Dominique Plihon, and Dhafer Saïdane. *Les banques, acteurs de la globalisation financière*. Paris: La documentation française, 2006.

Dal Maso, Giulia. *Risky Expertise in Chinese Financialisation: Returned Labor and the State-Finance Nexus*. Singapore: Palgrave Macmillan, 2020.

Dambrin, Claire, and Keith Robson. "Tracing the Performance in the Pharmaceutical Industry: Ambivalence, Opacity and the Performativity of Flawed Measures." *Accounting, Organizations and Society* 36, no. 7 (2011): 428–55.

Davies, Howard, and David Green. *Global Financial Regulation: The Essential Guide*. Cambridge: Polity Press, 2011.

De Certeau, Michel. *L'invention du quotidien 1: Arts de faire*. Paris: Gallimard, 1990 [1980].

De Goede, Marieke. *Virtue, Fortune and Faith: A Genealogy of Finance*. Minneapolis: University of Minnesota Press, 2005.

Deleuze, Gilles, and Félix Guattari. *Capitalisme ou Schizophrénie 2: Mille Plateaux*. Paris: Les Editions de Minuit, 1980.

Dewey, John. *Theory of Valuation*. Chicago: University of Chicago Press, 1939.

Dodd, Nigel. *The Social Life of Money*. Princeton, NJ: Princeton University Press, 2014.

Doganova, Liliana. "Discounting and the Making of the Future: On Uncertainty in Forest Management and Drug Development." In *Uncertain Futures: Imaginaries, Narratives and Calculation in the Economy*, ed. Jens Beckert and Richard Bronk, 278–97. Oxford: Oxford University Press, 2018.

——. "Discounting the Future: A Political Technology." *Economic Sociology_ The European Electronic Newsletter* 19, no. 2 (2018): 4–9.

Doshi, Sudeep, Ju-Hon Kwek, and Joseph Lai. "Advanced Analytics in Asset Management: Beyond the Buzz." MacKinsey & Company, March 20, 2019. https://www.mckinsey.com/industries/financial-services/our-insights/advanced-analytics-in-asset-management-beyond-the-buzz.

Dumont, Louis. *Homo Hierarchicus: The Caste System and Its implications*. Translated by Mark Sainsbury, Louis Dumont, and Basia Gulati. Oxford: Oxford University Press, 1990 [1970].

Eichengreen, Barry. *Globalizing Capital: A History of the International Monetary System.* Princeton, NJ: Princeton University Press, 1996.

Erturk, Ismail, Julie Froud, Sukhdev Johal, Adam Leaver, and Karel Williams. "Against Agency: A Positional Critique." *Economy and Society* 36, no. 1 (2007): 51–77.

Escalona Victoria, José Luis. "Anthropology of Power: Beyond State-Centric Politics." *Anthropological Theory* 16, no. 2–3 (2016): 249–62.

Ezzamel, Mahmoud, Hugh Wilmott, and Frank Worthington. "Manufacturing Shareholder Value: The Role of Accounting in Organizational Transformation." *Accounting, Organizations and Society* 33, no. 2–3 (2008): 107–40.

FAO, IFAD, UNICEF, WFP, and WHO. *The State of Food Security and Nutrition in the World 2018: Building Climate Resilience for Food Security and Nutrition.* Rome: FAO, 2018. http://www.fao.org/policy-support/tools -and-publications/resources-details/en/c/1152267/.

Fichtner, Jan, Eelke Heemskerk, and Javier Garcia Bernardo. "Hidden Power of the Big Three? Passive Index Funds, Re-concentration of Corporate Ownership, and New Financial Risk." *Business and Politics* 19, no. 2 (2017): 298–326.

Fisher, Melissa. *Wall Street Women.* Durham, NC: Duke University Press, 2012.

Fligstein, Neil. *The Architecture of Markets: An Economic Sociology of Twenty-First-Century Capitalist Societies.* Princeton, NJ: Princeton University Press, 2001.

——. *The Transformation of Corporate Control.* Cambridge, MA: Harvard University Press, 1990.

Foucault, Michel. *Discipline and Punish: The Birth of Prison.* Translated by Alan Sheridan. New York: Vintage, 1995 [1975].

——. *Histoire de la sexualité 1 La volonté de savoir.* Paris: Gallimard, 1976.

——. *History of Madness.* Translated by Jonathan Murphy and Jean Khalfa. New York: Routledge, 2006 [1972].

——.——. *The History of Sexuality.* Vol. 1, *An Introduction,* translated by Robert Hurley. New York: Pantheon, 1978 [1976].

——. *Les mots et les choses.* Paris: Gallimard, 1966.

——. *Naissance de la Biopolitique: Cours au Collège de France, 1978–1979.* Paris: Gallimard, Seuil, 2004.

Fourcade, Marion. "Cents and Sensibility: Economic Valuation and the Nature of 'Nature.'" *American Journal of Sociology* 116, no. 6 (2011): 1721–77.

——. "Ordinalization." *Sociological Theory* 34, no. 3 (2016): 175–95.

——. "State Metrology: The Rating of Sovereigns and the Judgment of Nations." In *The Many Hands of the State: Theorizing Political Authority and Social Control*, ed. Kimberly Morgan and Ann Orloff, 103–27. Cambridge: Cambridge University Press, 2017.

——. "Theories of Markets and Theories of Society." *American Behavioral Scientist* 50, no. 8 (2007): 1015–34.

Fourcade, Marion, and Rakesh Khurana. "From Social Control to Financial Economics: The Linked Ecologies of Economics and Business in Twentieth Century America." *Theory and Society* 42, no. 2 (2013): 121–59.

——. "The Social Trajectory of a Finance Professor and the Common Sense of Capital." *History of Political Economy* 49, no. 2 (2017): 347–81.

Gabor, Daniela, "The Wall Street Consensus," *Development and Change*, first published online (2021): doi: 10.1111/dech.12645.

Godechot, Olivier. "Financialization Is Marketization! A Study of the Respective Impact of Various Dimensions of Financialization on the Increase in Global Inequality." *Sociological Science* 3, no. 30 (2016): 495–519.

——. *Les Traders: Essai de sociologie des marchés financiers*. Paris: La Découverte, 2001.

——. *Wages, Bonuses and Appropriation of Profit in the Financial Industry: The Working Rich*. New York: Routledge, 2016.

——. "What Do Heads of Dealing Rooms Do? The Social Capital of Internal Entrepreneurs." *Sociological Review* 56, no. 1 (2008): 145–61.

Godechot, Olivier, and Paul Lagneau-Ymonet. "D'un rapport salarial favorable à un autre: Les professionnels de la bourse 1970–2000." In *Le salariat bancaire: Enjeux sociaux et pratiques de gestion*, ed. Patrice Baubeau, Chantal Cossalter, and Catherine Omnès, 193–220. Nanterre: Presses de l'université Paris Ouest, 2009.

Graeber, David. "It Is Value That Brings Universes Into Being." *HAU: Journal of Ethnographic Theory* 3, no. 2 (2013): 219–43.

Guyer, Jane. "The Eruption of Tradition: On Ordinality and Calculation." *Anthropological Theory* 10, no. 1–2 (2010): 121–31.

——. *Legacies, Logics, Logistics: Essays in the Anthropology of the Platform Economy*. Chicago: University of Chicago Press, 2016.

——. *Marginal Gains: Monetary Transactions in Atlantic Africa*. Chicago: University of Chicago Press, 2004.

Guyer, Jane, Naveeda Khan, Juan Obarrio, Caroline Bledsoe, Julie Chu, Souleymane Bachir Diagne, Keith Hart et al. "Introduction: Number as Inventive Frontier." *Anthropological Theory* 10, no. 1–2 (2010): 36–61.

Hart, Keith. "Heads or Tails? The Two Sides of the Coin." *Man*, n.s., 21, no. 4 (1986): 637–56.

——. "Introduction." In *Economy for and Against Democracy*, ed. Keith Hart, 1–15. New York: Berghahn Press, 2015.

——. *The Memory Bank: Money in an Unequal World*. London: Profile, 2000.

——. "Models of Statistical Distribution: A Window on Social History." *Anthropological Theory* 10, no. 1–2 (2010): 67–74.

Hart, Keith, and Horacio Ortiz. "The Anthropology of Money and Finance: Between Ethnography and World History." *Annual Review of Anthropology* 43 (2014): 465–82.

Heilbron, Johan, Jochem Verheul, and Sander Quak. "The Origins and Early Diffusion of 'Shareholder Value' in the United States." *Theory and Society* 43, no. 1 (2014): 1–22.

Helleiner, Eric. *The Making of National Money: Territorial Currencies in Historical Perspective*. Ithaca, NY: Cornell University Press, 2003.

——. "The Southern Side of Embedded Liberalism: The Politics of Postwar Monetary Policy in the Third World." In *Monetary Orders: Ambiguous Economics, Ubiquitous Politics*, ed. Jonathan Kirshner, 57–77. Ithaca, NY: Cornell University Press, 2003.

Hertz, Ellen. *The Trading Crowd: An Ethnography of the Shanghai Stock Market*. Cambridge: Cambridge University Press, 1998.

Higgins, Robert. *Analysis for Financial Management*. Boston: Irwin McGraw-Hill, 2001[1984].

Ho, Karen. *Liquidated: An Ethnography of Wall Street*. Durham, NC: Duke University Press, 2009.

Hoag, Colin. "Assembling Partial Perspectives: Thoughts on the Anthropology of Bureaucracy." *PoLAR: Political and Legal Anthropological Review* 34, no. 1 (2011): 81–94.

Hopwood, Anthony. "On Trying to Study Accounting in the Contexts in Which It Operates." *Accounting, Organizations and Society* 8, no. 2–3 (1983): 287–305.

International Institute for Sustainable Development. *Ending Hunger: What Would It Cost?* October 2016. https://www.iisd.org/sites/default/files/publications/ending-hunger-what-would-it-cost.pdf..

James, Deborah. *Money from Nothing: Indebtedness and Aspiration in South Africa*. Stanford, CA: Stanford University Press, 2014.

James, William. "Pragmatism and Common Sense." In *The Writings of William James*, ed. John McDermott, 418–28. Chicago: University of Chicago Press, 1977 [1907].

——. "Pragmatism's Conception of Truth." In *The Writings of William James*, ed. John McDermott, 429–43. Chicago: University of Chicago Press, 1977 [1907].

Kennedy, Liam. "Top 400 Asset Managers." *Investment and Pensions Europe*, June 2018, 21–23. https://www.ipe.com/reports/special-reports/top-400 -asset-managers/top-400-asset-managers-2018-10-years-of-asset -growth/10025004.article.

Keynes, John. *The General Theory of Employment, Interest and Money*. New York: Prometheus, 1997 [1936].

Khan, Shamus. "The Sociology of Elites." *Annual Review of Sociology* 38 (2012): 361–77.

Klossowski, Pierre. *La monnaie vivante*. Paris: Payot & Rivages, 1997 [1970].

Kornberger, Martin, Lise Justensen, Anders Koed Madsen, and Jan Mouritsen. "Introduction: Making Things Valuable." In *Making Things Valuable*, ed. Martin Kornberger, Lise Justensen, Anders Koed Madsen, and Jan Mouritsen, 1–22. Oxford: Oxford University Press, 2015.

Krippner, Greta. *Capitalizing on Crisis: The Political Origins of the Rise of Finance*. Cambridge, MA: Harvard University Press, 2011.

Lambek, Michael. "The Value of (Performative) Acts." *HAU: Journal of Ethnographic Theory* 3, no. 1 (2013): 141–60.

Lambert, Caroline, and Eric Pezet. "The Making of the Management Accountant—Becoming the Producer of Truthful Knowledge." *Accounting, Organizations and Society* 35, no. 1 (2010): 10–30.

Lange, Ann-Christina, Marc Lenglet, and Robert Seyfert. "Cultures of High-Frequency Trading: Mapping the Landscape of Algorithmic Developments in Contemporary Financial Markets." *Economy and Society* 45, no. 2 (2016): 149–65.

Langley, Paul. *Liquidity Lost: The Governance of the Financial Crisis*. Oxford: Oxford University Press, 2015.

Lawrence, Geoffrey, Sarah Sippel, and David Burch. "The Financialisation of Food and Farming." In *Handbook on the Globalisation of Agriculture*, ed. Guy Robinson and Doris Carson, 309–27. Cheltenham, UK: Edward Elgar, 2015.

Lazonik, William, and Mary O'Sullivan. "Maximizing Shareholder Value: A New Ideology for Corporate Governance." *Economy and Society* 29, no. 1 (2000): 13–35.

Leins, Stefan. *Stories of Capitalism: Inside the Role of Financial Analysts.* Chicago: University of Chicago Press, 2018.

Lemoine, Benjamin. *L'ordre de la dette: Enquête sur les infortunes de l'état et la prospérité du marché.* Paris: La Découverte, 2016.

Lépinay, Vincent. *Codes of Finance: Engineering Derivatives in a Global Bank.* Princeton, NJ: Princeton University Press, 2011.

Levy, Jonathan. "Accounting for Profit and the History of Capital." *Critical Historical Studies* 1, no. 2 (2014): 171–214.

Leyshon, Andrew, and Nigel Thrift. "The Capitalization of Almost Everything: The Future of Finance and Capitalism." *Theory, Culture and Society* 24, no. 7–8 (2007): 97–115.

Lezaun, Javier, and Fabian Muniesa, "Twilight in the leadership playground: subrealism and the training of the business self," *Journal of Cultural Economy* 10, no. 3 (2017): 265–79.

Lin, Ken-Hou, and Donald Tomaskovic-Devey. "Financialization and U.S. Income Inequality, 1970–2008." *American Journal of Sociology* 118, no. 5 (2013): 1284–329.

Lordon, Frédéric. "La 'création de valeur' comme rhétorique et comme pratique: Généalogie et sociologie de la 'valeur actionnariale.'" *L'Année de la régulation* 4 (2000): 117–65.

MacKenzie, Donald. "The Credit Crisis as a Problem in the Sociology of Knowledge." *American Journal of Sociology* 116, no. 6 (2011): 1778–841.

——. *An Engine, Not a Camera: How Financial Models Shape Markets.* Cambridge, MA: MIT Press, 2006.

Marcuse, Herbert. *Eros and Civilization: A Philosophical Enquiry Into Freud.* Boston: Beacon Press, 1955.

Marx, Karl. *Capital: A Critique of Political Economy*, vol. 1, trans. Ben Fowkes. London: Penguin and New Left Review, 1992 [1972].

——. *Capital: A Critique of Political Economy*, vol. 3, trans. David Fernbach. London: Penguin and New Left Review, 1992 [1894].

——. *Economics and Philosophical Manuscripts of 1844.* Moscow: Progress, 1977 [1844].

Marx, Karl, and Friedrich Engels. *The Communist Manifesto.* Translated by Eric Hobsbawm. London: Verso, 1998 [1848].

Maurer, Bill. "The Anthropology of Money." *Annual Review of Anthropology* 35 (2006): 15–36.

———. "Credit Crisis Religion." *Religion and Society: Advances in Research* 1 (2010): 146–55.

———. *How Would You Like to Pay? How Technology Is Changing the Future of Money*. Durham, NC: Duke University Press, 2015.

———. "Repressed Futures: Financial Derivatives' Theological Unconscious." *Economy and Society* 31, no. 1 (2002): 15–36.

Mauss, Marcel. *The Gift*. Translated by W. D. Halls. London: Routledge, 2002 [1923–1924].

Mazouz, Sarah. "Faire des differences. Ce que l'ethnographie nous apprend sur l'articulation des modes pluriels d'assignation." *Raisons Politiques* 58, no. 2 (2015): 75–89.

McMichael, Philip. "A Food Regime Analysis of the 'World Food Crisis.'" *Agriculture and Human Values* 26, no. 4 (2009): 281–95.

Mennicken, Andrea, and Peter Miller. "Accounting, Territorialization and Power." *Foucault Studies*, no. 13 (2012): 4–24.

Miller, Daniel. "The Uses of Value." *Geoforum* 39 (2008): 1122–32.

Miller, Peter. "Calculating Economic Life." *Journal of Cultural Economy* 1, no. 1 (2008): 51–64.

Miller, Peter, and Ted O'Leary. "Mediating Instruments and Making Markets: Capital Budgeting, Science and the Economy." *Accounting, Organizations and Society* 32, no. 7–8 (2007): 701–34.

Miller, Peter, and Nikolas Rose. "Governing Economic Life." *Economy and Society* 19, no. 1 (1990): 1–31.

———. "Political Power Beyond the State: Problematics of Government." *British Journal of Sociology* 43, no. 2 (1992): 173–205.

Miyazaki, Hirokazu. "Between Arbitrage and Speculation: An Economy of Belief and Doubt." *Economy and Society* 36, no. 3 (2007): 396–415.

———. "Economy of Dreams: Hope in Global Capitalism and Its Critiques." *Cultural Anthropology* 21, no. 2 (2006): 147–72.

Miyazaki, Hirokazu, and Annelise Riles. "Failure as Endpoint." In *Global Assemblages: Technology, Politics, and Ethics as Anthropological Problems*, ed. Stephen Collier and Aihwa Ong, 320–31. Oxford: Blackwell, 2005.

Montagne, Sabine. *Les Fonds de Pension: Entre protection sociale et spéculation financière*. Paris: Odile Jacob, 2006.

——. "Go-go managers contre futurs prix Nobel d'économie: genèse de l'investisseur professionnel moderne." *Sociétés Contemporaines* 93, no. 1 (2014): 9–37.

——. "Investing Prudently: How Financialization Puts a Legal Standard to Use." *Sociologie du travail* 55, no. 1 (2013): 48–66.

——. "Pouvoir financier vs. pouvoir salarial: Les fonds de pension américains; contribution du droit à la légitimité financière." *Annales: Histoire, sciences sociales* 60, no. 6 (2005): 1299–325.

Montagne, Sabine, and Horacio Ortiz. "Sociologie de l'agence financière: enjeux et perspectives." *Sociétés Contemporaines* 92, no. 4 (2013): 7–33.

Müller, Lúcia. *Mercado Exemplar: um estudo antropológico sobre a Bolsa de Valores*. Porto Alegre, Brazil: Zouk, 2006.

Muniesa, Fabian. "A Flank Movement in the Understanding of Valuation." *Sociological Review* 59, no. 2 (2011): 24–38.

——. "Market Technologies and the Pragmatics of Prices." *Economy and Society* 36, no. 3 (2007): 377–95.

——. "On the Political Vernaculars of Value Creation." *Science as Culture* 26, no. 4 (2017): 445–54.

——. *The Provoked Economy: Economic Reality and the Performative Turn*. New York: Routledge, 2014.

Muniesa, Fabian, Liliana Doganova, Horacio Ortiz, Álvaro Pina-Stranger, Florence Paterson, Alaric Bourgoin, Véra Ehrenstein et al. *Capitalization: A Cultural Guide*. Paris: Presses des Mines, 2017.

Neiburg, Federico. "Inflation: Economists and Economic Cultures in Brazil and Argentina." *Comparative Studies of Society and History* 48, no. 3 (2006): 604–33.

Neiburg, Federico, and Jane Guyer. "The Real in the Real Economy." *HAU: Journal of Ethnographic Theory* 7, no. 3 (2017): 261–79.

Ortiz, Horacio. "Anthropology—of the Financial Crisis." In *Handbook of Economic Anthropology*, ed. James Carrier, 585–96. Cheltenham, UK: Edward Elgar, 2012.

——. "Financial Value: Economic, Moral, Political, Global." *HAU: Journal of Ethnographic Theory* 3, no. 1 (2013): 64–79.

——. "Hedge Funds and the Limit of Market Efficiency as a Regulatory Concept." In *Financial Cultures and Crisis Dynamics*, ed. Bob Jessop, Brigitte Young, and Christoph Scherrer, 191–207. New York: Routledge, 2015.

———. "Investir: une décision disséminée; Enquête de terrain sur les dérivés de crédit." *Sociétés Contemporaines* no. 92 (2013): 35–57.

———. "The Limits of Financial Imagination: Free Investors, Efficient Markets and Crisis." *American Anthropologist* 116, no. 1 (2014): 38–50.

———. "Marchés efficients, investisseurs libres et Etats garants: trames du politique dans les pratiques financières professionnelles." *Politix* 95, no.3 (2011): 155–80.

———. "A Political Anthropology of Finance: Profits, States and Cultures in Cross-Border Investment in Shanghai." *HAU: Journal of Ethnographic Theory* 7, no. 3 (2017): 325–45.

———. "A Political Anthropology of Finance: Studying the Distribution of Money in the Financial Industry as a Political Process." *Anthropological Theory* 21, no. 3 (2021): 3–27.

———. "Political Imaginaries of the Weighted Average Cost of Capital. A Conceptual Analysis", *Valuation Studies* (2021, in press)

———. "What Financial Crisis? The Global Politics of the Financial Industry: Distributional Consequences and Legitimizing Narratives." In *Economy for and Against Democracy*, ed. Keith Hart and John Sharp, 39–57. New York: Berghahn Press, 2015.

———. "Wittgenstein's Critique of Representation and the Ethical Reflexivity of Anthropological Discourse." In *Reflecting on Reflexivity: The Human Condition as an Ontological Surprise*, ed. Terry Evens, Don Handelman, and Christopher Roberts, 124–41. New York: Berghahn Press, 2016.

Ortiz, Horacio, and Fabian Muniesa. "Business Schools, the Anxiety of Finance and the Order of the 'Middle Tier.'" *Journal of Cultural Economy* 11, no. 1 (2018): 1–19.

Parry, Jonathan, and Maurice Bloch. "Introduction: Money and the Morality of Exchange." In *Money and the Morality of Exchange*, ed. Jonathan Parry and Maurice Bloch, 1–32. Cambridge: Cambridge University Press, 1989.

Pedersen, David. "Introduction: Towards a Value Theory of Anthropology." *Anthropological Theory* 8, no. 1 (2008): 5–8.

Peebles, Gustav. "The Anthropology of Credit and Debt." *Annual Review of Anthropology* 39 (2010): 225–40.

Petry, Johannes. "Financialization with Chinese Characteristics? Exchanges, Control and Capital Markets in Authoritarian Capitalism." *Economy and Society* 49, no. 2 (2020): 213–38.

Petry, Johannes, Jan Fichtner, and Eelke Heemskerk. "Steering Capital: The Growing Private Authority of Index Providers in the Age of Passive Asset Management." *Review of International Political Economy* 28, no. 1 (2019): 152–76. https://doi.org/10.1080/09692290.2019.1699147.

Piketty, Thomas. *Capital in the XXIst Century.* Translated by Arthur Goldhammer. Cambridge, MA: Harvard University Press, 2014.

Pitluck, Aaron. "Watching Foreigners: How Counterparties Enable Herds, Crowds, and Generate Liquidity in Financial Markets." *Socio-economic Review* 12, no. 1 (2014): 5–31.

Plihon, Dominique, and Jean-Pierre Ponssard, eds. *La montée en puissance des fonds d'investissement.* Paris: La Documentation Française, 2002.

Polillo, Simone. "Market Efficiency as a Revolution in Data Analysis." *Economic Anthropology* 5, no. 2 (2018): 198–209.

——. "Money, Moral Authority and the Politics of Creditworthiness." *American Sociological Review* 76, no. 3 (2011): 437–64.

Polillo, Simone, and Mauro F. Guillén. "Globalization Pressures and the State: The Worldwide Spread of Central Bank Independence." *American Journal of Sociology* 110, no. 6 (2005): 1764–802.

Power, Michael. "Accounting and Finance." In *The Oxford Handbook of the Sociology of Finance,* ed. Karin Knorr Cetina and Alex Preda, 291–314. Oxford: Oxford University Press, 2012.

Pradier, Pierre-Charles. *La notion de risque en économie.* Paris: La Découverte, 2006.

Preda, Alex. *Framing Finance: The Boundaries of Markets and Modern Capitalism.* Chicago: University of Chicago Press, 2009.

——. "The Investor as a Cultural Figure of Global Capitalism." In *The Sociology of Financial Markets,* ed. Karin Knorr Cetina and Alex Preda, 141–62. Oxford: Oxford University Press, 2005.

Quattrone, Paolo. "Books to Be Practiced: Memory, the Power of the Visual, and the Success of Accounting." *Accounting, Organizations and Society* 34, no. 1 (2009): 85–118.

——. "Governing Social Orders, Unfolding Rationality, and Jesuit Accounting Practices: A Procedural Approach to Institutional Logics." *Administrative Science Quarterly* 60, no. 3 (2015): 411–45.

Reddy, Yaga. *India and the Global Financial Crisis: Managing Money and Finance.* London: Anthem Press, 2009.

Reinsberg, Bernhard, Thomas Stubbs, Alexander Kentikelenis, and Lawrence King. "The World System and the Hollowing Out of State Capacity: How Structural Adjustment Programs Affect Bureaucratic Quality in Developing Countries." *American Journal of Sociology* 124, no. 4 (2019): 1222–57.

Riles, Annelise. *Collateral Knowledge: Legal Reasoning in the Global Financial Markets.* Chicago: University of Chicago Press, 2011.

Robbins, Joel. "Monism, Pluralism, and the Structure of Value Relations: A Dumontian Contribution to the Contemporary Study of Value." *HAU: Journal of Ethnographic Theory* 3, no. 1 (2013): 99–115.

Roberts, Adrienne. "Gender, Financial Deepening and the Production of Embodied Finance: Towards a Critical Feminist Analysis." *Global Society*, 29, no. 1 (2015): 107–27.

Roberts, John, Paul Sanderson, Richard Barker, and John Hendry. "In the Mirror of the Market: The Disciplinary Effects of Company/Fund Manager Meetings." *Accounting, Organizations and Society* 31, no. 3 (2006): 277–94.

Robson, Keith. "Accounting as 'Inscription': Action at a Distance and the Development of Accounting." *Accounting, Organizations and Society* 17, no. 7 (1992): 685–708.

Roitman, Janet. *Anti-Crisis.* Durham, NC: Duke University Press, 2014.

——. *Fiscal Disobedience: An Anthropology of Economic Regulation in Central Africa.* Princeton, NJ: Princeton University Press, 2004.

Roth, Louise. *Selling Women Short: Gender and Inequality on Wall Street.* Princeton, NJ: Princeton University Press, 2006.

Rudnyckyj, Daromir. *Beyond Debt: Islamic Experiments in Global Finance.* Chicago: University of Chicago Press, 2019.

Sahlins, Marshall. "On the Culture of Material Value and the Cosmography of Riches." *HAU: Journal of Ethnographic Theory* 3, no. 2 (2013): 161–95.

Salzinger, Leslie. "Re-making Men: Masculinity as a Terrain of the Neoliberal Economy." *Critical Historical Studies* 3, no. 1 (2016): 1–25.

Sassen, Saskia. "Global Finance and Its Institutional Spaces." In *The Oxford Handbook of the Sociology of Finance*, ed. Karin Knorr Cetina and Alex Preda, 13–32. Oxford: Oxford University Press, 2012.

Scott, James. *The Moral Economy of the Peasants: Rebellion and Subsistence in South-East Asia.* New Haven, CT: Yale University Press, 1976.

Sen, Amartya. *Development as Freedom.* Oxford: Oxford University Press, 1999.

Simmel, Georg. *The Philosophy of Money*. New York: Routledge, 1978 [1900].

Sinclair, Timothy. *The New Masters of Capital: American Bond Rating Agencies and the Politics of Creditworthiness*. Ithaca, NY: Cornell University Press, 2005.

Smith, Adam. *An Inquiry Into the Nature and Causes of the Wealth of Nations*. New York: Prometheus, 1991 [1776].

Smith, Charles. *Success and Survival on Wall Street: Understanding the Mind of the Market*. New York: Roman & Littlefield, 1999.

Souleles, Daniel. *Songs of Profit, Songs of Loss. Private Equity, Wealth and Inequality*. Lincoln: University of Nebraska Press, 2019.

Stark, David. "For What It's Worth." In *Research in the Sociology of Organizations*, vol. 52, ed. Charlotte Cloutier, Jean-Pascal Gond, and Bernard Leca, 383–97. Bingley, UK: Emerald, 2017.

——. "What's Valuable." In *The Worth of Goods: Valuation and Pricing in the Economy*, ed. Patrick Aspers and Jens Beckert, 319–38. Oxford: Oxford University Press, 2011.

Stiglitz, Joseph. *Making Globalization Work*. London: Penguin, 2006.

Stout, Noelle. *Dispossessed: How Predatory Bureaucracy Foreclosed on the American Middle Class*. Oakland: University of California Press, 2019.

Strathern, Marilyn. "Naturalism and the Invention of Identity." *Social Analysis* 61, no. 2 (2017): 15–30.

Swedberg, Richard. "Conflicts of Interests in the US Brokerage Industry." In *The Sociology of Financial Markets*, ed. Karin Knorr Cetina and Alex Preda, 187–203. Oxford: Oxford University Press, 2005.

Takatera, Sadao, and Norio Sawabe. "Time and Space in Income Accounting." *Accounting, Organizations and Society* 25, no. 8 (2000): 787–98.

Therborn, Göran. *The Killing Fields of Inequality*. Cambridge: Polity Press, 2013.

Trouillot, Michel-Rolph. *Global Transformations: Anthropology and the Modern World*. New York: Palgrave Macmillan, 2003.

Tsing, Anna. "Sorting Out Commodities: How Capitalist Value Is Made Through Gifts." *HAU: Journal of Ethnographic Theory* 3, no. 1 (2013): 21–43.

Van der Zwan, Natascha. "Making Sense of Financialization." *Socio-economic Review* 12, no. 1 (2014): 99–129.

Venugopal, Rajesh. "Neoliberalism as Concept." *Economy and Society* 44, no. 2 (2015): 165–87.

Vernimmen, Pierre, Pascal Quiry, Maurizio Dallocchio, Yann Le Fur, and Antonio Salvi. *Corporate Finance: Theory and Practice*. London: Wiley, 2011.

Vollmer, Hendrik. "How to Do More with Numbers: Elementary Stakes, Framing, Keying, and the Three-Dimensional Character of Numerical Signs." *Accounting, Organizations and Society* 32, no. 6 (2007): 577–600.

Walter, Christian. "Une histoire du concept d'efficience sur les marchés financiers." *Annales: Histoire, sciences sociales* 51, no. 4 (1996): 873–905.

Wang, Yingyao. "The Rise of the 'Shareholding State': Financialization of Economic Management in China." *Socio-economic Review* 13, no. 3 (2015): 603–25.

Weber, Max. *Economy and Society: An Outline of Interpretive Sociology.* Edited by Guenther Roth and Claus Wittich. Translated by Ephraim Fischoff et al. Berkeley: University of California Press, 1978 [1922].

——. "Politics as a Vocation." In *From Max Weber, Essays in Sociology*, ed. and trans. Hans Gerth and C. Wright Mills, 77–128. Oxford: Oxford University Press, 1958 [1917].

——. *Wirtschaft und Gesellschaft: Grundriss der Verstehenden Soziologie.* Edited by Johannes Winckelmann. Tübingen: J. C. B. Mohr (Siebeck P), 1990 [1922].

White, Ben, Saturnina Borras, Ruth Hall, Iain Scoones, and Wendy Wolford. "The New Enclosures: Critical Perspectives on Corporate Land Deals." *Journal of Peasant Studies* 39, no. 3–4 (2012): 619–47.

Whitley, Richard. "The Transformation of Business Finance Into Financial Economics: The Roles of Academic Expansion and Changes in U.S. Capital Markets." *Accounting, Organizations and Society* 11, no. 2 (1986): 171–92.

Wilkis, Ariel. *The Moral Power of Money: Morality and Economy in the Life of the Poor.* Stanford, CA: Stanford University Press, 2018.

Williams, James. "Regulatory Technologies, Risky Subjects, and Financial Boundaries: Governing 'Fraud' in the Financial Markets." *Accounting, Organizations and Society* 38, no. 6–7 (2013): 544–58.

World Bank Group. "Database." Accessed December 20, 2018. https://data.worldbank.org/indicator/NY.GDP.MKTP.CD.

——. *Reaching the Global Target to Reduce Stunting: How Much Will It Cost and How Can We Pay for It?* Accessed December 20, 2018. http://pubdocs.worldbank.org/en/460861439997767818/Stunting-Costing-and-Financing-Overview-Brief.pdf.

World Federation of Exchanges. *Statistics.* Accessed December 20, 2018. https://www.world-exchanges.org/our-work/statistics.

Young, Brigitte, Isabella Bakker, and Diane Elson. *Questioning Financial Governance from a Feminist Perspective.* London: Routledge, 2011.

Young, Joni. "Making Up Users." *Accounting, Organizations and Society* 31, no. 6 (2006): 579–600.

Zaloom, Caitlin. "The Evangelical Financial Ethic: Double Forms and the Search for God in the Economic World." *American Ethnologist* 43, no. 2 (2016): 325–38.

——. *Out of the Pits: Traders and Technology from Chicago to London.* Chicago: University of Chicago Press, 2006.

Zelizer, Viviana. *Economic Lives: How Culture Shapes the Economy.* Princeton, NJ: Princeton University Press, 2009.

——. *Morals and Markets: The Development of Life Insurance in the United States.* New York: Columbia University Press, 1979.

——. *The Purchase of Intimacy.* Princeton, NJ: Princeton University Press, 2005.

——. *The Social Meaning of Money: Pin Money, Paychecks, Poor Relief, and Other Currencies.* Princeton, NJ: Princeton University Press, 1997.

INDEX

accounting: companies with categories of, 62; company activities in, 200–201; as mediating instruments, 39; salespeople knowing, 108; stock prices and, 61–62; valuation with knowledge of, 120

algorithms, in valuation and investment, 247

alternative investments, 63, 206, 213

analysts' consensus, 171

Arjaliès, Diane-Laure, 36–37, 42, 210

Association of Certified International Investment Analyst, 78, 160

back-office employees, 48, 80–81

Bank of International Settlements (BIS), 170

bankruptcy, of companies, 252–53

Beckert, Jens, 53

beta, of listed companies, 171

big cap stocks: in brokerage houses, 44; Brokers Inc. and, 44–45;

for investment management companies, 97

BIS. *See* Bank of International Settlements

Bloomberg company, 170–71

bonds, 7, 11, 64; inequalities and, 13; sovereign, 151; in United States, 19–20

bonus, valuation linked to, 133–35

Bretton Woods agreement, 10

brokerage houses, 41; assets turnover in, 219–20; big cap stocks in, 44; outings financed by, 120–21; research published of, 99–100. *See also* trading

Bronk, Richard, 53

budgetary disciplines, 23

buy-and-hold approach, 60, 63, 160

buy and sell orders, 187–88, 211–12

buy-side analyst, 176; financial analysis, 50–51; for fund managers, 91–92; from fund managers, 47

buy-side traders, 188

Callon, Michel, 145
capital asset pricing model, 64, 154
capitalism, 232–33, 235, 241
capitalization: of financial assets,
    150, 256n6; of listed companies, 7;
    returns reinvestment in, 273n84;
    stock prices in, 267n23; of stocks,
    43
cash flow, 221, 273n84; fundamental
    valuation and, 58, 61; future, 58;
    of listed companies, 249; present
    value of, 56–57; stock prices and,
    74–75. *See also* discounted cash
    flow method
certified international investment
    analyst (CIIA), 17, 54, 230
CFA. *See* Chartered Financial
    Analyst Institute
Chartered Financial Analyst
    Institute, 54, 78, 173; chartered
    financial analyst (CFA) program,
    17, 54, 101, 173; CIIA, 17, 54, 74,
    230chartism, 66
China: Communist Party of, 227,
    248; company funding in, 19–20;
    financial industry in, 247–48;
    GDP of, 7; manufacturing in, 10;
    shareholder value in, 72–73
Chong, Kimberly, 227
CIIA. *See* certified international
    investment analyst
classical investment method,
    154, 163–64; beat market by,
    150–51, 187; conflicting views
    on, 191; diversification in,
    205–6; employees using, 205–6;
    fund managers using, 158–59,

162; market efficiency in, 158;
    modern financial theory in,
    155–56; MPT applied in, 204;
    personal opinions and, 246;
    personal valuation influence in,
    184; as professional standard,
    178–79; relative valuation in,
    249–50; salespeople's role in,
    185–86
Colonial empires, 9, 251
commodities, 11
communication technologies, 4
Communism, 9–10
Communist Manifesto, The (Marx),
    233
Communist Party, 227, 248
company value: convictions about,
    129; money invested in, 94; in
    stock valuation, 67
contradictions, 76; epistemological
    and ontological, 198–99; fund
    managers facing, 157–58, 195–96;
    in value, 66–71
convictions, 92, 118, 129, 140
cost of equity, 57
Covid-19 pandemic, 243
creditors, power relations of, 141
crisis. *See* financial crisis

DCF. *See* discounted cash flow
    method
debt securities, 203
De Goede, Marieke, 22
Deleuze, Gilles, 20–21
derivatives, 11, 256n9; Europe and
    U.S. collapse of, 12; hedge funds
    using, 162; inequalities and, 13

discounted cash flow (DCF)
method, 157, 165; company
lifespan and, 184; financial
analysis using, 102; fundamental
value from, 101–2; internet
bubble and, 217; prices in, 203–4;
rejection of, 105; short-term
price changes and, 104; true
value from, 57–58; for valuation,
103, 170–72
discount rates, 57, 270n48
discrimination, 11
diversification: alternative
investments in, 206; in classic
investment methods, 205–6;
by fund managers, 181; by
investment management
companies, 76–77; with market
efficiency, 213; MPT with
investment, 148; of mutual funds,
220–21; value from, 241; volatility
and, 154
dot.com crisis, 214, 222

EBITDA, 60–61
economy: real, 27; stock exchanges
representing, 144; technologies
transforming, 222; true value
of, 59
educational institutions, 172–73,
225–26
efficient markets: figure of investor
and, 142; investments and, 55–56;
investors role in, 140; prices in,
60; relative valuation in, 58; true
value in, 141; value in, 58–59, 82
elite academic institutions, 275n10

elitism, 226–27
emerging markets, 150
Employee Retirement Income
Security Act (1974), 84
Enron, 252
epistemological presuppositions,
244; in financial theory, 198–99;
in power relations, 201–2; in
valuation and investment, 205,
206–9, 248–49
ETFs. See exchange traded funds
ethics, 235
Eurodollars, 10
Europe: company funding in, 19–20;
equities in, 179; Eurozone GDP
in, 7; financial institution profits
in, 253–54; financial regulation in,
14, 41; fund managers stocks in,
3–4; mortgage derivative collapse
in, 12; regulatory transformations
in, 41; stock exchange of, 1, 45;
stock prices in, 4; U.S. balance of
power with, 10
everyday practices, 31, 76–78; of
employees, 239–40; of market,
169, 191–92; political meaning
and morality in, 209–10; true
value in, 79–80; in valuation and
investment, 81–82; value and, 238
exchange traded funds (ETFs),
159–60
expected return (Er), 65

factory workers, 234
Fama, Eugene, 272n74
FCFF. See free cash flow to the firm
Federal Reserve, 214

fees: customers paying, 107–8, 133–34, 137; fund managers paying, 114–15, 127–28, 189, 280n45

fieldwork, 17, 29–30

figure of investor: absence of, 235–36; efficient market and, 142; employees and, 196; in financial industry, 15–16; information sought by, 139; market efficiency with, 144, 196–97; money distribution and, 241; in relative valuation, 65–66; in valuation and investment, 86; valuation and multiple, 88–89

financial bureaucracy, 235

financial crisis, 4, 79, 197; erroneous valuation in, 215–16; financial regulations and, 35, 252–53; market efficiency and, 215–16; regulatory reform from, 232; stock prices in, 251–53; subprime, 243, 252–53

financial regulations, 6–7, 247–48; in Europe, 14, 41; financial crisis and, 35, 252–53; in market efficiency, 42, 168–69; market efficiency ensured by, 89; money allocation and, 244; principal-agent relation and, 84–85; regulatory reform, 232; state, 48; of stock trades, 15; in United States, 14

financial theory, 52, 81–82, 143; epistemological and ontological contradictions in, 198–99; for investments, 53–54; investors freedom in, 202; legal owners

of money in, 245; modern, 72, 155–56; speculative valuation in, 144; valuation in, 75–76

"the float," 184

food crisis (2007–2008), 12

foreign currency, 11–12

Foucault, Michel, 22, 229, 236–38

Fourcade, Marion, 145

France, 9

free cash flow to the firm (FCFF), 57

free market prices, 143, 230

free will: of investors, 202; in valuation, 198–99

front-office employees, 49, 80, 129, 172–73, 225–26

fundamental valuation, 166; cash flow and, 58, 61; of companies, 71; from DCF method, 101–2; of listed companies, 105–6, 218; listed prices in, 69–70; market efficiency in, 158; market prices in, 143–44; in MPT, 70; personal opinion in, 216; relative valuation integrated with, 63, 67, 70; risk in, 63; short-term price in, 104

fund managers: analysis technical content and, 117–18; of Brokers Inc., 100–101; buy and sell side analysis for, 91–92; buy-side from, 47; classical investment method used by, 158–59, 162; contradictory demands faced by, 157–58, 195–96; costs of, 159; diversification by, 181; for European stocks, 3–4; fees paid by, 114–15, 127–28, 189, 280n45; income produced by,

99; independence of, 96–97; index legitimacy and, 182–83; for investments, 15; investments balanced by, 152; legitimacy of, 94; listed companies discussed by, 175; listed companies specialty of, 114; loyalty of, 97–98; market feel of, 174; MPT used by, 63–64; mutual funds and, 118; personality of, 123; personal opinion of, 92–93; power relations of, 120–21; regular interval trading of, 107; salary of, 50; salespeople remunerated by, 49–50; salespeople's dialogue with, 115, 174; salespeople's relationship with, 93–94, 110–13, 116–17, 125–26, 176, 189–90; salesperson's analysis to, 90–91; satellite funds of, 154; sell-side analysis and, 91–92, 186; synergy created by, 153–54; true value and, 186; in United States, 188–89; valuations by, 46–47, 119–20; volatility understood by, 163

futures, 154–55, 277n20

GDP. See gross domestic product
gender identities, 122–23, 255n2
geographies, financial industry, 8–9
global hierarchies: financial industry and, 225; financial valuation and investment of, 19; money in, 254
globalization: exchanges in, 251; financial industry and, 222; money distribution in, 18–19, 24–25

global political institution, 18–23
global resource distribution, 5–6
Godechot, Olivier, 226
gold standard, 9
grandes écoles (elite academic institutions), 275n10
Greenspan, Alan, 214
gross domestic product (GDP), 7
Guattari, Félix, 20–21
Guyer, Jane, 23, 26, 53, 145

Hart, Keith, 53
hedge funds, 45, 224; beat market with, 163–64; derivatives used by, 162; income from, 268n30; in market efficiency, 162; short selling by, 278n27; speculation in, 163; in valuation and investment, 161–62
hierarchy, 23–26, 28–29, 49
Ho, Karen, 129, 173

IMF. See International Monetary Fund
income statement, 56
index-based method, 159
indexes: companies using, 148–49, 184–85; fund managers and legitimacy of, 182–83; investment management companies beating, 185; investment portfolio beating, 155, 182; investment portfolio return to, 153; performance of, 281n11; software-based replication of, 161, 163–64, 167; stock prices in, 279nn40–42; valuation and investment role of, 144, 226

inequalities: from discrimination, 11;
on monetary distribution, 8–9;
stocks, bonds and derivative, 13;
subprime crisis with, 253–54
information: companies, sold,
267n25; erroneous, 68–69;
figure of investor seeking, 139;
investment management sources
of, 45–46; investors seeking, 142–
43; listed prices from efficiency
of, 85; market with reliable, 172,
193; news analysis for, 169–70
infrastructure, technologies in, 231
intellectual superiority, 225–26
intentionality, 238
interdependence, 66–71, 76, 195–96
interest rates: Federal Reserve
increasing, 214; London
interbank, 271n70; risk-free, 201;
risk-free rate of return, 64, 73–74
International Monetary Fund
(IMF), 12, 170
internet: bubble, 186, 214–18, 221–23,
243, 252; stocks, 45; technologies,
214
investments: alternative, 63, 206,
213; capitalization of, 273n84;
diversification of, 206; efficient
markets and, 55–56; financial
theory for, 53–54; index-based
method of, 159; methods of,
154–55; MPT with diversification
of, 148; performance of, 152–53;
personal opinion decisions for,
211; power relations in, 71–76;
present value of, 270n48; pressure
in, 219; returns from, 52, 62–64;

risks and, 52, 62–64; U.S. process
of, 45, 180–81; value in, 82. *See also*
valuation and investment
investment universe, 59, 147, 184, 192
investors: convictions of, 140;
definition of, 83; efficient market
role of, 140; free will of, 202;
information sought by, 142–43; as
legal money owners, 84, 212, 233–
34, 246; market efficiency from
valuation of, 245–46; monetary
gain of, 230–31; personal opinion
of, 111; sophisticated, 260n38;
value and, 146
Islamic finance, 247

James, William, 29

Keynes, John, 65, 233–34

labor, 28
Langley, Paul, 22
language, 49, 255n2
Lehman Brothers, 253
life insurance, 219
liquidity, market, 184
listed prices: in fundamental
valuation, 69–70; informational
efficiency for, 85; true value in, 147
London interbank interest rates,
271n70

margins, 105, 275n14, 277n20
market efficiency: companies true
value in, 148–49; diversification
with, 213; with figure of investor,
144, 196–97; financial assets

bought and, 151; financial crisis
and, 215–16; in financial industry,
192; financial regulations in, 42,
168–69; financial valuation and,
34–35, 68–69; in fundamental
valuation, 158; hedge funds in,
162; independent valuation for,
143; informationally efficient,
55; investor valuation for,
245–46; personal valuation
balance with, 190–91; personal
valuation conflict with, 179;
personal valuation in, 157,
178; price movements and,
147–48, 203–4, 221–22; regulations
ensuring, 89; rejection of, 213;
returns maximized from, 193;
in speculative valuation, 110;
speculative valuation rejecting,
67; valuation from, 166–68,
192–93; valuation methods for,
177. *See also* efficient markets
market risk (Mr), 64
Markovitz, Henri, 272n74
Marx, Karl, 27, 232–33
Marxism, 25
mathematical circularity, 70
mathematical expertise, 109–10
mathematical formulations, 52–53
Maurer, Bill, 53
Mauss, Marcel, 25–26, 233
mediating instruments, 39
Merton, Robert C., 275n18
middle class, 84
Miller, Peter, 21, 38–39, 85, 146
modern portfolio theory
(MPT), 211–12; capital asset

pricing model from, 64; in
classical investment method,
204; employees using,
149–50; financial assets in, 77;
fundamental valuation in, 70;
fund managers using, 63–64;
investment diversification in,
148; returns maximized by, 60;
strategies with, 154
money: approaches to, 25; Brokers
Inc. managing, 4; commercial
relations with owners of, 42;
company value and investment
of, 94; concentration of, 8;
distribution of, 10–11, 38; figure
of investor and distribution
of, 241; in financial industry,
220–21; financial regulations
and allocation of, 244; financial
theory and legal owners of,
245; in financial valuation,
231–32, 254; global distribution
of, 18–19, 24–25; in global
hierarchies, 254; hierarchies
from, 6–7; inequalities in
distribution of, 8–9; investors
as legal owners of, 84, 212,
233–34, 246; investors gaining,
230–31; narrow monetary mass
and, 256n11; power relations
around, 19–20; practices
used with, 24; prices and
distribution of, 240–41, 244–45;
resources, 87; salespeople
motivated by, 130–31; social
hierarchies from, 146; U.S.
owners of, 42

morality, 25; in everyday practices, 209–10; political imaginaries and, 197, 208–28; religious, 23; of valuation and investment, 228; values and, 27–28

MPT. *See* modern portfolio theory

multiplicity, 20, 76, 240; in monetary practices, 24; of positions, 141; of power relations, 21, 24; in valuation practices, 31–32

Muniesa, Fabian, 60

mutual funds, 118, 220–21

Nasdaq Composite Index, 214

neoliberalism, 223, 241

news analysis, 169–70

OECD. *See* Organization for Economic Cooperation and Development

ontological presuppositions, 244; in financial theory, 198–99; in power relations, 201–2; in valuation and investment, 205–9, 248–49

operational field, 21

Organization for Economic Cooperation and Development (OECD), 170

outings: activity discrimination during, 124–25; brokerage houses financing, 120–21; gender identities during, 122–23; personal choices in, 125; personal connections through, 174–75; professional relations and, 124; quality of, 123–24; salespeople

personalities for, 121–22; social identities during, 122

ownership, socialization of, 232–33; owner, 233–34; property, 140, 232

Paris Stock Exchange, 17

P/E. *See* price to earnings ratio

peer recognition, 37

pension funds, 83–84, 118, 156

performance, 152–53, 181, 281n11

personal capacity, 85

personal character, 87, 119–20, 125, 130

personal connections, 174–75

personal experience, 95–96

personal expertise, 240

personality, of fund managers, 123

personal opinion, 174; classical investment method and, 246; about financial valuation, 127–28; in fundamental valuation, 216; of fund managers, 92–93; investment decisions based on, 211; of investors, 111; in market, 199–200; procedures for, 138; on stock price, 110; on true value, 87; valuation as, 128; on value, 86

personal valuation: classical investment method influence of, 184; in market efficiency, 157, 178; market efficiency balance with, 190–91; market efficiency conflict with, 179

P/FCF. *See* price to free cash flow

political imaginaries, 194; elitism with, 226–27; of financial valuation, 38–39; morality and,

197, 208–28; of valuation and investment, 228, 236–37

politics: everyday practices in, 209–10; in financial industry, 23; financial industry role of, 223–24; financial role in, 27; global institutions for, 18–23; power relations in institutions of, 19–20; technologies with, 53

power relations: of employees, 96–97; epistemologies and ontologies with, 201–2; in financial industry, 20, 241–42; of fund manager, 120–21; in investments, 71–76; around money, 19–20; multiplicity of, 21, 24; of political institution, 19–20; of salespeople, 120–21; shareholder and creditor, 141; social activities and, 77–78; specific territory of, 21–22; in valuation, 71–76; in valuation and investment, 249–50

present value: of cash flows, 56–57; future forecasts for, 69, 71; income and, 73; of investment, 270n48

prices: averages of, 59; daily, 59; in DCF method, 203–4; DCF method and short-term changes in, 104; in efficient markets, 60; financial analysis of, 70–71; of futures, 277n20; listed, 69–70, 85, 147; of listed companies, 164; listed companies short-term, 106–7; market and, 143–46; market efficiency and,

147–48, 203–4, 221–22; money distribution influencing, 240–41, 244–45; movement of, 60; real estate, 253; short-term, 104, 106–7; social value for, 236; speculative valuation variations of, 65, 70, 143–44; statistical processing of, 200; on stock exchanges, 69; trading with short-term, 110; true value and, 199, 212, 217–18, 223; value defined by, 167; variation of, 65

price to earnings (P/E) ratio, 61, 104, 185

price to free cash flow (P/FCF), 61

principal-agent relations, 42, 84–85, 252

private equity funds, 12

probabilities, 59–60, 66

professional lives, of employees, 132, 246–47

professional rules, 209–10

professional standards, 178–79

psychiatry, 237

public administration, 13

public offering, of stocks, 43

real economy, 27

real estate prices, 253

relative valuation, 89, 166; Brokers Inc. independence and, 118; in classical investment method, 249–50; companies ranked in, 60; DCF method and, 103; in efficient market, 58; figure of investor in, 65–66; financial value as, 56; fundamental valuation

relative valuation (*continued*)
  integrated with, 63, 67, 70;
  market corrections in, 62;
  problems with, 103–4; risk in, 63
relative value, 58–59
religious morality, 23
reports, from financial analysis, 90
research, of brokerage houses,
  99–100
returns: expected, 65; financial
  assets with high, 221; investment
  portfolio, 153; from investments,
  52, 62–64; market efficiency
  maximizing, 193; MPT
  maximizing, 60; reinvestment
  of, 273n84; risk-free rate of, 64;
  shareholder, 41–42; standard
  deviation of, 60
revenue: of Brokers Inc., 16, 47,
  115–16; cost reduction or,
  72; customers paying, 51; in
  free markets, 73; in income
  statement, 56–57; salespeople
  source of, 95; from stocks, 43. *See
  also* income
Rf. *See* risk-free rate of return
risk: in fundamental valuation,
  63; of investments, 52, 62–64;
  market, 64; performance and,
  181; in relative valuation, 63;
  of securities, 271n71; volatility
  creating premiums from, 64
risk-free interest rate, 201
risk-free rate of return (Rf), 64,
  73–74
Roitman, Janet, 239
Rose, Nikolas, 38, 85

salespeople: accounting known
  by, 108; back-office employees
  and, 80–81; of Brokers Inc., 50;
  Brokers Inc. hierarchy of, 183;
  Brokers Inc. revenue source
  of, 95; classical investment
  method role of, 185–86; client
  contact with, 113; DCF method
  rejection by, 105; expertise of,
  189; fund manager analysis from,
  90–91; fund manager's dialogue
  with, 115, 174; fund manager's
  relationship with, 93–94, 110–13,
  116–17, 125–26, 176, 189–90;
  fund managers remunerating,
  49–50; intellectual valuation by,
  106; legitimacy of, 136; money
  motivating, 130–31; outings
  and personalities of, 121–22; as
  overpaid, 108; power relations
  of, 120–21; revenue source of,
  95; traders conflict with, 175–76;
  true value conveyed by, 102–3;
  valuation quality by, 119–20, 124;
  valuations by, 46–47, 116–17
sanctions, 87, 127
Sassen, Saskia, 21
Scholes, Myron, 275n18
sell-side analysis, 47, 185, 188, 211;
  financial analysis, 50–51; for
  fund managers, 91–92, 186; in
  valuation, 100
shareholders, 11, 234; China and
  value to, 72–73; financial
  valuation, 6; listed companies
  returns for, 41–42; finance theory
  maximizing value to, 72; power

relations of, 141; value to, 51–52,
    55–56, 75, 236
Sharpe, William, 272n74
short selling, 278n27
short-term gains, 187
short-term prices, 104, 106–7
Simmel, Georg, 25–26, 234
slavery without master, 235
small cap stocks, 43
Smith, Adam, 143, 230, 232
social activities, 223; financial value of,
    242; power relations and, 77–78; Rf
    and, 73–74; true value of, 56, 75–76;
    in valuation and investment, 201
social hierarchies, 73, 146, 229, 248
social identities, 123; of employees,
    239; during outings, 122;
    valuation with, 129, 138–40
social justice, 229
social space: employees and, 178–79,
    225; of financial industry, 168–78;
    market and, 146–47; in valuation
    and investment, 198
social value, 236
software, 247; fund management
    costs reduced by, 159; for
    valuation and investment, 206–7
software-based index replication,
    161, 163–64, 167
sophisticated investors, 260n38
sovereign bond, 151
speculation: in hedge funds, 163;
    trading and, 186
speculative valuation, 106, 140;
    Brokers Inc. independence and,
    118; DCF method and, 103,
    166; erroneous information in,

68–69; in financial theory, 144;
    market efficiency in, 110; market
    efficiency rejected by, 67; methods
    of, 66; price variations in, 65, 70,
    143–44; short-termism of, 105
standard deviation of returns, 60
state: power, 202–3; regulations, 48;
    rich, 251; sovereignty, 204, 250
statistical processing, 200
statistics, 60, 62, 64, 200
stockbrokers: at investment
    management companies, 50–51;
    stock's public offering by, 43;
    transactions by, 40–41
stock exchanges, 11, 40–41; economy
    represented by, 144; ETFs on,
    159–60; of Europe, 1, 45; prices
    on, 69
stock prices: accounting numbers
    and, 61–62; in capitalization,
    267n23; cash flows and, 74–75;
    collapse of, 215; in Europe, 4;
    evolution of, 155; in financial
    crisis, 251–53; in indexes,
    279nn40–42; personal opinion
    on, 110; true value of, 59–60; in
    United States, 4, 251–53
stocks, 11; buying and selling, 211–12;
    capitalization of, 43; financial
    regulations of, 15; fund managers
    European, 3–4; inequalities and,
    13; internet, 45; public offering of,
    43; purchase of, 47–48; revenue
    from, 43; small cap, 43; in United
    States, 19–20; valuation of, 46–47,
    67. See also listed stocks
subprime crisis, 243, 252–53

technologies: for communications,
4; economic transformations
from, 222; in infrastructure, 231;
internet, 214; political, 53
track record, 156
traders, 46–51
trade unions, 210–11
trading: Brokers Inc. relations in,
176–77; buy and sell orders in,
187–88; expertise in, 189; fund
manager's regular interval,
107; mathematical expertise
in, 109–10; salespeople conflict
and, 175–76; short-term price
movements in, 110; speculation
and, 186; teams for, 108–9;
transactions in, 279n34
true value, 34; of companies, 148–49;
customer fees in, 107–8; from
DCF method, 57–58; of economy,
59; in efficient markets, 141;
employees contributions to, 88;
in everyday practices, 79–80;
in financial industry, 244–48;
free market prices in, 143; fund
managers and, 186; of listed
companies, 81, 101, 128, 164–65; in
listed prices, 147; personal opinions
on, 87; prices and, 199, 212, 217–18,
223; salespeople conveying, 102–3;
of social activities, 56, 75–76; of
stock prices, 59–60; in valuation
and investment, 229

United Kingdom, 9
United States (U.S.): Europe's
balance of power with, 10;
financial institution profits in,
253–54; financial regulation in, 14;
fund managers in, 188–89; GDP
of, 7; investment management
companies in, 17, 45; investment
process in, 180–81; investments
from, 45, 180–81; money owners
in, 42; mortgage derivative
collapse in, 12; regulatory
transformations in, 41; stock
prices in, 4, 251–53; stocks and
bonds in, 19–20

valuation: accounting knowledge
in, 120; bonus linked with,
133–35; Brokers SA quality
of, 97; in classical investment
method, 249–50; company value
in, 67; DCF method for, 103,
170–72; employees activities of,
39, 86–87; employee's quality
of, 133–34; erroneous, 215; in
financial analysis, 89; financial
crisis and erroneous, 215–16; in
financial theory, 75–76; free will
in, 198–99; by fund managers,
46–47, 119–20; listed stock, 18,
36, 152; from market efficiency,
166–68, 192–93; market
efficiency from investor, 245–46;
market efficiency methods
of, 177; market efficiency with
independent, 143; methods of,
48; multiple figure of investors
in, 88–89; multiplicity in, 31–32;
personal character in, 119–20, 130;
personal experience in, 95–96;

as personal opinion, 128; power relations in, 71–76; quality of, 119–20, 124; by salespeople, 46–47, 116–17; salespeople's intellectual, 106; sell-side analysis in, 100; short-term price movements in, 110; social identity and, 129, 138–40; state's power in, 202–3; of stocks, 46–47, 67. *See also specific valuation*

valuation and investment: Acme's methods of, 31, 205; algorithms in, 247; by Brokers Inc., 39–40, 149; daily practices in, 81–82; employees consideration of, 38; epistemological and ontological, 205–9, 248–49; figure of investor in, 86; by Frédéric, 6; of global hierarchies, 19; hedge funds in, 161–62; indexes role in, 144, 226; methods of, 21–23; personal expertise in, 240; political imaginaries of, 228, 236–37; power relations in, 249–50; practices related in, 16; professional rules on, 37–38; in public administration, 13; social activities in, 201; social spaces in, 198; software for, 206–7; true value in, 229

value: in analytic hierarchy, 28–29; contradictions in, 66–71; creation, 214–15; defining, 52, 67–68, 109–10; destruction of, 215; from diversification, 241; in efficient markets, 58–59, 82; everyday practices and, 238; of financial assets, 29, 51, 64, 229–30; interdependence in, 66–71; in investments, 82; investors and, 146; labor as source of, 28; of listed companies, 5, 57–58; listed companies creation of, 214–15; of listed stock, 46; morality and, 27–28; personal opinion on, 86; prices defining, 167; relative, 58–59; to shareholders, 51–52, 55–56, 75, 236

volatility: diversification and, 154; fund managers understanding, 163; risk premiums from, 64; satellite funds and, 154; small bets minimizing, 153; as standard deviation of returns, 60

WACC. *See* weighted average cost of capital

wages, 130, 214, 245; of fund managers, 50

Weber, Max, 28, 234–37

weighted average cost of capital (WACC), 57, 69, 71

WorldCom, 252

Zaloom, Caitlin, 129

Zelizer, Viviana, 145